AF210489

Studies in the Phonology and Morphology
of Modern Icelandic

Janez Orešnik

Studies in the Phonology and Morphology of Modern Icelandic

A selection of essays

Edited by
Magnús Pétursson

HELMUT BUSKE VERLAG HAMBURG

Im Digitaldruck »on demand« hergestelltes, inhaltlich mit der ursprüng-
lichen Ausgabe identisches Exemplar. Wir bitten um Verständnis für un-
vermeidliche Abweichungen in der Ausstattung, die der Einzelfertigung
geschuldet sind. Weitere Informationen unter: www.buske.de/bod.

Bibliographische Information der Deutschen Nationalbibliothek

Die Deutsche Nationalbibliothek verzeichnet diese Publikation
in der Deutschen Nationalbibliographie; detaillierte bibliographische
Daten sind im Internet über ‹http://portal.dnb.de› abrufbar.
ISBN 978-3-87118-683-7

www.buske.de

© Helmut Buske Verlag GmbH, Hamburg 1985. Alle Rechte vorbehalten. Dies
gilt auch für Vervielfältigungen, Übertragungen, Mikroverfilmungen und die
Einspeicherung und Verarbeitung in elektronischen Systemen, soweit es nicht
§§ 53 und 54 URG ausdrücklich gestatten. Gesamtherstellung: BoD, Norder-
stedt. Gedruckt auf alterungsbeständigem Werkdruckpapier, hergestellt aus
100% chlorfrei gebleichtem Zellstoff. Printed in Germany.

CONTENTS

PREFACE

Old Norse is well known as one of the most important languages for the study of old Germanic culture and traditions. It is an indispensable element for the reconstruction of Proto-Germanic, and hence important for our knowledge of Indo-European. Owing to the key positon that Old Norse occupies in comparative linguistics it is only natural that it has been the object of intensive study and research ever since Rasmus Kristjan Rask (1787–1832) began to investigate it in 1811. Old Norse data are quoted in textbooks, and as examples in studies devoted to general linguistics. They are therefore often well known to linguists working even with quite unrelated languages.

The case of modern Icelandic is different. Although modern Icelandic is derived directly from Old Norse and has retained many of its characteristics, particularly in morphology, it is much less well known. What, however, makes modern Icelandic so exciting for the linguist is the fact that some processes, like i-umlaut and u-umlaut, which are known only as historically attested changes in other Germanic languages, are here still alive.

This selection of twelve essays on modern Icelandic by Professor Janez Orešnik is published with the aim of making his pioneer work known to wider circles of linguists than those working only with modern Icelandic. With an unusually fine touch Professor Orešnik has opened a new page in the study of modern Icelandic by investigating some of the phonetic/phonological processes which are alive in daily speech. The selection includes his excellent articles on i- and u-umlaut, on the Epenthesis Rule, and on the devoicing rules.

One of the myths often heard is that modern Icelandic spoken language is very regular and shows much less variation than other European tongues. This is an intuitive feeling based on the fact that in Iceland there are no dialects in the sense of geographical variants of speech, as in Europe. But the scientific investigation of modern Icelandic has only just begun, and nobody really knows how much variation there is in speech, and how great the gap is between the spoken and the written language. From the preliminary investigations conducted so far it seems clear that that gap is much greater than has been supposed. It is even surprisingly great, so that in some cases there exists an impressive number of variants which have not been recognized in normative grammars as correct, and hence have not been registered anywhere, but continue, as it were, a subterranean existence in the spoken language.

Here too Professor Orešnik has done the work of a pioneer. In patient field work he has collected data on the imperative and other verb forms as used in the spoken language. The imperative is typical of speech and therefore perhaps less stable than many other members of the verbal paradigm. As the reader will see, its shapes are many. Professor Orešnik tries to reconstruct the ways in which they are formed by speakers, and he has discovered some unexpected analogies, which show how extremely variable the spoken language is. Professor Orešnik's research on the clipped imperative is absolutely the first attempt to describe this phenomenon. – According to the data collected so far on Icelandic speech, the verb seems to show greater variation than other grammatical categories, but before anything definitive can be said about this matter we must wait to see the results of research in progress.

In summary, this is an unusual book on an unusual subject. Hopefully there will be many linguists who will appreciate having these careful studies on modern Icelandic gathered in one volume. It is our conviction that they will be of interest to everyone trying to learn more about the nature of human language.

Hamburg   Magnús Pétursson
January 1984

JANEZ OREŠNIK

On Some Weak Preterite Subjunctives of Otherwise Strong Verbs in Modern Icelandic

This paper studies a hitherto neglected morphological problem of the Modern Icelandic strong preterite: those of its subjunctives which are — unlike its indicatives — characterized by the presence in them of the so-called dental suffix, e.g., pret. subj. *dœði* of *deyja* 'die', strong verb VI (normal pret. subj. *dœi*, cf. preterite indicative stem *dó-*). Section 1 contains the philological evidence for such subjunctives. In section 2 an attempt is made to account for these strange forms in the broader context of the Modern Icelandic preterite subjunctive in general. Some forms that should perhaps have been accounted for in this paper are mentioned in section 3.—1.1.2, 1.2.2, and 2.3 are the summarizing sections.*

1. Nine preterite subjunctive forms are dealt with in this section, each is discussed in its own subsection containing the evidence for the particular preterite subjunctive form (a) in the printed texts of the post-Reformation

* My thanks are due to the Icelandic Ministry of Cultural Affairs, to the Foundation »Sklad Borisa Kidriča», Ljubljana, and to the Yugoslav Commission for Cultural Relations with Foreign Countries, which have made it possible for me to spend 1965—66 in Iceland, where I was able to work in the locale of the University of Iceland Dictionary Project, whose staff I am grateful for their extensive and frequent help. My thanks are also due to the International Research and Exchanges Board sponsored by the American Council of Learned Societies, New York, and to Harvard University, Cambridge, Mass., for enabling me to spend 1969—70 in the United States; the present paper is a partial result of this stay. The University of Ljubljana granted me a sabbatical year in both these cases. I am especially indebted to Einar Haugen, Stefán Karlsson, and John Weinstock, who have criticized an earlier version of this paper. The persons listed in footnote 17 and/or in (21) below have helped me in many ways. Sigrid Valfells and Stephen Anderson have kindly furnished me with copies of their respective unpublished dissertations. Kerstie Andersen and Kenneth Naylor improved the style of the paper. All errors are my own.

centuries (no forms of the kind discussed here are to be found before the sixteenth century), (b) in the grammatical literature, and (c) in the dialect file of the OHÍ.[1]

1.1. In 1.1.1 the following preterite subjunctive forms are discussed: *dœði* of *deyja* 'die' (1.1.1.1), *drœði* of *draga* 'draw' (1.1.1.2), *hlœði* of *hlœja* 'laugh' (1.1.1.3), *lœði* of *liggja* 'lie' (1.1.1.4), *sjœði* of *sjá* 'see' (1.1.1.5), and *slœði* of *slá* 'strike' (1.1.1.6). —1.1.2 contains a summary of the findings presented in 1.1.1.

1.1.1.1. *Deyja* 'die' strong verb VI, has inherited two preterite indicatives from pre-Reformation Icelandic, *dó-* and *deyð-*.[2] The preterite subjunc-

---

[1] OHÍ = University of Iceland Dictionary Project. I found many of the examples reported below in the main and the dialect files of the OHÍ in 1965—66, when the main file was to a large extent completed so far as excerpts from the non-twentieth century literature are concerned, while the dialect file was still incomplete, although the work necessary to enlarge it was well under way. My descriptions of the files of the OHÍ refer to these files as they were in the summer of 1966. The following examples, adduced below, are not yet recorded in the OHÍ, mostly because they appear in the grammatical literature: (6) to (10), (12) (thus *drœð-* of *draga* 'draw, pull' is not at all recorded in the OHÍ), (17), (20), the first example of (31), and (33).

[2] I agree with Sturtevant 1940: 48 that pret. *deyð-* is a genuine analogical formation of Old Icelandic, the result of a derivational process in which the present stem *deyj-* was the basic form and the weak verbs supplied the rule for the formation of the weak preterite out of the present stem: *deyj-* + *ð* + endings. To my knowledge, this view on the origin of *deyð-* is at variance with the opinions of all the other scholars who have committed themselves on the matter: Cleasby-Vigfusson 1874 s.v. *deyja*; Westergård-Nielsen 1946: LV, LXXXVIII, and s.v. *deyði*; Bandle 1956: 405; Jóhannesson 1956: 968; etc. According to them, *deyð-* is borrowed from Danish (*døde*), possibly through Norwegian. The arguments for this position have been best stated by Westergård-Nielsen and Bandle: (a) A genuine analogical weak formation would gain entry into the spoken language —*deyð-* has not done so; (b) a genuine weak formation would not only survive but also prevail upon its strong counterpart — but *deyð-* has not prevailed upon *dó-*. Neither of these arguments is conclusive. Pret. *deyð-* WAS a form of the spoken language, as instances of *deyð-* in, for instance, Árnason 1862—64 (folk tales) attest. It is not the case that weak analogical preterites that enter into competition with their strong counterparts always prevail over the latter. As I have argued in Orešnik 1964 and in my lecture in Félag íslenzkra fræða, Reykjavík, in May 1966, the strong preterite has always occupied an extremely strong position in Icelandic (quite apart from the fact that the normative grammar has in many cases favored the strong forms in the last century or so), and there are a great many instances of weak analogical formations that have failed to prevail upon their respective strong preterites in spite of the fact that the competition has lasted long. The weak pret. *hangd-* of *hanga* 'hang', strong

tives correlated with these are *dœ-* and *deyð-*, respectively. In addition to
these subjunctives, there is a pret. subj. *dœð-*, with the root vowel of the
regular pret. subj. *dœ-* and with the dental suffix. Here follows my complete evidence for the existence of *dœð-* in the texts, see (1)—(3), in the
grammatical literature, see (4)—(10), and in the OHÍ, see (11):

(1) Campe 1800: 185. en ef sálin mín dædi undir eins og minn líkami á ad
deyja, þá gjæti Gud ecki framar látid mér lída vel, af því eg væri þá ecki
lengur til. 'and if my soul should die ...'

The German work was translated into Icelandic via Danish by the   Reverend Bjarni Arngrímsson (1768—1821), who was connected with Bor-
garfjarðarsýsla practically all his life, see ÍslÆv 1: 156—57.

(2) Brynjúlfsson 1952: 208. Mamma hélt, að fyrri vísuna hefði einhver
aumingja mæðumaðurinn eða kona kveðið áður en dæði. '... before
he/she died.'

Brynjúlfsson 1952 is the poet Gísli Brynjúlfsson's diary, edited after the
author's own manuscript, now Ny kgl. Saml. 3262, 4to, Royal Library,
Copenhagen. Gísli Brynjúlfsson (1827—1888) spent most of his life outside
Iceland, in Copenhagen, where he constantly met educated Icelanders
from all parts of Iceland. No conclusions concerning the origin or
geographical distribution of *dœð-* can be drawn from what is known about
his linguistic experience.

(3) "Séra Magnús og séra Illugi" in Árnason III 1955: 560. Er það sagt
að hann hafi margar glettingar gert séra Magnúsi meðan Illugi var uppi,
og var sagt að hann hefði ekki gleymt þessum fjandskap þó hann dæði.
'... even if he had died.'

---

verb VII, is still dialectally limited although it has existed since Classical times and
been supported by the dissyllabic present stem *hangi-*, somewhat unusual for a
strong verb (Halldórsson 1950: 152). *Hrinda* 'push', strong verb III, has also had
weak preterite forms (*hrint-*) in post-Reformation times, but the weak forms have
not replaced the strong preterite of this verb in all of its meanings, in spite of the
support of the very frequent dissyllabic present stem *hrindi-* (Þorkelsson 1888—94:
238—40). *Hefja* 'lift', strong verb VI, has often had a weak preterite *hafð-* in the
post-Reformation centuries, which form has in addition been supported by a *j*-pre-
sent stem *hefj-*, and by the past part. *hafin-*, contracted cases *hafð-*; yet the strong
pret. ind. *hóf-* still prevails (Bandle 1956: 405—06). These random examples of verbs
beginning with *h* could be easily multiplied. Bandle also thinks that *deyð-*, if a
genuine Icelandic form, would have had a better chance to replace the strong *dó-*
than similar formations of other strong verbs, because *deyja* is such a common verb.
This argument is, of course, inconclusive: it is the commonest words of the language
that usually retain some irregularity.

Árnason is a collection of Icelandic folk tales. The source of the story from which the above quotation is taken, is ms. Landsbókasafn 536, B I 36, where our text is in the handwriting of Páll í Árkvörn. In Árnason VI 1961: 50, 54, 148 this person is identified as Páll Pálsson (1853—1876, son of Páll alþingismaður Sigurðarson), who lived at Árkvörn, Fljótshlíð, Rangárvallasýsla, South Iceland, and wrote the above mentioned manuscript as a child in 1862—63 and 1865. The story is connected with the adjacent Vestur-Skaftafellssýsla, where the two persons mentioned in the title of the story lived.

(4) Rask in Helgason 1960: 297. Datiden af nogle Gjærningsord af anden Forandringsmaade dannes paa *œdi* for *œi* v. *œgi*, f Eks. dædi, hlædi, slædi, siædi (for sægi), þædi (af þádi), men ikke af Ordet liggja.

According to Helgason 1960: 290—91, this quotation is found in a manuscript in the handwriting of Rasmus Rask and preserved among his papers in the Royal Library, Copenhagen, under no. Add. 627 c, 4to. The manuscript was written during Rask's stay in Iceland, most probably during his travels in the summers of 1814 and 1815. It contains dialectal data, mostly lexicological. The above quotation appears in the section on *Østerlandet* (= East Iceland).

(5) Vigfússon 1857: 163. Mig furðar að eins, að menn skuli ekki vera farnir að rita sjæju, dæðu, ferð, ljærð, sjerð, spyrð, komustum o.s.fr. /.../, því eg sè ekki að þetta sè neinu verra en hitt. 'I am only astonished to see that people have not begun to write *sjœju, dœðu, ferð, ljœrð, sjerð, spyrð, komustum*, etc. /.../, for I cannot see that this is worse than what I mentioned earlier.'

The quotation is from a philological paper by Guðbrandur Vigfússon (1827—1889). What the author had 'mentioned earlier', is the replacement of the old preterite subjunctive endings -*im*, -*ið*, -*i* by -*um*, -*uð*, -*u*, cf. pret. subj. *dœjum, dœjuð, dœju* of *deyja*, as against the older *døim, dóið, dói*. Guðbrandur Vigfússon advocates the reintroduction of the old endings and goes on to say that if the endings -*um*, -*uð*, -*u* have been adopted, why not adopt the forms listed in the quotation as well. The relevant implication here is that forms like pret. subj. *dœðu* existed in the spoken language at the time when the paper from which our quotation is taken was written. No information on the geographical distribution of forms like *dœð*- can be deduced from the above quotation, or from any other part of the paper in which the quotation appears.

(6) Cleasby-Vigfusson 1874: 99, s.v. *deyja*. pret. subj. dæi; in the south of Iceland people say dæði, inserting a spurious ð.

(7) Þorkelsson 1888—94: 124—25. Til eru í alþýðumáli ýmsar aðrar veikar myndir af sterkum sagnorðum, t.d. vth. þátíðar *dœði, drœði*,

hlœði, sjœði, slœði, þœði af sagnorðunum *deyja, draga, hlœja, sjá, slá, þiggja*; enn þessar veiku myndir finnast naumlega allar í prentuðum bókum. 'In the popular language there exist also several other weak forms of strong verbs, e.g., pret. subj. *dœði, drœði, hlœði, sjœði, slœði, þœði* of the verbs *deyja, draga, hlœja, sjá, slá, þiggja*; but these weak forms are hardly all to be found in printed books.'

(8) Hægstad 1942: 17. Innskot av ð er der ofte i daglegtalen i *haiðstýr* for hæstur superl., *aiðstýr* for æztur, *staiðstýr* Reykj. for stærstur. Ogso i maalføri millom vokalar *daiði, slaiði* ofl. for dæi, slæi, fort. konj. av deyja, slá.—Ibidem, p. 47: Fraa Seyðisfj. og Fáskrúðsfj. hev eg skrive upp fortidsformer i konj. som *sjaiði* (sæi) og *slaiði* (slæi) av sjá and slá.

Marius Hægstad made the observations reported in these quotations during a stay in Iceland in the summer of 1907 (Hægstad 1942: 1). The latter quotation appears in the section on *Austlandsmaal*. Jón Helgason has added the following comment to it, see Hægstad 1942: 47, fn. 2: "Formene dæði, sjæði, slæði osfr. høyrer ein jamt paa Austlandet og Sudlandet, men, so vidt eg veit, ikkje paa Nordlandet. Det finst ei herma fraa Nordlandet der dei nett spottar desse formene, som dei hev høyrt hjaa austlendingane."

(9) Blöndal 1920—24: 129, s.v. *deyja*. I Stedet for imp. conj. *dœi* forek. i Syd- og Øst-Island af og til Formen *dœði* [dai:ðı].

(10) Smári 1923: 107. Af nokkrum sterkum sögnum myndast viðth. þát. veikt í talmáli, t.d. dræði, dæði, slæði (f. drægi, dæi, slægi), en slíkt þykir fegurst að varast í ritmáli. 'Certain strong verbs have weak forms of the preterite subjunctive in the spoken language, e.g. *drœði, dœði, slœði* (for *drœgi, dœi, slœgi*), but it is considered best [literally: most beautiful] to avoid such forms in the written language.'

(11) On the only pertinent card in the dialect file of the OHÍ, dated Febr. 21, 1963, a person from Kelduhverfi, Norður-Þingeyjarsýsla, North Iceland, states that he remembers that a man who had moved to Kelduhverfi from somewhere else always used to say *dœði* for *dœi*, *lœði* for *lœi*, and *sjœði* for *sœi*.

1.1.1.2. Besides *drœgj-*, the normal pret. subj. of *draga* 'pull, draw', strong verb VI, there is a rare preterite subjunctive stem *drœð-*, with the dental suffix, attested in the grammatical literature only. See (7) and (10) above, and (12):

(12) Jónsson 1908: 120. Í þát. viðth. finst í daglegu máli oft ð f. g (t.d. 'dræði, hlæði'), en ekki þykja það bókhæfar myndir. 'In the preterite subjunctive there is often *ð* instead of *g* (e.g. *drœði, hlœði*) in the colloquial language, but these are not considered literary forms.'

1.1.1.3. Beside *hlœgj*-, the regular preterite subjunctive of *hlœja* 'laugh', strong verb VI, there is a rare pret. subj. *hlœð*-, with the dental suffix. It is attested in the grammatical literature only, see (4), (7), and (12).

1.1.1.4. Beside the regular pret. subj. *lœgj*- of *liggja* 'lie', strong verb V, a single instance of pret. subj. *lœð*-, with the dental suffix, is attested in the OHÍ dialect file, see (11).

1.1.1.5. Beside the normal pret. subj. *sœ*- of *sjá* 'see', strong verb V,[3] there is a peculiar pret. subj. *sjœð*-, with *j* as in the present stem, and with the dental suffix. Subj. *sjœð*- is amply attested:
(13) Hallgrímsson 1932: 82. Nú er eftir að vita, hvort hann séra Benedikt Eiríksson myndi gera sig ánægðan með þetta bréf, ef hann "sjæði" það. '... if he saw it.'

This quotation is taken from a letter from Jónas Hallgrímsson (1807—1845) to Konráð Gíslason; the part of the letter that contains the quotation is dated on June 13, 1841. If Jónas Hallgrímsson is mimicking, as is probable, the Reverend Benedikt Eiríksson when he uses *sjœði* instead of *sœi*, this instance of *sjœði* can be located to South Iceland, where Benedikt Eiríksson lived at Kálfholt, Rangárvallasýsla, from 1833 to 1847, after having attended school, together with Jónas Hallgrímsson, at Bessastaðir in the twenties; see ÍslÆv 1: 123.

(14) "Papeyjarbuxur og fleiri fébrögð" in Árnason III 1955: 456. Annað ráð til að ná fólgnu fé úr jörð átti að vera að gæta að hvar eldsbirta sjæðist á nætur og kasta þangað einhvörju og leita þess að morgni. '... where the light of fire could be seen at night, ...'

The source of the account from which the above quotation is taken is Landsbókasafn 420, 8vo, p. 260. Pp. 259—74 of this manuscript are in the hand of Runólfur Runólfsson (1806—1884), who lived at Holtar, Mýrum, Austur-Skaftafellssýsla, South Iceland. (See Árnason III 1955: 648; VI 1961: 52, 152.)

---

[3] In post-Reformation Icelandic the main forms of *sjá* have been *sé*-/*sjá*- in the present, *sá*- in the preterite, and *sén*-/*séð*- in the past participle. In the past participle the form with the dental suffix (masc. *séður*, fem./neuter/supine *séð*) has now completely prevailed.

(15) "Mín hefur augu og mitt hefur nef" in Árnason IV 1956: 246. karl var að hossa reifaða barninu út við gluggann og tók úr skjáinn so hann sjæði útlit og yfirbragð barns þessa. '... in order to see the appearance of this child.'

The source of the story from which the quotation is taken is Landsbóka-safn 423, 8vo, p. 215. See Árnason IV 1956: 674, and VI 1961: 53, where this source is characterized as an East Icelandic folk tale manuscript, with pp. 65—128 and 145—230 in the hand of the Rev. Sigurður Gun-narsson (1812—1878), who served at Desjamýri, Norður-Múlasýsla, and at Hallormsstaður, Suður-Múlasýsla, both East Iceland (see Árnason VI 1961: 158), and our story thus likely originates from the East of Iceland.

(16) "Með morgunkaffinu" in daily *Morgunblaðið*, no. 230, Oct. 12, 1943, p. 11, column 3. Og ef Kristur væri kominn hingað og sjæði hvernig með mál hans væri farið, myndi hann nota fyrsta tækifæri til þess að verða krossfestur aftur. 'And if Christ ... saw how his cause fares ...'

This quotation is taken from an anecdote published in the column of anecdotes and jokes in the daily *Morgunblaðið*. Most of the material pub-lished in the column is translated from foreign languages. Neither the translator's nor the author's name is given.

Subj. *sjæð*- appears in the grammatical literature as well. See (4), (7), (8) above, and (17):

(17) Blöndal 1920—24: 1047, s.v. 2. *sjá*. imp. conj. ogs. undert. *sjæði* (Skaft., Af.).

Moreover, there are two instances of *sjæð*- found in the OHÍ dialect file, see (11) above, and (18):

(18) A person originating from Borgarfjörður, East Iceland, but living in Reykjavík, is reported to have given the following example of how people from the Southern fjords mimic the inhabitants of the East: "Ég jæti þig, ef ég sjæði þig." ('I would eat you if I saw you.')

1.1.1.6. In addition to the regular pret. subj. *slægj*- of *slá* 'strike', strong verb VI, there is a much less usual pret. subj. *slæð*-, with the dental suffix, attested in

(19) "Jón í Næfurholti og draugurinn" in Jónsson IX 1951: 45. var það og líka, að það lá við sjálft, að Jóni slæði fyrir brjóst af svælunni upp úr djöfsa. '... the choking smoke from the devil almost made Jón vomit.'

Jónsson IX 1951 is the ninth volume of a collection of folk tales. According to a note on p. 53 of the volume, the tale which contains the above quotation is edited from a manuscript of Bjarnhéðinn Jónsson járnsmiður. The manuscripts of this and two other tales also published in the aforementioned collection are kept in Landsbókasafn, Reykjavík, under nos. 2083 and 2084, both 8vo. The two manuscripts were written in 1905 and 1910, respectively, see Ólason 1927: 404. As concerns Bjarnhéðinn Jónsson, I know only that he lived in Reykjavík in the first quarter of the twentieth century.—The story takes place in Rangárvallasýsla, South Iceland.

Slæð- is also recorded in the grammatical literature; see (4), (7), (8), (10) above, and (20):

(20) Blöndal 1920—24: 748, s.v. 3. *slá.* [phonetic transcription of the preterite subjunctive:] slai:jı (pop. slai:ðı).

1.1.2. In section 1.1.1 six somewhat unusual preterite subjunctive forms have been presented: *dæð-, dræð-, hlæð-, læð-, sjæð-,* and *slæð-.* All six forms rhyme with each other, although their preterite indicatives and, still less, their non-preteritival forms do not necessarily do so. The strong verbs in whose paradigms these preterite subjunctives appear all belong to the fifth or the sixth class. Only *deyja* and *sjá* have known forms containing the dental suffix (pret. and past part. *deyð-,* and past part. *séð-*), but these have had nothing to do with the origin of the preterite subjunctives under discussion. In particular, there have been no relevant weak forms in the critical preterite indicative of the six verbs. It is because of this circumstance that these verbs have been chosen for treatment in the present paper. There would obviously be nothing strange about, say, *sjæð-* if there existed a pret. ind. *sjáð-.* In no case is the preterite subjunctive of the type *dæð-* the only preterite subjunctive of the verbs in question. In fact, the regular formations and those like *dæð-* even appear in the same texts.[4]

The reliability of the examples adduced can only be questioned in the case of pret. subj. *læð-,* because of the lack of examples and because the source of its only example is a subset of the sources of *dæð-* and *sjæð-.* With *dæð-, sjæð-,* and *slæð-* the sources are varied, relatively many, and, as will presently be seen, well defined in terms of their geographical

---

[4] See, for instance, Campe 1800. On the 192 pages of this translation, there are, 1 pret. ind. *dó-* (p. 71), 2 pret. ind. *deyð-* (pp. 151, 181), 1 pret. subj. *dæ-* (p. 100), 1 pret. subj. *dæð-* (p. 185), and 9 past part. *dá(i)n-.* (Spelling normalized here.)— Although similar statistical surveys were prepared for almost all sources of our quotations, only a few of these surveys were found to be of potential interest, and thus worthy of incorporation into the present paper.

distribution. With *drœð-*, *hlœð-*, and *lœð-* the sources are limited to the grammatical literature or to the OHÍ dialect file, relatively few, and on the whole of vague geographical distribution.

Subj. *dœð-* can be assumed to exist, or to have existed, in Borgarfjarðar-sýsla, cf. (1); in Rangárvallasýsla and Vestur-Skaftafellssýsla, cf. (3); in South Iceland in general, cf. (6), Helgason in (8), and (9); in Múlasýslur = East Iceland, cf. (4), (8), and (9). The geographical distribution of subj. *sjœð-* is similar to that of *dœð-*. *Sjœð-* can be assumed to exist, or to have existed, in Rangárvallasýsla, cf. (13); in Skaftafellssýslur, cf. (14) and (17); in Múlasýslur = East Iceland, cf. (4), (8), (15), (17), and (18); in East and South Iceland in general, cf. Helgason in (8). Subj. *slœð-* can be assumed to exist, or to have existed, in Rangárvallasýsla, cf. (19) (uncertain); in South Iceland in general, cf. Helgason in (8); in Múlasýslur = East Iceland, cf. (4) and (8). There are no indications in my references as to the geographical distribution of *drœð-*. The only pertinent information on *hlœð-* is in (4): Rask states that he has heard *hlœð-* in the East of Iceland. The geographical distribution of *lœð-* is given in negative terms only.

(11) expressly denies the existence of autochthonous *dœð-*, *lœð-*, and *sjœð-* in Kelduhverfi, Norður-Þingeyjarsýsla, North Iceland, and Helgason in (8) states that *dœð-*, *sjœð-*, and *slœð-* are not autochthonous in the North of Iceland in general.

Whatever positive and negative information there is on the geographical distribution of these preterite subjunctives points unanimously to the South and the East of Iceland. We are on this basis entitled to draw a morphological isogloss that separates South and East Iceland from the rest of the country. The exact course of the isogloss is still to be determined by field work and investigations of twentieth century dialect texts unaccounted for in the present paper. The preterite subjunctives under discussion are autochthonous at least as far to the North as the southernmost parts of Norður-Múlasýsla in the East, and at least as far to the West as Rangárvallasýsla in the South, and very probably beyond this district. On the other hand, the evidence presented in this paper is not sufficient to decide the question as to whether the spread, within the area indicated by the isogloss, of the preterite subjunctives treated here is the same or different for each given form.

That the preterite subjunctives of the type *dœð-* belong to the dialects is beyond doubt; they either do not appear in the literary texts, or typically appear in texts from times before the establishment of the modern literary norm, and in texts in which dialect forms are to be expected (folk tales, texts originally not intended for publication, etc.).[5] The grammatical literature stamps these forms as colloquial or dialect, cf. (4) to (12), (17), (18), (20); the normative grammar anathemizes them, cf. (5) and (10). Their dialect status is further corroborated by the circumstance that instances of them are recorded in the OHÍ dialect file.

No example of the preterite subjunctives of the type *dœð*- is older than the beginning of the nineteenth century, and all of them have been reported to exist in the twentieth century. Preterite subjunctives *drœð*- and *lœð*- may be younger than the rest of the forms; at any rate they are reported later.[6]

1.2. In 1.2.1 the preterite subjunctive forms *berð*- of *bera* 'carry' (1.2.1.1), *nemd*- of *nema* 'take, learn' (1.2.1.2), and *syngd*- of *syngja* 'sing' (1.2.1.3) are discussed. Subsection 1.2.2 contains a summary of the findings presented in 1.2.1.

1.2.1.1. Beside the regular pret. subj. *bœr*- of *bera* 'carry', strong verb IV, one instance of subj. *berð*-, with the vowel of the present stem and with the dental suffix, is recorded:

(21) "Tólfskildínga skattrinn, vestra" in the periodical *Þjóðólfr*, twelfth year, no. 10—11, 1860: 43. ekki heldr í amtsbrèfi því af 21. maí, er nokkrir

---

[5] At the beginning of the nineteenth century the Icelandic written norm was still in the making with the writers drawing upon the resources of the spoken language much more readily than is the case today. This accounts for (1). The text of (2), being a diary, was never meant for publication, and is hence less polished than printed work of the same period (i.e. the middle of the nineteenth century). Quotations (3), (14), and (15) are from a collection of folk tales; the original recordings of the tales were prepared by compilers who were instructed to make as faithful recordings as possible; some compilers were not necessarily well educated. (19) is from another collection of folk tales, not edited so as to fully conform to the literary norm. (13), appearing in a private letter to a friend, was not meant for publication; besides it is most probable that the author mimics the dialect of his acquaintance when he writes *sjœði*. As to quotation (16), from *Morgunblaðið*, Stefán Karlsson, to whom I am grateful for this information, has pointed out to me that Valtýr Stefánsson, who was the editor-in-chief of the newspaper in 1943, was nicknamed *fjólupabbi*, approx. = 'father of barbarisms', because of the many non-standard forms that he permitted to be printed in *Morgunblaðið*.

[6] The oldest and the most recent examples of *dœð*- are (1) and (11), respectively; of *drœð*-, (7) and (10), respectively; of *hlœð*-, (4) and (12), respectively; of *sjœð*-, (4) and (11), respectively; of *slœð*-, (4) and (10), respectively. Subj. *lœð*- is only recorded in the twentieth century, and Rask explicitly denies its existence at the beginning of the nineteenth century, see (4).

amtsbúar berðu út sem laga ástæðu fyrir kröfunni. 'not even in the letter from the administrative authorities of the *amt* of May 21, which [letter] some inhabitants of the *amt* are disseminating as a lawful reason for the claim.'

My thanks are due to Ásgeir Blöndal Magnússon and Jakob Benediktsson of the OHÍ, who in 1966 kindly identified for me *berðu* of this quotation as a preterite subjunctive form of *bera* (*bera út* = 'deliver, disseminate, distribute'). Ásgeir Blöndal Magnússon has also provided me with a translation of the quotation.—The quotation is taken from a newspaper article dated on Nov. 8, 1859, and written by Indriði hreppstjóri Gíslason, varaþingmaður, from Vestfirðir. The article is about conditions in North-West Iceland.

1.2.1.2. One of the preterite subjunctives of *nema* 'take, learn', strong verb IV,[7] is, or was, *nemd-*, with the vowel of the present stem and with the dental suffix. Here follows my complete list of examples of *nemd-*. (22) "Prestastefnusamþykt Odds biskups Einarssonar og klerka hans á Alþingi við Öxará 1592" in *Alþingisbækur* 1915: 266. þa villdum vier ad þad skyllde vera þeirra not. þo nockrum peningum nemde. '... although it cost some money.'

According to *Alþingisbækur* 1915: 264, the original "Prestastefnusamþykt" of 1592 is not preserved, although three later copies of it are: the manuscripts Landsbókasafn 1319, 4to and MSteph. 47, 4to were written about 1650: Landsbókasafn 68, 4to is a concise version ('ágrip') from about 1690; The hand of the two manuscripts from about 1650 is the hand of Halldór Guðmundsson, from Eyjafjarðarsýsla, North Iceland, see Stefán Karlsson in Bibliotheca arnamagnæana vol. XXX, 1970, pp. 83 ff. The

---

[7] *Nema* has undergone a number of morphological changes in the post-Reformation period. Its history is further complicated by the fact that its paradigm may have been at least to some extent modified according to its various meanings. A separate investigation into this problem is still a desideratum. Another desideratum is an investigation into which forms of *nema,* in what meanings and idioms, are still in colloquial use nowadays. However, for the purposes of the present discussion it suffices to present a survey of the preterite forms in the files of the OHÍ: 31 exx. of sg. pret. ind. *nam-,* from all post-Reformation centuries; 3 pret. pl. ind. *nám-,* from the second half of the nineteenth and from the twentieth century; 21 pl. pret. ind. *num-* from all post-Reformation centuries; 33 pret. ind. *numd-,* from all post-Reformation centuries; 3 exx. of pret. ind. *namd-,* one of these in the dialect file (1 ex. from the second half of the eighteenth century, 1 from the nineteenth century, and 1 from modern dialect. All 3 exx. in the idiom *nema af hljóði/veini* 'stop crying/screaming'); 2 pret. subj. *næm-,* one from the second half of the nineteenth century, one from the twentieth century; 6 pret. subj. *nymd-,* all from the nineteenth century; 11 pret. subj. *nemd-,* see below.

basic source of the above quotation is 1319, with variants from the other two manuscripts noted in the footnotes. The punctuation of the quotation is that of 1319. There is one variant: *þeirra not* of 1319 is *not kyrknanna* in 47.

In all probability the document from which the above quotation is taken was composed by the energetic bishop Oddur Einarsson mentioned in the title of the document. See Helgason bishop 1927: 121 ff. Bishop Oddur (1559—1630) was born and lived in the North of Iceland till 1588, except when he was a student at the University of Copenhagen. In 1592, the year of the above document, he had been the bishop of Skálholt and living in South Iceland for only three years. Since there is strong independent evidence, to be adduced below, that *nemd-* is a Northern form, the natural explanation of its appearance in a text of Southern origin is that the text had been written by a Northern man living in the South. Bishop Oddur is an obvious candidate.

(23) Arndt 1731: L 1 recto. Þess hærra sem soddann eirn Madur klifrar, þess diupara hlytur hann nidur adsteipast. Og þo ad Høfuded a soddan einum nemde vid Skyenn, ja, hanns Hæd næde allt upp til Himna, þa forgeingur hann þo med þad sijdsta sem Skarn. '... And even if such a person's head reached to the clouds, ...'

The work from which this quotation is taken is an Icelandic version of a German work by J. Arndt. The translator, Þorleifur Árnason (1630—1713), used a Danish translation of the German work, as he explicitly points out in his introduction to the translation. He spent the first 25 years of his life in North Iceland, and during his mature years lived in Austur-Skaftafellssýsla, South-East Iceland, see ÍslÆv 5: 172—73. The translation was published posthumously.

(24) "Annáll Þorláks stúdents Markússonar í Gröf á Höfðaströnd og síðar á Sjávarborg eða Sjávarborgarannáll" in *Annálar* IV 1940—48: 324. Varð hvorki því né öðru bjargað það munum nemdi, þar loginn lék svo geysilega um alt húsið í einu. 'Neither the former nor the latter were rescued to any significant extent ...'

This quotation is from Þorlákur Markússon's annals, the entry for A. D. 1709. On Þorlákur Markússon (ca. 1692—1736), see ÍslÆv 5: 164, and the introduction, by Jón Jóhannesson, to his "Annáll". Þorlákur spent all his life in North Iceland. His annals are preserved in Landsbókasafn 290, fol., mostly in his own handwriting.

(25) Milton 1828: 239. Eigi svo vanvirðt / hún væri þó, / eðr almenn gjörð, / ef í sèr hefðu / not hennar nokkut, / sem nemdi því, / eða verðt væri, / at við þat yrði / sál ok sinni manns / sært ok þvingat. 'It would not be disregarded, or made common, if there were anything in its use that would be so important, or would be of such worth, that the human

soul and mind should be affected [literally: wounded] and oppressed by it.'[8]

This quotation is taken from the poet Jón Þorláksson's Icelandic translation of Milton's *Paradise Lost*. On Jón Þorláksson (1744—1819), see ÍslÆv 3: 316—17. He lived in West Iceland (Dalasýsla and to the North of it) till 1778, whereupon he moved to Eyjafjarðarsýsla, North Iceland, where he translated *Paradise Lost*.[9]

(26) *Ármann* 1829: 41—42. þegar vinnumennirnir heyrdu það, settu þeir upp spekíngs svip, og søgdu ad mikill heimskíngi væri eg ad vilja fara ad selja saudinn, það nemdi svo engu, sem eg fengi fyrir hann. '... what I would get for it would amount to nothing.'

It is expressly stated in the preface to the annual volume from which the quotation is taken that practically the whole volume had been written by Balduin Einarsson, one of the two editors. (An exception to this is Eggert Ólafsson's "Búnaðarbálkur", reprinted in *Ármann* 1829.) Balduin (Baldvin) Einarsson (1801—1833) spent most of his adolescent life in South Iceland, and lived afterwards in Copenhagen, see ÍslÆv 1: 111.

(27) *Frèttir* 1840: 31. Á umliðnu vori ætluðu 2 eða 3 kaupmenn að semja við hið almenna brunabótafèlag, um að taka að sèr ábyrgð á varnaði og öðrum munum, er nemdi hèrumbil 100,000 ríkisdala virði. '... which would amount to a value of about 100,000 rix-dollars.'

Frèttir contains the proceedings of a series of meetings. The names of the recorder(s) and of the editor(s) are not stated in the publication.

(28) *Tiðindi* 1842: 68. Líksaungseyrir virðtist sanngjarnlegt að meta 6 álnum; þó skyldi eingva borgun greiða fyrir líksaung yfir hreppslimum, ef dánarbú þeirra ekki nemdi meiru enn svaraði skuld þeirra til fátækra sjóðsins. '... if the estates of the deceased did not amount to more than ...'

---

[8] The 'it' (twice) and 'its' of this translation are anaphoric for what is in the English original referred to as 'the sense of touch whereby mankind is propagated'. The corresponding lines of the English original, viii, 582—85: ...; which would not be/ To them made common and divulg'd, if aught / Therein enjoy'd were worthy to subdue / The soul of Man, or passion in him move. —Here 'which' and the 'it' of 'therein' = 'in it' refer to 'the sense of touch whereby mankind is propagated', and 'them' is anaphoric for 'Cattle and each Beast'.

[9] On pages 1—408 of the translation (including the footnotes, which were almost without exception prepared by the translator himself, see the preface to the book) I have found the following instances of non-present forms of *nema*: 13 pret. ind. sg. *nam-* (pp. 25, 34, 56, 70, 90, 93, 104, 115, 123, 136, 234, 304, 348), 1 pret. ind. pl. *nám-* (p. 17), 1 pret. ind. pl. *num-* (p. 112), 1 pret. ind. pl. *numd-* (p. 381), 1 pret. subj. *nemd-* (p. 239), and 18 past part. *numin-, numd-*.

Tíðindi 1842 contains the proceedings of a series of meetings, parliamentary in character; a number of the speakers' statements are recorded in addition to the recorder's own account, and it is in most cases not clear whether the recorder is paraphrasing the actual statements, or presenting a verbatim report of them. On the recorder, Kristján Kristjánsson (1806—1882), see ÍslÆv 3: 378. Before 1840, the only period of his life of interest here, Kristján Kristjánsson had lived in North Iceland (in the districts of Suður-Þingeyjarsýsla and Eyjafjarðarsýsla), except that he attended the the Bessastaðaskóli in the South and spent some time in Copenhagen.

(29) Grímsson 1925: 138. Að eg sé hér frá inn til fullra 20 ára úthlaups, ef svo lengi lifi, frí við að gjalda kongstíund, skatt, þó þeim fjárhlut næði, er honum nemdi, gjaftoll og lögmannstoll, en greiði jafnan árlega svokallaðan sakamálskostnað, eða þá peninga, sem undir því nafni alþjóðlega eptir tiltölu gjaldast þurfa. '... so much property as it amounted to ...'

This passage is from a letter by Guðmundur Guðmundsson 'læknir', whose life is discussed in Grímsson 1925. The letter, dated on August 2, 1843, is a legal document addressed to Eggert O. Briem. Its original is preserved. As stated in Grímsson 1925, Guðmundur Guðmundsson spent most of his life in North Iceland.

(30) *Norðri* 1855: 32. rjeði því það af, að skipta skuldabrjefum mínum í 15 staði, þannig, að hver þeirra nemdi 1000 fraunkum og sagði við sjálfan mig. '... so that each of these amounted to 1,000 franks, ...'

This quotation is taken from a short note under the heading of "Smásögur", published in the Northern periodical *Norðri*. The note is obviously translated from a foreign language; the translator's name is not given.

(31) "Sparnaðarsjóðir" in *Norðanfari* 1866: 31. af menn ættu kost á að koma því á óhultann geymslu- og leigustað, er þeir gætu dregið til muna af daglaunum sínum eða kaupi, og fengið svo upphæð þessa, hvort hún nemdi litlu eða miklu út aptur þegar þeir vildu. '... without regard to whether the amount were small or large ...'—Ibidem: Hver /.../ þyrfti að /.../ fá /.../ leigu /.../ fyrir það hann leigði inní sjóðinn, hvort það nemdi 1 eða fleirum dölum. '... no matter whether the amount were equal to one or more *dalir*.'

Both quotations are found in the same unsigned editorial in the Northern periodical *Norðanfari*.

(32) "Úr Dakota í Vesturheimi" in *Norðanfari* 1881: 69. Mikið er þessi flækingur okkar landa hjer hörmulegur yfir öll þessi ár, og óskandi að hjer nemdi nú staðar, enda lítur út fyrir, að nýlenda þessi verði töluvert stór og mannmörg innan fárra ára. '... it would be desirable that it stopped now, ...'

The quotation is from an unsigned letter published in *Norðanfari*.

While subj. *nemd-* is not recorded in the OHÍ dialect file, it is once discussed in the grammatical literature:
(33) Jón Magnússon, "Grammatica Islandica" in Jónsson 1933: 105. [in preterite subjunctive] u. in y., ut kynne, ynne, ynnte, ylle. Excipe numdum, qvod facit nemde. '... Make exception for *numdum*, which becomes *nemde*.'—Ibidem, p. 109: Nem in Præterito Subjunctivi facit nemde. '*Nem* becomes *nemde* in the preterite subjunctive.'

Jón Magnússon (1662—1738) wrote his "Grammatica Islandica" between 1733 and 1738, see Jónsson 1933: 11—14. Finnur Jónsson characterizes Jón Magnússon's linguistic background as follows: "The author's language contains many 'Vestfirðir'-elements, which is natural in view of the fact that he was born and reared in West Iceland." The author spent his youth in Dalasýsla, which is immediately South of Vestfirðir, and most of his adult life in the North-West or not very far from it; see ÍsL/Ev 3: 219—20.[10]

1.2.1.3. Beside the regular pret. subj. *syngj-* of *syngja* 'sing', strong verb III, there is one instance of pret. subj. *syngd-*, with the dental suffix:
(34) Holberg 1948: 60. Einusinne sagða eg þeim, at vjer beiddumst optsinnis fyrer, og jafnvel í voru hússerfiðe og handverkum, og sýngdum andlig ljóð og psálma. '... and sang spiritual songs and psalms.'—Ibidem, p. 307: (Jón Helgason's comment) *syngja,* þát. vth. *sýngdum* (!) 60[31]. '*syngja,* pret. subj. *sýngdum* (!) 60[31].'

The first of these quotations is from Jón Ólafsson's eighteenth century Icelandic translation of a German work by L. Holberg. Jón Ólafsson (1705—1779), on whom see ÍsL/Ev 3: 238—39, was born in Vestfirðir, North-West Iceland, grew up there and in Skagafjarðarsýsla, North Iceland, left for Copenhagen in 1726, and lived there to his death; his only long stay in Iceland after 1726 was from 1743 to 1751, during which time he, living in Húnavatnssýsla and Suður-Þingeyjarsýsla, both North Iceland, translated *Nikulás Klím* from German making some limited use of the Danish translation as well. See Holberg 1948:xi.

---

[10] The complete list of the non-present forms of *nema* in "Grammatica Islandica" is as follows: 3 pret. ind. sg. *nam* (pp. 99, 101 twice), 4 pret. ind. *numde, numdum* (pp. 100, 101, 105 twice), 1 pret. pl. ind. *nämum* (p. 103), 2 pret. subj. *nemde* (pp. 105, 109), 1 past part. *numinn* (p. 126). To these 11 examples we can add 5 that are implied: sg. pret. ind. *nam* on p. 110, pl. pret. ind. *nämum* on pp. 101 and 110, pret. subj. *næmum* on pp. 103 and 110. The only semantic information given is the gloss 'capio' to *nem* on p. 110.

1.2.2. In section 1.2.1 three preterite subjunctive forms, *berð-*, *nemd-*, and *syngd-*, have been added to the six of section 1.1.1. While *bera* and *syngja* have never known any weak forms in their paradigms, *nema* can boast several: pret. *numd-*, *namd-*, and past part. *numin-*, contracted cases *numd-*. Of these only *namd-* could theoretically be considered as a source of the pret. subj. *nemd-*, but has to be discarded for the following reasons. Subj. *nemd-* appears as early as the sixteenth century, ind. *namd-* only in the second half of the eighteenth century. In view of the fact that preterite indicatives tend to be more frequent in the texts than their respective preterite subjunctives, we would expect more, and earlier, examples of ind. *namd-* than of subj. *nemd-*. However, as is pointed out in fn. 7, there are 11 instances of subj. *nemd-* in the files of the OHÍ, and only 3 of ind. *namd-*. Compare this to the opposite situation with the pair of ind. *numd-*, subj. *nymd-*: there are 33 examples of ind. *numd-* from all post-Reformation centuries in the files of the OHÍ, as against 6 examples of subj. *nymd-*, all from the nineteenth century. There is also a considerable semantic discrepancy between ind. *namd-* and subj. *nemd-*: the former appears only in the idiom *nema af hljóði/veini*, the latter is never found in this idiom, although it is once found used in the possibly semantically related *nema staðar* 'come to a halt', see (32).[11] The conclusion is that the preterite subjunctives *berð-*, *nemd-*, and *syngd-* are not correlated with any weak preterite indicatives, and therefore are qualified for treatment in the present paper.

The reliability of the examples adduced cannot be questioned, although it would be difficult to draw any very serious conclusions on the basis of just one instance of *berð-* and *syngd-*.

While *berð-* is known from the nineteenth century only, and *syngd-* from the eighteenth century only, the oldest example of *nemd-* is from 1592, preserved in manuscripts dating from the middle of the seventeenth century, see (22). The most recent instance of *nemd-* given above is from 1881, see (32). I know of no examples of *berð-*, *nemd-*, and *syngd-* from the twentieth century.

Geographically, *berð-* is a North-Western, and *syngd-* a Northern, form. The oldest examples of *nemd-*, (22) and (23), cannot be located to the North with absolute certainty. We have no relevant data on (26) and (27). All the other texts containing *nemd-*, however, point to North Iceland,

---

[11] There is a clear preponderance of the examples of *nemd-* meaning 'amount to', 'be equivalent to', 'be of such and such importance', and the like. Exceptions: *nema staðar* of (32), and *nema við skýin* of (23).

possibly with North-West as the focal point, thus roughly to those regions complementary to the geographical area assumed in 1.1.2 to be the home of the preterite subjunctives of 1.1.1.

There is no indication of *berð-*, *nemd-*, and *syngd-* being considered dialectal forms avoided in the written language, except that we are free to consider the aforementioned geographical distribution as indicating dialect. Of the texts quoted in 1.2.1 only the legal document (29) was not intended for the wider public according to the standards of its time.

1.3. Here follows a list of the differences and the similarities—some more, some less relevant—between the preterite subjunctive forms treated in 1.1.1 and those discussed in 1.2.1.

The differences: (a) *Berð-*, *nemd-*, and *syngd-* are older than the type *dœð-*, known only from the nineteenth and twentieth centuries. On the other hand, I know of no examples of *berð-*, *nemd-*, and *syngd-* from the twentieth century. (b) While *berð-*, *nemd-*, and *syngd-* are dialectal forms only in the sense of having limited geographical distribution within Iceland, the type *dœð-* is dialectal in the stylistical sense as well. (In the nineteenth century, *nemd-* [*syngd-* was probably non-existent then, and I dare not say anything about *berð-* in this connection] must have been felt as provincial, and the type *dœð-* as true dialect.) (c) While *berð-*, *nemd-*, and *syngd-* are Northern forms, the type *dœð-* is Southern and Eastern. (d) *Berð-*, *nemd-*, and *syngd-* do not rhyme either with each other or with the forms of the type *dœð-*, which rhyme among themselves.

The similarities: (a) All preterite subjunctives treated here are found only marginally in the modern literary language. (b) All of them belong to such strong verbs which either have never had any weak forms, or have had weak forms that could not possibly be the synchronic or the diachronic source of the preterite subjunctives under discussion here.

1.4. There are some indications that other preterite subjunctives of the type discussed above have existed, but there is no way of proving it, because the corresponding weak preterite indicatives have been in existence since the same time as the weak preterite subjunctives. Consider just one example: *hefja* 'lift', strong verb VI. Jón Magnússon in Jónsson 1933: 115 gives the complete paradigm of this verb in the following way (spelling normalized here): pres. *hefj-*, pret. ind. *hóf-*, pret. subj. *hefð-*. The point about ind. *hóf-* vs. subj. *hefð-* is repeated on p. 104. The editor of Jón Magnússon's grammar, Finnur Jónsson, adds the following note (his note 146, p. 139): "It is almost incomprehensible that the author adduces *hefði* as the subjunctive of *hóf*." The reason why *hefja* has not been discussed above is that there is also a complete weak paradigm of this verb, with pret. ind. *hafð-*. In fact, Jón Magnússon mentions this himself on p. 107, stating that "hef (elevo)" is inflected like *seðja* (*saddi*). If subj. *hefð-* is, from the diachronic point of view, not derived from the weak preterite indicative *hafð-*, it probably originally belonged to the same type of preterite subjunctives as *berð-*, *nemd-*, and *syngd-*.

2. Here an attempt will be made at placing the preterite subjunctives treated in section 1 above into the broader context of the Modern Icelandic preterite subjunctive in general. In 2.1 the ways of forming the Icelandic preterite subjunctive are investigated. In 2.2 the same matter is studied from the standpoint of the preterite subjunctives discussed in section 1. A summary of the findings is presented in 2.3.[12]

---

[12] A part of the discussion of section 2 is in the framework of the so-called 'generative phonology'. For those readers unfamiliar with this approach, I would like to point out that the generative phonology is exclusively concerned with descriptive, not historical, grammar. This means that what are below referred to as 'rules', 'derivations', 'phonological representations', 'orderings of rules', 'applications of rules', etc. are formal devices designed to describe the regularities of a language at a given point of time. For practical reasons some of the rules formulated below bear mnemonic names reminiscent of the corresponding phenomena in the historical grammar of Icelandic. For instance, there is an i-umlaut rule. With this name I am below not referring to the phonetic change(s) that took place in the Scandinavian languages many centuries ago. I am just describing certain vocalic alternations as they exist in the modern language, and subsume them under the easy-to-remember name of i-umlaut, because the historical i-umlaut happens to be the main source of these alternations. Similarly, the rule orderings postulated in the derivations of phonetic forms from phonological representations do not necessarily reflect the chronological order in which the roughly corresponding historical processes took place.

The phonological representations are bounded by the obliques, //, with the pluses in the representations acting as morpheme boundaries. However, since the phonological representations commit the author on many points of Icelandic phonology which have been so far inadequately studied (a prominent example of this being the underlying vowel inventory), their use has been avoided as much as possible, in favor of the more informal italicized orthographic representations.

A note on unstressed [i]. In orthographic representations it is invariably spelled *i*. In the phonological representations, however, /i/ is used when the i-umlauting vowel is meant, and /e/ when the vowel is not i-umlauting. (On the term 'i-umlauting' see 2.1.1.) Both unstressed /i/ and unstressed /e/ are [i] on the phonetic level. See Anderson 1969.

2.1. It will be shown that there are two ways of forming the preterite subjunctive in Modern Icelandic. The 'preteritival' formations are discussed in 2.1.1. The 'present stem' formations are described in 2.1.2. In 2.1.3 some evidence is adduced in favor of the existence of 'present stem' formations. Their origin (in the diachronic sense of the word) is studied in 2.1.4.

2.1.1. We will say that a given preterite subjunctive is a 'preteritival' formation if it is formed according to rule (35):

RULE (35). Take the preterite indicative stem of the verb, and add to it one of the i-umlauting preterite subjunctive personal endings, sg. 1.3. -*i*, 2. -*ir*, pl. 1. -*um*, 2. -*uð*, 3. -*u*; middle voice, sg. -*ist*, pl. 1. -*umst* or -*ustum*, 2. -*uzt*, 3. -*ust*.

Notes to rule (35): (1) In the present paper, 'X i-umlauts Y', implied in the adjective 'i-umlauting' of rule (35), means, 'X co-occurs with the i-umlauted Y immediately after the application of the i-umlaut rule, if the structural description of the i-umlaut rule is satisfied at the time when this rule applies.' (2) If a verb has two preterite indicative stems, as is the case with many strong verbs, choose the one that is used with those preterite indicative personal endings beginning with a vowel. See Orešnik 1966—68. (3) In the case of the strong verbs whose root ends in a velar consonant (spelled *k*, *g*), the velar is invariably palatalized in preterite subjunctive, even if an *u* follows it. The palatalized velar is spelled *kj*, *gj* before non-front vowels. Cf. *taka* 'take', strong verb VI: pret. subj. sg. 1.3. *tœki*, 2. *tœkir*, pl. 1. *tœkjum*, 2. *tœkjuð*, 3. *tœkju*. This question, interesting from the standpoint of both the diachronic and the synchronic grammar, is discussed in Orešnik (forthcoming).

Examples of 'preteritival' formations: *biðja* 'ask', strong verb V, prevocalic preterite indicative stem *báð*-, pret. subj., e.g., *báð*- + i-umlauting -*i* > *bœði*; *kunna* 'know how to', preterite-present verb, preterite indicative stem *kunn*-, pret. subj., e.g., *kunn*- + i-umlauting -*um* > *kynnum*; *þykja* 'seem', irregular weak verb, preterite indicative stem *þótt*-, pret. subj., e.g., *þótt*- + i-umlauting -*u* > *þœttu*.

A 'preteritival' formation is so called here because the basic form from which it is formed by aid of rule (35) is the preterite indicative stem of the verb in question. The existence of 'preteritival' formations has always been recognized in Icelandic grammar, and in fact most relevant handbooks imply that all Icelandic preterite subjunctives are 'preteritival' formations. See Guðmundsson 1922: 117, 158—59 (implied); Einarsson 1949: 94; Halldórsson 1950: 166, 168; Kress 1963: 178—79. This, however, is not the view taken in the present paper. Here only those preterite sub-junctives are considered to be 'preteritival' formations which are parts of verbal paradigms that lack the simple morphological relation between the present and preterite stems observed in the regular weak verbs.[13] The following two sets of verbs lack this morphological relation: (1) The ablauting verbs, i.e. the strong verbs, the preterite-present verbs, and verbs with ablauting or quasi-ablauting weak preterites. For the examples, see *biðja, kunna,* and *þykja* above. Of these, *þykja* has a quasi-ablauting root vowel. A true-ablauting weak preterite is found in e.g. *þiggja* 'accept', also strong verb V, pret. ind. *þáð-,* pret. subj. *þæð-.* (2) The non-ablauting verbs in which the pre-dental and/or the dental suffixes are not distri-buted in accordance with the formal characteristics of the present tense stem. Example: *meina* 'mean', present stem *meina-* (cf. *hann meinar*), preterite indicative stem usually *meint-,* not *meinað-,* as expected on the basis of the present stem *meina-.* Preterite subjunctive is a 'preteritival' formation, *meint-.*

The root vowel of a 'preteritival' formation is invariably i-umlauted if the root vowel is umlautable and the predesinential part of the formation is monosyllabic.

2.1.2. We will say that a given preterite subjunctive is a 'present stem' formation if it is formed according to rule (37):

RULE (37). Take the present stem of the verb, and add to it the dental suffix and one of the i-umlauting preterite subjunctive personal endings.—For the inventory of the endings, see 2.1.1 above.

A 'present stem' formation is so called here because the basic form from which it is formed by aid of rule (37) is the present stem of the verb in question. The present stem consists of the verbal root, sometimes followed by a derivational suffix and/or a present suffix.[14] The examples in (38) are representative of the four classes of the regular weak verbs.

---

[13] This morphological relation exists if the preterite indicative stem can be con-ceived as formed from the present stem by rule (36):

RULE (36). Take the present stem of the verb, and fill the slot of the present suffix with the dental suffix, thus replacing the present suffix, if there is one, in the process.

Examples. *Kalla* 'call', present stem /kall + a/, no present suffix, preterite in-dicative stem /kall + a + ð/. *Krefja* 'request', present stem /krav + j/, present suffix /j/, preterite indicative stem /krav + ð/. *Færa* 'bring, move', present stem /fǣr + e/, present suffix /e/, preterite indicative stem /fǣr + ð/. *Blasa* 'lie open be-fore the eyes', present stem /blas + e/, present suffix /e/, preterite indicative stem /blas + ð/. On the suffixes of the weak verbs, see 2.1.2.

(38)	present stem		
	verbal root	derivational suffix	present suffix
kalla 'call'	/kall/	/a/	—
krefja 'request'	/krav/	—	/j/
fœra 'bring, move'	/fǣr/	—	/e/
blasa 'lie open'	/blas/	—	/e/

We have to recognize the existence of the following morphonological rules:

RULE (39). An 'elidible' unstressed vowel is elided if it is followed by one consonant and another vowel, with optional segments following this consonant and vowel.

Under what conditions a vowel is 'elidible', remains unclear. Benediktsson 1969: 394 suggests that a necessary (but certainly not sufficient) condition imposed on 'elidible' vowels is that they are immediately followed by *l*, or *r*, or *n*. This condition is too strong. Cf. dat. sg. *höfði* of *höfuð* 'head', with *u* elided before *ð*.—Rule (39) applies, e.g., in *farnir* from /far + en + er/, nom. pl. masc. of *farinn*, past participle of *fara* 'go, travel'.[15]

RULE (40). The glides /j/ and /w/ are elided if preceded by a consonant and followed by at least a consonant or a word boundary (#).

This is a part of Benediktsson's (1969: 394) rule stated in his footnote 3. Two of his implied examples are *nið*, acc. sg. of *niður* 'descendant', from /niðj # / and *söngur* nom. sg. 'song', from /söngw + r/. (The epenthetic *u* of the latter example is generated by another rule after the elision of /w/ before /r/.)—The few exceptions to this rule constitute a clearcut subregularity: they are verbal nouns derived from verbs whose roots end in a /j/ or /w/, and are followed by the derivational suffix /a/. Cf. *grenj*, verbal noun of *grenja* (pret. *grenjaði*) 'wail, scream'; *bölv*, verbal noun of *bölva* 'curse'.

RULE (41) = the i-umlaut rule. In spite of the insights of Valfells 1967 and Anderson 1969, the structural change of this rule remains unclear. Fortunately, we need here only consider a part of the structural description of the rule. A stressed vowel is i-umlauted if it is followed by an i-

[14] The present suffixes are a property of the present stem. The derivational suffixes are found throughout the verbal paradigm. The suffix /j/ is i-umlauting.

[15] Rule (39) does not cover the deletion of unstressed vowel immediately followed by another unstressed vowel. It is not yet clear to me whether rule (39) and the rule that would perform the vowel truncation just described can be collapsed.

umlauting segment (segments), with one or more optional consonants, but no vowels, intervening between the vowel to be umlauted and the umlauting segment(s).—The endings of the preterite subjunctive are i-umlauting. When no vowel intervenes between these endings and an umlautable vowel of the verbal root, the root vowel is umlauted. Example: pret. subj. *kallaði* of *kalla* 'call', without the i-umlaut of the root vowel in *kall-*, as against *feldi*, preterite subjunctive of *fela* 'hide, entrust', cf. pret. ind. *faldi*.[16]

Examples of 'present stem' formations: *kalla* 'call', weak verb, present stem /kall + a/, pret. subj. /kall + a/ + dental suffix /ð/ + i-umlauting preterite subjunctive personal endings, e.g., /kall + a + ð + i/ > *kallaði*: no i-umlaut is evident in /kall/, because a vowel intervenes between /kall/ and the i-umlauting segment /i/, so that the structural description of the i-umlaut rule (41) is not satisfied. The derivational suffix /a/ is not 'elidible'.—*Krefja* 'request', weak verb, present stem /krav + j/, pret. subj., e.g., /krav + j + ð/ + i-umlauting /uð/ > *krefðuð*. Here it cannot be determined from the phonetic representation whether the i-umlaut of the root vowel is due to the present suffix /j/ or to the i-umlauting ending /uð/. The suffix /j/ disappears by the j/w-rule (40).—*Færa* 'bring, move', weak verb, present stem /fǣr + e/ (where the /e/ is 'elidible'), pret. subj., e.g., /fǣr + e + ð/ + i-umlauting /ir/ > *færðir*. The present suffix /e/ is elided by rule (39).—*Blasa* 'lie open before the eyes', weak verb, present stem /blas + e/ (where /e/ is 'elidible'), pret. subj., e.g., /blas + e + ð + i/ > *blasti*. The ending /i/ cannot i-umlaut the root vowel because of the intervening vocalic present suffix /e/. The latter is later elided by rule (39), and still later rules assimilate /sð/ to render the surface string *st*.

To ensure the correct phonetic results in these examples, it is here suggested that the i-umlaut rule (41) precede the elision rule (39). A large class of examples which require this ordering is constituted by the preterite subjunctives of the *lifa* verbs. See the discussion of *blasa* above. (The inventory of the *lifa* verbs is studied in 2.1.3.1.) The claim about this ordering cannot be substantiated, or disproved, by another homogeneous class of examples: no comparable class seems to exist if the search for it is limited to the field of flectional paradigms. However, there is at least one, lexicalized, exception to the postulated ordering (Anderson 1969): *ketill* masc. 'kettle', contracted cases *katl-*, where the elision rule (39) must

---

[16] Rule (41) does not cover the umlaut of *e* to *i* (e.g. in *biðja* 'ask'). In my opinion a separate rule is needed in the descriptive grammar of Icelandic to account for this phenomenon.

precede the i-umlaut rule (41), otherwise we would expect *ketl-* in the contracted cases. As long as such exceptional cases are non-systematic, they cannot be used as counterexamples with respect to the ordering postulated here.

Looking now at the 'preteritival' and the 'present stem' formations together, we can say that the grammar proceeds in the following way when it generates the preterite subjunctive forms. It first compares the present stem to the corresponding preterite indicative stem(s), and measures the complexity of the morphological relation between them. Suppose it finds that the relation is of the simple kind characteristic of the regular weak verbs. In such a case the grammar decides that the corresponding preterite subjunctive be a 'present stem' formation. In all the other cases the preterite subjunctive is a 'preteritival' formation.

We have shown that it is possible to account for the morphology of the Modern Icelandic preterite subjunctives with the assumption that some of them are 'preteritival', and others 'present stem', formations. As already pointed out, the grammarians have always operated with 'preteritival' formations only. The evidence in favor of the 'present stem' formations will be adduced in 2.1.3.

2.1.3. A case in favor of the existence of the 'present stem' formations can be made using the following evidence: (1) the origin of the preterite subjunctives like those studied in section 1; (2) the peculiarities of the preterite subjunctives of the regular weak verbs of the type *lifa;* and (3) the peculiarities of the preterite subjunctive of the irregular weak verb *sœkja.*—Point (1) is discussed in 2.2. Points (2) and (3) are studied in 2.1.3.1 and 2.1.3.2, respectively.

2.1.3.1. Most preterite subjunctives of the *lifa* type lack the i-umlaut even if their root vowel is umlautable. (Recall that the preterite subjunctive of *blasa* 'lie open', is *blasti*, not *blesti*.) This fact is recognized in the grammars of Modern Icelandic. See Guðmundsson 1922: 132, 158; Einarsson 1949: 87; Kress 1963: 179. The details, however, are unclear. There is no exhaustive list of the Modern Icelandic *lifa* verbs, although partial lists are given in the three grammars just referred to. There is considerable fluctuation in the paradigms of some of the verbs, and such fluctuation is not recorded consistently; when it is, there is little or no information on the regional distribution, stylistic value, or semantic differentiation of the alternative paradigms. The most extensive list of the Modern Icelandic *lifa* verbs is in Guðmundsson 1922: 145—50, which work lists 104 *lifa* verbs, as opposed to 93 *krefja* verbs, and several hundreds of *færa* and *kalla* verbs, respectively. (Not all verbs have been correctly classified.)

The existing partial lists of *lifa* verbs do not give exhaustive information on the i-umlaut in the preterite subjunctive. The most complete information on this question is to be found in Einarsson 1949: 87—89, although Einarsson's data is unfortunately not always reliable or consistent. In view of this, a field investigation of the morphology and membership of the *lifa* class is a desideratum.

According to the traditional view, which is nowhere explicitly stated to the best of my knowledge, those preterite subjunctives of the *lifa* type without the i-umlaut of the umlautable root vowel are exceptions to the rule that generates the 'preteritival' formations, i.e., to rule (35). The only regular preterite subjunctives of the *lifa* type are those with the i-umlaut of the umlautable root vowel. Consequently the number of exceptions to rule (35) is much greater than the number of regular preterite subjunctives formed by this rule. I estimate the number of verbs which would have to be considered exceptional in the sense under discussion to be over one hundred, and I suspect that this is a very low estimate; but even with this low estimate the exceptions outnumber of whole— true enough, the smallest—class of regular weak verbs, that of *krefja*. The regular cases, on the other hand, could be given in the form of a list of 20—30 verbs.

Quite the opposite situation obtains when one takes the view advocated in the present paper. Almost all umlautless preterite subjunctives of the *lifa* type become regular formations according to rule (37); of the preterite subjunctives of the *lifa* type with the i-umlaut of the root vowel some are regular, and some exceptions. A list of exceptions and quasi-exceptions will now be extracted from Einarsson 1949: 87—89, and from the results of a poll which I conducted in Iceland in the summer of 1966 using a questionnaire containing sixty *lifa* verbs.[17]

[17] The questionnaire was submitted to the following persons: Árni Böðvarsson, editor of *Íslenzk orðabók* 1963, Ásgeir Blöndal Magnússon of the OHÍ, Halldór Halldórsson and Hreinn Benediktsson, professors at the University of Iceland, Jón Aðalsteinn Jónsson of the OHÍ, Ólafur Halldórsson of the Handritastofnun Íslands, Stefán Karlsson, then of the Arnamagnæan Institute in Copenhagen, and Svavar Sigmundsson, then student at the University of Iceland. These informants, to whom I am grateful for their knowledge, time, and energy generously expended in answering the questionnaire, were asked to mark the non-obsolete verbs in the list, and to add the following forms to their infinitives: third p. sg. pres. ind., third p. sg. pret. ind., third p. sg. pret. subj., and the supine. In responding, one of the

(a) Seven *lifa* verbs have, at least alternatively, preterite subjunctives that are 'preteritival' formations: *duga* 'help, avail', when its present is *dugi-*, its preterite indicative *dugð-*, and its preterite subjunctive *dygð-*; *lafa* 'hang, dangle', when its preterite subjunctive is *lefð-*; *segja* 'say', pret. subj. *segð-*; *stara* 'stare' when its preterite subjunctive is *sterð-*; *una* 'be satisfied', pret. subj. *ynd-*; *vaka* 'be awake', pret. subj. *vekt-*; and *þegja* 'keep silent', pret. subj. *þegð-*.[18]

(b) Eight *lifa* verbs are irregular not only in the sense that their preterite subjunctives are not the expected formations, but also display additional complications (e.g. i-umlaut of /o/ to /i/). This makes it difficult to include these verbs under (a). The eight verbs are: *loða* 'stick, cleave to', when its preterite subjunctive is *lydd-*; *sk(r)olla* 'hang loosely' when its preterite subjunctive is *sk(r)oll-*; *skorta* 'lack' when its preterite subjunctive is *skyrt-*; *tolla* 'stick, cleave to' when its preterite subjunctive is *tylld-*; *trúa* 'believe', pret. subj. *tryð-*, with unexplained lax /i/; *þola* 'suffer', pret. subj. *þyld-*; and *þora* 'dare', pret. subj. *þyrð-*.[19]

informants declined almost consistently to give the information about the preterite subjunctive stating that he felt too uncertain about it. Therefore only seven, instead of eight, answers will sometimes be reported below.

[18] Subj. *lefð-* is given by 2 of my informants, by one of these hesitatingly. 5 informants (one hesitatingly, stating that he has heard children use subj. *lefð-*) list subj. *lafð-*, which is the expected 'present stem' formation.—One might be tempted to think that subj. *segð-* is a regular 'present stem' formation, its present stem being /sag + e/, and the corresponding 'present stem' formation, e.g., /sag + e + ð + i/; whatever causes the i-umlaut in the present, would cause it in the preterite subjunctive as well, giving *segð-*. However, as follows from Orešnik forthcoming, the expected result would be *seigð-*, not *segð-*, through the same processes that yield, e.g., *sleignir* (usually spelled *slegnir*), nom. pl. masc. of the past part. *sleg(i)n-* of *slá* 'strike' VI. The same argument is valid for pret. subj. *þegð-* of *þegja* 'keep silent'.— Subj. *sterð-* is listed by one of my informants, hesitatingly. All the others indicate that the subjunctive is *starð-*, a regular 'present stem' formation.

[19] Subj. *lydd-* is adduced by Einarsson. All my informants list *lodd-*, the expected 'present stem' formation.—Pret. subj. *sk(r)oll-* is listed in Einarsson and Guðmundsson 1922: 148. It is neither a 'present stem' formation (there being no dental suffix), nor a 'preteritival' one (no i-umlaut). In my poll, all the informants deny that *skolla* is used in spoken Modern Icelandic. 5 informants say the same about *skrolla*, one adduces the paradigm, pres. *skrollir*, pret. *skrollaði*, and 2 mention just the pres. *skrollir*. I have been trying to find the ultimate source of pret. *sk(r)olli* in the grammatical literature. So far I have only found pret. *skolli* in Cleasby-Vigfusson 1874: 554, in Old Icelandic texts.—Subj. *skyrt-* is given by one of my informants. Another informant lists both *skyrt-* and *skort-*, the latter being the expected 'present stem' formation. The remaining informants adduce subj. *skort-* only.—Subj. *tylld-* is listed by Einarsson and 6 of my informants. Two informants adduce the expected 'present stem' formation *tolld-*.

(c) Einarsson adduces *rýja* 'shear (wool)', pres. *rý(i)*-, pret. ind. and subj. *rúð*-. On the basis of the present stem *rý(i)*- the expected 'present stem' formation would be *rýð*-, which is not listed anywhere to the best of my knowledge. However, Einarsson gives an alternative paradigm as well: *rúa*, pres. *rúi*-, pret. ind. and subj. *rúð*-. Subj. *rúð*- is the expected 'present stem' formation. I assume that subj. *rúð*- of *rýja* in reality belongs to *rúa*, and Einarsson's description is confused because of the coexistence of the alternative paradigms. Einarsson lists a number of similar verbs beside *rýja* ∼ *rúa*: *dýja* ∼ *dúa* 'shake, quiver', pret. subj. *dúð*-; homonymous *dýja* ∼ *dúa* 'angle, fish', pret. subj. *dúð*-; *heyja* ∼ *há* 'hold a meeting', pret. subj. *hœð*-; *hlýja* ∼ *hlúa* 'warm, cover up', pret. subj. *hlúð*-; *lýja* 'tire', pret. subj. *lúð*-; *spýja* ∼ *spúa* 'spit', pret. subj. *spúð*-; and *œja* ∼ *á* 'bait, rest', pret. subj. *áð*-.[20]

(d) The expected preterite subjunctive of *hafa* 'have' is *hefð*-, a 'present stem' formation.[21] The preterite subjunctive *tœð*- of *tœja* 'pick (wool)' is likewise a regular 'present stem' formation. Pret. subj. *yll*- of *valda* ∼ *olla* 'cause' is a 'preteritival' formation, as expected in view of the complicated morphological relation between the present and the preterite indicative stems.

To summarize, the above short lists contain a number of *lifa* verbs

[20] In the case of *dýja* ∼ *dúa* 'shake, quiver' my poll has yielded very different results from Einarsson's. Only one informant knows *dýja* from the spoken language, as a *kalla* verb: pres. *dýjar*, pret. *dýjaði*. All the informants know the alternative verb *dúa*, but again as a *kalla* verb: pres. *dúar*, pret. *dúaði*. (The latter paradigm is listed in Einarsson 1949: 323.)—*Dýja* ∼ *dúa* 'angle, fish' was unfortunately not included in my questionnaire.—The pret. subj. *hœð*- of *heyja* is expected because of the complicated morphological relationship between the present stem *hey(i)*- and the preterite indicative stem *háð*-. However, the preterite subjunctive of *há* ought to be *háð*-, which form is not registered anywhere, to my knowledge.—*Hlúð*- is the expected subjunctive of *hlúa*. My poll indicates that the paradigm *hlýja, hlúði* is no longer in general use: one informant does not know this lexical item, the others use it as a *kalla* verb: *hlýjar, hlýjaði*. On the other hand, all the 8 informants list *hlúa, hlúi, hlúði*.—As to *lýja*, no alternative paradigm is adduced by Einarsson in this case. The expected 'present stem' formation *lýð*- is listed in Blöndal 1920—24: 496.—Subj. *spúð*- is a regular 'present stem' formation of *spúa*. The expected subj. *spýð*- of *spýja* is listed in Blöndal & Stemann 1959: 106, 116.—Subj. *áð*- is the expected 'present stem' formation to *á*. Subj. *œð*-, which we expect to be correlated with *œja*, is listed in Blöndal & Stemann 1959: 117, but the infinitive is *á*. Present stem *œ(i)*- is little used, if at all, according to my poll: 5 informants prefer, or know exclusively, present stem *ái*-. Only one informant lists *œi*- without qualifications.

[21] The present stem of *hafa* is /hav/, cf. pres. *hef(ur)*, *höfum*, etc. The irregular i-umlauting *i* of the bookish alternative pres. ind. sg. *hefi(r)* is not a present suffix, hence the present stem of the latter paradigm is likewise /hav/.

whose preterite subjunctives are counterexamples to the view that the preterite subjunctives of the regular weak verbs are 'present stem' formations. However, not even all of these verbs are equally reliable counterexamples. Some instances presumably reflect the confusion due to the fact that there are similar alternative paradigms, rather than the actual state of affairs in the spoken language. I also feel convinced that some of the counterexamples listed above exist in the written language only, while the spoken language uses regular formations. It is to be hoped that the field work which is under way to elicit dialect information for the files of the OHÍ will cast additional light on the morphology of the *lifa* verbs.

As pointed out above, the majority of the *lifa* verbs are exceptional if the view is espoused that all Icelandic preterite subjunctives are 'preteritival' formations. They become mostly regular if the views advocated in the present paper are adopted. In this sense the *lifa* verbs provide evidence in favor of the existence of rule (37), and thus of the existence of preterite subjunctives which are 'present stem' formations.

2.1.3.2. Additional evidence in favor of the existence of 'present stem' formations comes from the irregular weak verb *sœkja* 'seek, fetch'. The present stem of *sœkja* is here assumed to be /sōk + e/. This representation has the advantage of bringing *sœkja* nearest to the regular weak verbs (cf. present stems /blas + e/ and /fǣr + e/ of *blasa* and *fœra*, respectively), but it requires us to stipulate that *sœkja* is subject to the rule that palatalizes the velar consonants before non-round non-back non-low vowels and glides PRIOR to the operation of the i-umlaut rule (41), so that the i-umlaut rule applies to this lexical item. (Other exceptional cases of the same kind are, e.g., *dagur* 'day', dat. sg. *degi*; *tekinn*, past participle of *taka* 'take', etc. See Orešnik, forthcoming.)

The preterite indicative stem of *sœkja* is *sótt-* (also used in the past participle), with irregular *tt* instead of *kt*. (We would expect to find the latter if the preterite indicative were a regular formation.) Accordingly, we predict that the preterite subjunctive is a 'preteritival' formation, *sœtt-*. However, *sœtt-* is very rare, if not obsolete. The normal preterite subjunctive of *sœkja* is *sœkt-*. See Guðmundsson 1922: 154; Einarsson 1949: 87; Kress 1963: 179. (Blöndal 1920—24: 832 lists pret. ind. *sótti* and *sókti* as spelling variants, with the pronunciation that is predictable from the spelling variant *sótti*: [soᵘhdı]. Blöndal's only preterite subjunctive is *sœkti*, pronounced [saiχ·dı]. The supine is *sótt* [soᵘht].) Pret. subj. *sœkt-* can be generated as a 'present stem' formation: present stem /sōk + e/ +

dental suffix /ð/ + the i-umlauting preterite subjunctive endings, e.g., /sōk + e + ð + u/ > *sœktu*. The derivation proceeds in the following steps: /e/ palatalizes the /k/ of the root; by the i-umlaut rule (41) /ō/ is i-umlauted to /æ/ with the palatalized /k'/ as the umlauting segment; the elision rule (39) elides the /e/; the assimilation of /kð/ to [xt] takes place.

In Classical Icelandic the preterite stem of *sœkja* was *sótt-*, with pret. subj. *sótt-*, see Larsson 1891: 325. In the subsequent centuries, especially from the Reformation onwards, preteritival forms with *kt* instead of the lautgesetzlich *tt* occurred very frequently in both the preterite indicative and subjunctive: ind. *sókti*, subj. *sœkti*. See Helgason 1929: 86, 370; Bandle 1956: 414—15; Holberg 1948: 307—08. This state of affairs can be explained as an attempt at regularizing the paradigm of *sœkja*. The attempt was made in two directions. One was the regularization of the preterite stem through the replacement of *tt* by *kt*. This part of the attempt was ultimately not successful, which made Bandle guess that it may not have taken place at all in the spoken language ("möglicherweise nur schriftsprachlich und nicht in der Aussprache begründet"), but I cannot see that this assumption is necessary. The other direction of the regulariz-ing attempt was to render the preterite subjunctive of the verb a 'present stem' formation. This effort was actually triggered by the first mentioned one, in that all regular weak verbs tend to have preterite subjunctives that are 'present stem' formations. When the 'cause' was obliterated, the 'effect' remained—something that can be observed innumerable times in language history. By way of example, recall the nom. pl. masc. *teknir* of *tekinn*, past participle of *taka* 'take', strong verb VI: while *teknir* was still *takener* (or something similar), the middle *e* palatalized the *k*, which in turn caused the i-umlaut of the root vowel (*a > e*). Later, the ultimate 'cause' of this chain process, the vowel *e*, disappeared, so did the palatal feature of the velar consonant, but the 'effect', the i-umlaut of the root vowel, is still there, and as a consequence the past participle *tekinn*—in fact, the subclass of the past participles it is representative of—is slightly irregular. So is pret. subj. *sœkt-*, because we would expect a 'preteritival' formation in its place, in view of the irregular pret. ind. *sótt-*. In the case of *sœkt-* the 'cause' is the coming into being of the regular preterite stem *sókt-* by rule (36); one of the 'effects' of this 'cause' is the generation of a 'present stem' formation in the preterite subjunctive, *sœkt-*, by rule (37). When the 'cause' ceased to exist, for whatever reason, the 'effect', by virtue of its relative independence from the 'cause', remained. The essential point here is the relative independence of the 'effect' from the 'cause': they must not be parts of the same rule, so to speak. If the view is espoused that all Icelandic preterite subjunctives are 'preteritival' formations (so that the rule that generates the stem of the preterite indicative also generates the stem of the preterite subjunctive), the only way to explain the contrast of ind. *sótt-* vs. subj. *sœkt-* seems to be by maintaining that the *kt* of *sœkt-* is an accidental remainder of the formation, ind. *sókt-*, subj. *sœkt-*, which has ultimately not prevailed in the indicative. But then the development might just as well have been such that the ultimate result were pret. ind. *sókt-*, pret. subj. *sœtt-*, a paradigm of which there is no trace to my knowledge. On the other hand, if the existence of 'present stem' formations is admitted, situations like the ones described above (*sótt-* vs. *sœkt-*) are expected. It is therefore that pret. subj. *sœkt-* vs. ind. *sótt-* is here adduced as evidence in favor of the existence of the rule that generates 'present stem' formations, and thus of the existence of 'present stem' formations themselves.

2.1.4. There is general agreement, although this agreement is rarely explicitly stated, that all Old Icelandic preterite subjunctives are 'preteritival' formations whose production was governed by rule (35). It is hoped that the discussion in sections 2.1.3.1, 2.1.3.2, and 2.2.2 convinces the reader that this is no longer the case in Modern Icelandic, where the 'preteritival' formations have been partially, notably in the weak classes, replaced by 'present stem' formations. In the present section we will study those aspects of the history of Icelandic morphophonemics and verbal morphology which have brought about the modern state of affairs as far as the production of the preterite subjunctive is concerned. The study of these processes is the concern of this paper only in so far as it is necessary to check the chronology of the changes so as to ensure that no chronological arguments can be adduced against the views advocated in the present paper. Therefore this section is rather a set of notes than a consistent presentation of the historical development, which has unfortunately not yet been studied in sufficient detail.

The following are the two essential parts of the relevant development: (a) A 'conspiracy' which resulted in the creation of a number of exceptional preterite subjunctives with umlautable, but not umlauted, root vowels in positions that satisfied the structural description of the i-umlaut rule (41). (b) A restructuring of the grammar with the aim of accomodating these exceptions as normal cases, which was achieved through the addition, to the grammar, of rule (37) responsible for the production of 'present stem' formations.

Which historical circumstances have 'conspired' to create which exceptional preterite subjunctives? I can only supply a partial answer to this essential question.

(1) In Old Icelandic a number of *kalla* verbs (ten to twenty?) had roots ending in a tense *a* after which the suffixal lax *a*, typical of the *kalla* verbs, was not realized on the phonetic level because of the contraction rule. See Noreen 1923: 115, 342. Example: *spá* 'prophesy' < *spáa*, pret. ind. and subj. *spáð-* < *spáað-*, past part. nom. sg. masc. *spáðr* < *spáaðr*.[22] In the post-Classical centuries the present stem of the *spá* verbs gradually assumed the non-umlauting present suffix /e/. The new present indicative singular was *spái(r)*, whereas there were no changes in the other parts of the paradigm. The exact chronology and motivation of this process are poorly understood. Bandle (1956: 419) suggests that the change took place under the influence of the *lifa* class because of the partially equal morphological structures of the paradigms: "Der Übertritt ist vom Prät und Part-Prät veranlasst, wo sie [= the *spá* verbs] infolge der Kontraktion ganz mit schwVb IV [= the *lifa* verbs] wie *gá*, *ná* übereinstimmen (*spáði—spáð = náði—náð*)." The process took place mostly in the sixteenth century. Helgason (1929: 84—85) finds only one form possibly ascribable to this development in the New Testament of 1540: pres. ind. *sár*, itself a replacement of *sœr*, of *sá* 'sow', originally strong verb VII, alternates with *sáir*. In the Guðbrandsbiblía of 1584, Bandle (1956: 419) finds that the older present type *spá-* is still slightly more common than the new type *spái-*. The result of the replacement of the present stem *spá-* by *spái-* was that there were now a number of verbs, say thirty to forty, whose paradigm was exactly like the paradigm of the *lifa* verbs, except that there was no i-umlaut in the root vowel of the pret. subj. *spáð-*. In this way one aspect of the 'conspiracy' under discussion was realized.

(2) Some vocalic segments, either context-free or in certain contexts, have always displayed, or have developed, a resistance to i-umlauting. Cases in point might be the lax *o* (cf. *brosa* 'smile', pret. subj. *brosti*) and the combination *j* + lax *a* (cf. *hjara* 'live in poverty', pret. subj. *hjarði*). The reasons for this situation are poorly understood, and may be different from case to case in spite of superficial similarities. This will not be discussed here.

---

[22] The fact that the pret. subj. *spáð-* was not umlauted can be explained by assuming the following ordering of the rules in the descriptive grammar of Old Icelandic: i-umlaut first, contraction next. In other words, the lack of i-umlaut in the root vowel of the subj. *spáð-* is due to the circumstance that the structural description of the i-umlaut rule was not satisfied when the i-umlaut rule applied.

(3) Systemzwang may have been exerted by the many verbs whose respective preterite indicative and preterite subjunctive stems are wholly identical on the phonetic level. This is true of all regular weak verbs with the exception of the type *krefja* and of those *lifa* verbs with umlautable root vowels. Cf. *kallað-*, *fœrð-*, and *lifð-*, preterite indicatives and subjunctives of *kalla* 'call', *fœra* 'bring, move', and *lifa* 'live', respectively; on the other hand, pret. ind. *krafð-* ≠ subj. *krefð-* of *krefja* 'request', and pret. ind. *vakt-* ≠ subj. *vekt-* of *vaka* 'be awake'.

The 'conspiracy' some of whose aspects have just been briefly described would have resulted in a considerable number of exceptions had it not been accompanied by a restructuring of the grammar aimed at the reinterpretation of the basically open and homogeneous class of exceptions-to-be as regular formations. The restructuring consisted in the addition, to the grammar, of the morphophonemic rule (37), which produces 'present stem' formations and alternates with rule (35), which produces 'preteritival' formations. I cannot define the exact mechanism of the restructuring. The development must have been virtually completed, at least in some parts of Iceland, by the end of the sixteenth century. This follows from the circumstance that pret. subj. *nemd-*, which is the oldest of the preterite subjunctives studied in section 1, and whose coming into being is in 2.2.2 below explained to be a consequence of the existence of rule (37), appears at the end of the sixteenth century. The fact that the formations of section 1 make their debut in the North of the country would be accounted for if it could be shown that the restructuring of the grammar took place in the northern districts before it took place in the South. However, I have not so far found any evidence in favor of, or against, this assumption.

In the course of, and subsequent to, the restructuring of the grammar, all preterite subjunctives of the regular weak verbs, hitherto 'preteritival' formations, were reinterpreted as 'present stem' formations. The reinterpretation was covert in (a) the *kalla*, *fœra*, and *krefja* verbs; (b) those *lifa* verbs with non-umlautable root vowels; (c) other weak verbs, some of which had at least one paradigm of the *lifa* type (*tœja*, etc.); (d) in *ná* 'reach': the Classical forms were, according to Larsson 1891: 237, pres. *nái(r)*, pret. ind. *náði*, pret. subj. *nœði*. Subj. *nœði* has remained unchanged to this day. The reason for this is not difficult to see: about the sixteenth century pres. *nái(r)* was replaced by *nœ(r)*, an old alternative to *nái(r)* or an innovation, see Bandle 1956: 422. When the present stem is *ná-*, the expected 'present stem' formation is *nœð-*.

The reinterpretation failed to go into effect in a small number of common *lifa* verbs, see 2.1.3.1. On the other hand, the reinterpretation had repercussions on the surface forms of the majority of those *lifa* verbs with umlautable root vowels. Some verbs whose preterite subjunctives have changed (although the old forms may not yet be completely obsolete) are listed in (42).

(42) infinitive	Classical pret. subj.	Modern pret. ind. & subj.
gá 'look'	*gœð-*	*gáð-*
horfa 'look'	*hyrfð-*	*horfð-*
lafa 'hang limply'	*lefð-*	*lafð-* (see fn. 18)
loða 'stick to'	*lydd-*	*lodd-* (see fn. 19)
skorta 'lack'	*skyrt-*	*skort-* (see fn. 19)
spara 'save'	*sperð-*	*sparð-*
stara 'stare'	*sterð-*	*starð-* (see fn. 18)
tolla 'stick to'	*tylld-*	*tolld-* (see fn. 19)

The reinterpretation of the preterite subjunctives has gone on in all post-Reformation centuries and is not yet concluded. Its force can be judged by the fact that it has also affected some preterite subjunctives outside the domain of the regular weak verbs: the process is responsible for the changed shape of the preterite subjunctive of *sœkja* (see 2.1.3.2), and for the emergence of a number of the preterite subjunctives of section 1 (see 2.2.2 below).

2.2. We are now returning to the preterite subjunctives treated in section 1 above. An attempt will now be made, within the framework established in 2.1, to show how these preterite subjunctives are formed. This is done in subsection 2.2.2, preceded by subsection 2.2.1, which contains a survey of the history of this problem.

2.2.1. The quotations from the grammatical literature in section 1 report all scholarly discussion of the preterite subjunctives studied in section 1 that I know of. Here follows a survey of this discussion.

Of the Northern forms, *berð-*, *nemd-*, and *syngd-*, *syngd-* is mentioned by Helgason in (34), and *nemd-* is listed by Jón Magnússon in (33). The forms are not characterized as Northern, or discussed in any other way. Jón Magnússon's *nemd-* is to my knowledge the oldest recording of any of the preterite subjunctives treated in section 1, in the grammatical literature.

The Southern forms have oftener been mentioned, both in linguistic monographs, the grammars, and the dictionaries. The first scholar to discuss the preterite subjunctives of the type *dœð-* was Rasmus Rask in (4). He lists as many as four of the six forms known to me, and characterizes them as Eastern dialect. The recognition of the dialect status of these forms is general in the linguistic monographs and grammars that mention them. The normative grammar does not approve of them; see (5) and (10). The oldest dictionary that lists any of the Southern preterite subjunctives is Cleasby-Vigfusson, see (6), which quotes *dœð-* as a Southern form. Blöndal corrects this by stating that *dœð-* is both a Southern and Eastern form, and by adding *sjœð-*, which according to Blöndal is autochthonous in Skaftafellssýslur and in Austfirðir, and *slœð-*, see (9), (17), (20).

Cleasby-Vigfusson, see (6), and Hægstad, see (8), suggest an informal explanation of the origin of two of these preterite subjunctives. According to them, *dœð-* and *slœð-* are derived from the normal preterite subjunctives *dœ-* and *slœgj-* (where *g* is not pronounced) through the epenthesis of *ð*.

2.2.2. A classification of the preterite subjunctives of section 1 in terms of their geographical distribution and probable origin (the latter to be discussed now) yields (43).

(43)	Northern	Southern & Eastern
'present stem' formations	(A) *berð- nemd- syngd-*	(B) *hlœð- sjœð- slœð-*
rhyme words	(C) —	(D) *dœð- drœð- lœð-*

Sets (A) and (B) are 'present stem' formations, that is, formations according to rule (37): *bera*, present stem /ber/, pret. subj. /ber + ð + i/ > *berði*; *nema*, present stem /nem/, pret. subj. /nem + ð + i/ > *nemdi*; *syngja*, present stem /sing + j/, where /j/ is the present suffix, pret. subj. /sing + j + ð + i/ > *syngdi*; *hlœja*, present stem /hlǣ/, pret. subj. /hlǣ + ð + i/ > *hlœði*; *sjá*, present stem /sjā/ (itself from the descriptive point of view presumably the result of the breaking of /sē/, cf. pres. ind. sg. *sé-*), pret. subj. /sjā + ð + i/ > *sjœði* (Notice the *j*, not present in the preterite indicative stem *sá-* or in the strong pret. subj. *sœ-*.); *slá*, present stem /slā/, pret. subj. /slā + ð + i/ > *slœði*.

As the 'present stem' formations are a property of the regular weak verbs, the introduction of these formations into the paradigms of some strong verbs can only be interpreted as yet another way in which the regular weak verbs can influence the preterite of other verb classes. To the typical kinds of this influence[23] we can now add, (a) The preterite subjunctive of the strong verb competes with a 'present stem' formation. Cf. *sjá* 'see', pret. ind. *sá-*, pret. subj. *sœ-* and *sjœð-*. (b) The preterite subjunctive stem of the strong verb competes with this stem expanded with the dental suffix. Cf. *draga* 'draw', pret. ind. *dró(g)-*, pret. subj. *drægj-* and *drœð-*. This point will be dealt with below.

The conditions that brought sets (A) and (B) of (43) into existence have obtained everywhere in Iceland, so that there is—in absence of the evidence to the opposite—no reason why (A) and (B) should not be regarded as products of two distinct mutually independent processes. The time gap that separates the beginnings of (A) from those of (B) and the differences in the inventories of the resulting forms favor this assumption.

The coming into being of the oldest recorded preterite subjunctive of (43), *nemd-*, may have been accelerated by the circumstance that the preteritival system of *nema* was early disrupted. (See the inventory of the post-Reformation forms in fn. 7.) The reasons for the collapse are poorly understood, but may have been related to the fact that most verbs of the strong class IV have been idiosyncratically irregular from the beginning of literary Icelandic, and/or have undergone considerable changes in the post-Classical centuries.[24] Pret. subj. *nemd-* is presumably an

---

[23] The typical cases are: (a) The preterite stem of the strong verb is expanded with a dental suffix. Cf. preterite stem *þáð-* of *þiggja* 'accept', originally strong verb V, with strong pret. ind. *þá(g)-*. (b) The preterite of the strong verb is replaced by, or must compete with, a preterite containing a dental suffix. Cf. preterite stem *hangd-*, of *hanga* 'hang', also strong verb VII. (c) One of the preterite stems of the strong verb which has more than one preterite stem is replaced by, or must compete with, a preterite stem containing a dental suffix. Cf. *meta* 'esteem', strong verb V: one of its paradigms is, pret. *mat-* in the singular, *matt-* (replacing *mát-*) outside the singular, including the subjunctive, *mett-*. (Oral communication of Professor Hreinn Benediktsson, summer 1966.)

[24] Beside *nema* recall (a) *fela* 'hide, entrust': in pre-literary times switched from class III to class IV, in post-Classical times from class IV to class VI and to the weak verbs, pret. *fald-* and *fól-*; (b) *koma* 'come': irregular ablaut grade in the present and preterite stems, dialectal variation in the root vowel of the preterite stem, *kom-* vs. *kóm-*. The pret. subj. *kœm-* of the normal paradigm *koma*—pret. *kom(um)* is irregular from the descriptive point of view; (c) *sofa* 'sleep': irregular ablaut grade in the present stem and in pret. pl. *sváf-*, where the lautgesetzlich form would be *svof-*; (d) *svima* and *svimma* 'swim': now obsolete, irregular ablaut grade in the present stem, vacillation between classes III and IV; (e) *troða* 'tread': irregular ablaut grade in the present stem, switched from class IV to class VI (pret. *tróð-*) in the post-Reformation centuries. — This leaves only *bera* 'carry' (whose only irregularity, apart from what is discussed in 1.2.1.1, seems to be the dialectal pret. pl. *bórum*, reported in Hægstad 1942: 47 from Fljótsdalur in East Iceland), *skera* 'cut', and

attempt to replace the inherited subjunctive *næm-*, which, like pret. ind. pl. *nám-*, was losing ground. No similar argument could be true of the other forms of (43).

The following observations will help us account for the origin of the forms in (43D): (a) (43D) cannot be explained as 'present stem' formations; (b) They are not older than the forms of (43B); (c) They rhyme with the forms in (43B); (d) They have the same geographical distribution as the forms in (43B); (e) The forms in (43B) except *sjœð-* are structurally ambiguous: on the one side they can be considered to be 'present stem' formations, see above. On the other hand, they look like forms derived from their respective preterite indicative stems by aid of rule (44):

RULE (44). Take the preterite indicative stem ending in /Cō/, and add to it the dental suffix and the i-umlauting preterite subjunctive personal endings.

Examples: *hlœja*, preterite indicative stem /hlō/, preterite subjunctive according to rule (44) /hlō + ð + i/ > *hlœði*. *Slá*, preterite indicative stem /slō/, preterite subjunctive according to rule (44) /slō + ð + i/ > *slœði*.

In fact, *dœð-* and *drœð-* of (43D) can be explained by assuming that the forms of (43B) were interpreted as products of rule (44), and *deyja* and *draga* just followed the same rule: *deyja*, preterite indicative stem /dō/, preterite subjunctive according to rule (44) /dō + ð + i/ > *dœði*. *Draga*, preterite indicative stem /drō/, preterite subjunctive by rule (44) /drō + ð + i/ > *drœði*.

However, rule (44) does not account for *lœð-* of (43D), whose preterite indicative stem is /lā/ (*lá-* and *lág-* are just spelling variants). Subj. *lœð-* is essentially younger than all the other forms in (43), see fn. 6 above. Its origin can be accounted for by assuming that rule (44) has been replaced by rule (45) some time during the former's almost two hundred years old existence:

RULE (45). Take the preterite indicative stem ending in a consonant and a tense back vowel, and add to it the dental suffix and the i-umlauting preterite subjunctive personal endings.

The expression 'tense back vowel' of rule (45) refers to (strings of) segments spelled *á*, *ó*, *ú*. Alternatively, the rule could be limited to *á* and *ó* in such a manner that their diphthongal pronunciation would be at least implied. (There are no strong verbs whose preterite indicative stem/stems

---

stela 'steal', as the normal strong verbs of class IV.—These remarks are limited to some well-known facts. The details deserve separate treatment.

ends/end in *ú*.) Whichever formulation of rule (45) is chosen, the segments involved form a natural class, consequently the replacement of the earlier rule (44) by the later rule (45) is a case of rule simplification in the technical sense of the term usual in transformational generative grammar (Kiparsky 1968). Rule simplification is a very common historical phenomenon in languages.—Example of rule (45): *liggja* 'lie', preterite indicative stem /lā/, preterite subjunctive according to rule (45) /lā + ð + i/ > *lœði*.

Pret. subj. *lœð-* can either have come into being as a consequence of the simplification of the earlier rule (44), as has just been suggested above, or have contributed to the simplification of the rule by its very existence. In the latter case, a source other than rule (45) has to be found for *lœð-*. I suggest the rhyming verb *þiggja* 'accept', originally strong verb V, with its pret. subj. *þœð-* (normal in view of the pret. ind. *þáð-*). Cf. equation (46):

(46) *þiggj-* : *þœð-* = *liggj-* : X, where X = *lœð-*

This equation would of course be quite unrealistic if 'present stem' formations did not exist at the time of its operation. For 'present stem' formations guarantee the existence of a special morphological relationship between the present stem and the preterite subjunctive of the same paradigm without the preterite indicative being directly involved. In the absence of this relationship it would be difficult to explain, on the basis of equation (46), why a pret. ind. *láð-*, parallel to pret. ind. *þáð-*, was not created as well. At present I have no basis for choosing between the two described alternative sources of *lœð-*. If the aforementioned rule simplification is the true source of *lœð-*, equation (46) can still have been a catalyst in the process that yielded this form.

We can assume that (43D) would have been expanded to include (47), by rule (37) or (44) or (45), had not another process overtaken this development by the seventeenth century (see Þórólfsson 1925: 114—15), and produced preterite indicatives *fláð-*, *þvoð-*, and *þáð-*, respectively, to which the expected respective preterite subjunctives are exactly as given in (47). The subjunctives *flœð-* and *þvœð-* are 'present stem' formations,[25] whereas subj. *þœð-* is a 'preteritival' formation because of the complicated morphological relationship between the present stem *þiggj-* and the preterite

---

[25] Present stem *þvo-* must be /þvā/ underlyingly, cf. pres. ind. sg. *þvœ-* and pret. subj. *þvœð-*.

(47) *flá* 'flay', strong verb VI   pret. ind. *fló(g)-*   pret. subj. *flæð-*
    þvo 'wash', strong verb VI   *þó(g)-*   *þvæð-*
    þiggja 'accept', strong verb V   *þá(g)-*   *þæð-*

indicative stem *þáð-*. Thus no currently used verbs whose preterite indicative ends now, or ended in older Icelandic, in /Cā/ or /Cō/ have escaped the influence of the regular weak verbs in the Eastern and Southern dialects.

2.3. In Modern Icelandic the preterite subjunctive is formed in two ways: (a) The 'present stem' formations typically occur in the regular weak verbs, and are produced by rule (37) from the present stems by the addition of the dental suffix and of the i-umlauting preterite subjunctive personal endings. (b) The 'preteritival' formations typically occur in verbal classes other than the regular weak verbs, and are produced by rule (35) from the preterite indicative stems by the addition of the i-umlauting preterite subjunctive personal endings. All Old Icelandic preterite subjunctives were 'preteritival' formations. The preterite subjunctives of the regular weak verbs were reinterpreted as 'present stem' formations in the post-Reformation centuries, in order that a growing number of exceptions from the old rule (35) could be accomodated as regular formations.

Rule (37), which produces 'present stem' formations, helps to explain (1) why in the majority of the *lifa* verbs the umlautable root vowels of the preterite subjunctives are not i-umlauted; (2) why the preterite subjunctive of *sækja* 'fetch, seek' is *sækt-*, with *kt* = [xt], whereas the usual preterite indicative is *sótt-*, with *tt* = [ʰt]; and (3) what the origin of the preterite subjunctives of section 1 is. As to point (3), the answer is that the Northern subjunctives *berð-*, *nemd-*, and *syngd-*, as well as the Southern *hlæð-*, *sjæð-*, and *slæð-*, are 'present stem' formations, evidence of yet another way in which the weak verbs influence the less regular formations. The Southern subjunctives *dæð-*, *dræð-*, and *læð-* are essentially an extension of the type represented by the rhyming Southern subjunctives *hlæð-*, *sjæð-*, and *slæð-*.

3. In (5) above an interesting pret. subj. *sjæju* of *sjá* 'see' is mentioned. In (18) an equally interesting pret. subj. *jæti* of *éta* 'eat' is recorded. Since I have no information on these forms other than what is said in (5) and (18), I do not wish to speculate about them.—The preterite subjunctive of *slökkva* 'extinguish', weak verb, is sometimes *slekkti*, with *e*. Similarly in some other verbs which rhyme with *slökkva*. Since the problem of the i-umlaut and u-umlaut before /w/ has not yet been solved in the descriptive grammar of Modern Icelandic, I leave these verbs unaccounted for.

University of Ljubljana
  Jugoslavija

References

Alþingisbækur Íslands II, 1 = Sögurit IX. Reykjavík, 1915.

Anderson, Stephen. *West Scandinavian Vowel Systems and the Ordering of Phonological Rules*. Unpublished M.I.T. dissertation. Cambridge, Mass., 1969.

Annálar 1400—1800 gefnir út af Hinu íslenzka bókmenntafélagi. Vol. IV. Reykjavík, 1940—48.

Armann á Alþingi eda almennur Fundur Islendinga. Arsrit fyrir búhølda og bændafólk á Islandi. Editors: Þorgeir Gudmundsson and Balduin Einarsson. Copenhagen, 1829.

Árnason, Jón. *Íslenzkar þjóðsögur og æfintýri*. Vol. I—II. Leipzig, 1862—64.

Árnason, Jón. *Íslenzkar þjóðsögur og ævintýri*. Second (augmented) edition. Edited by Árni Böðvarsson and Bjarni Vilhjálmsson. Vol. III, 1955. Vol. IV, 1956. Vol. VI, 1961. Reykjavík.

Arndt, Johan. *Þridia Bok um iñ sanna Christendom, og Innra Mannenn, /.../ Sammanskrifud af /.../ Doctor Johan Arndt, /.../ Enn i Norrænu utløgd af /.../ Sira Þorleife Arnasyne, Firrum Profaste yfer Skaptafells Syslu*. Copenhagen, 1731.

Bandle, Oskar. *Die Sprache der Guðbrandsbiblía*. Bibliotheca arnamagnæana, vol. XVII. Copenhagen, 1956.

Benediktsson, Hreinn. "On the Inflection of the ia-Stems in Icelandic" in *Afmælisrit Jóns Helgasonar 30. júní 1969*. Reykjavík, 1969.

Blöndal, Sigfús. *Íslenzk-dönsk orðabók*. Reykjavík, 1920—24.

Blöndal, Sigfús, and Stemann, Ingeborg. *Praktisk Lærebog i islandsk Nutidssprog*. Third edition. Copenhagen, 1959.

Brynjúlfsson, Gísli. *Dagbók í Höfn*. Reykjavík, 1952.

[Campe, J. H.] *J. H. Campes Sálar = Frædi, ætlud námfúsum Unglingum, einkum Kénnslu Børnum*. Translated from Danish by Bjarni Arngrímsson, sóknarprestur til Mela og Leirár í Borgarfjarðarsýslu. Leirárgørdum vid Leirá, 1800.

[Cleasby-Vigfusson.] *An Icelandic-English Dictionary*. Initiated by Richard Cleasby subsequently revised, enlarged and completed by Gudbrand Vigfusson. Oxford, 1874. Here quoted from the second edition with a supplement by Sir William A. Craigie. Oxford, 1957.

Einarsson, Stefán. *Icelandic Grammar Texts Glossary*. Baltimore, 1949.

Frèttir frá Fulltrúa-þinginu í Hróarskeldu, viðvíkjandi málefnum Íslendinga, gefnar út af nokkrum Íslendingum. Copenhagen, 1840.

Grímsson (Borgfirðingur), Sighvatur. "Æfiágrip Guðmundar "læknis" Guðmundssonar norðlenzka" in *Blanda* III, 2 = Sögurit XVII. Reykjavík, 1925.

Guðmundsson, Valtýr. *Islandsk Grammatik. Islandsk Nutidssprog*. Copenhagen, 1922.

47

Hægstad, Marius. *Nokre ord um nyislandsken.* Skrifter utgitt av Det Norske Videnskaps-Akademi i Oslo II. Hist.-Filos. Klasse, 1942. No number. Oslo, 1942.

Halldórsson, Halldór. *Íslenzk málfrœði handa œðri skólum.* Reykjavík, 1950.

Hallgrímsson: see Þórðarson, Matthías.

Helgason, Jón. *Málið á Nýja Testamenti Odds Gottskálkssonar.* = Safn fræðafjelagsins um Ísland og Íslendinga gefið út af Hinu íslenska fræðafjelagi í Kaupmannahöfn, vol. VII. Copenhagen, 1929.

Helgason, Jón. "Fem islandske ordsamlinger fra 18. og 19. århundrede. 5. En ordsamling af Rasmus Rask" in Bibliotheca arnamagnæana, vol. XX. Copenhagen, 1960.

Helgason, bishop Jón. *Kristnisaga Íslands frá öndverðu til vorra tíma.* Vol. II. Reykjavík, 1927.

Holberg, Ludvig. *Nikulás Klím.* Translated into Icelandic by Jón Ólafsson úr Grunnavík (1745). Edited by Jón Helgason. Íslenzk rit síðari alda gefin út af Hinu íslenzka fræðafélagi í Kaupmannahöfn. Vol. 3. Copenhagen, 1948.

ÍslÆv: see Ólason 1948—52.

Jóhannesson, Alexander. *Isländisches etymologisches Wörterbuch.* Bern, 1956.

Jónsson, Finnur. *Málfræði íslenskrar tungu og helstu atriði sögu hennar í ágripi.* Copenhagen, 1908.

Jónsson, Finnur. *Den islandske grammatiks historie til o. 1800.* Det Kgl. Danske Videnskabernes Selskab, Historisk-filologiske Meddelelser, vol. xix, 4. Copenhagen, 1933.

Jónsson, Guðni, ed. *Íslenzkir sagnaþættir og þjóðsögur.* Vol. IX. Reykjavík, 1951.

Kiparsky, Paul. "Linguistic Universals and Linguistic Change" in Emmon Bach and Robert T. Harms, eds., *Universals in Linguistic Theory.* New York, 1968.

Kress, Bruno. *Laut- und Formenlehre des Isländischen.* Halle/Saale, 1963.

Larsson, Ludvig. *Ordförrådet i de älsta isländska handskrifterna.* Lund, 1891.

[Milton, John.] *Ens enska skálds, J. Miltons, Paradísar missir.* Translated into Icelandic by Jón Þorláksson. Copenhagen, 1828.

[daily] *Morgunblaðið.* Reykjavík.

Norðanfari. Hálfsmánaðar blað Íslendinga. Edited by Björn Jónsson. Fifth year, 1866. Twentieth year, 1881. Akureyri.

Norðri, hálfsmánaðar-rit handa Íslendingum. Edited by B. Jónsson and J. Jónsson. Third year, 1855. Akureyri.

Noreen, Adolf. *Altisländische und altnorwegische Grammatik (Laut- und Flexionslehre) unter Berücksichtigung des Urnordischen.* Sammlung kurzer Grammatiken germanischer Dialekte. IV. Altnordische Grammatik I. Fourth edition. Halle/Saale, 1923.

Ólason, Páll Eggert, ed. *Skrá um handritasöfn Landsbókasafnsins.* Vol. II. Reykjavík, 1927.

Ólason, Páll Eggert. *Íslenzkar æviskrár frá landnámstímum til ársloka 1940.* Vol. 1—5. Reykjavík, 1948—52.

Orešnik, Janez. *Menjava sprege v zgodovini islandskega glagola.* [= Change of Conjugation in the History of the Icelandic Verb] Unpublished doctoral dissertation. Ljubljana, 1964.

Orešnik, Janez. "On the Perfect Stem of the Strong and the Preterit-Present Verbs in Late Proto-Germanic and in the Old Germanic Languages" in *Linguistica* 8: 123—39. Ljubljana, 1966—68.

Orešnik, Janez. "Morphophonemic Notes on the Modern Icelandic Imperative Singular." Forthcoming.

Smári, Jakob Jóh. *Íslenzk málfræði*. Reykjavík, 1923.

Sturtevant, Albert Morey. "Analogic Weak Preterite Forms in Old Icelandic" in *Language* 16 (1940): 48—52.

Tíðindi frá nefndarfundum íslenzkra embættismanna í Reykjavík árin 1839 og 1841. Síðari deild. Tíðindi frá nefndarfundinum 1841, samin af kandídatus júris Kr. Kristjánssyni. Edited by Þorsteinn Jónsson. Copenhagen, 1842.

[periodical] *Þjóðólfr.* Twelfth year, 1860. Reykjavík.

[Þórðarson, Matthías, ed.] *Rit eftir Jónas Hallgrímsson. II. Sendibréf, umsóknir o. fl.* Reykjavík, [1932].

Þorkelsson, Jón. *Beyging sterkra sagnorða í íslensku.* Reykjavík, 1888—94.

Þórólfsson, Björn Karel. *Um íslenskar orðmyndir á 14. og 15. öld og breytingar þeirra úr fornmálinu.* Reykjavík, 1925.

Valfells, Sigrid. *"Umlaut"—Alternations in Modern Icelandic.* Unpublished Harvard doctoral thesis. Cambridge, Mass., 1967.

Vigfússon, Guðbrandur. "Um stafrof og hneigíngar" in *Ný félagsrit gefin út af nokkrum Íslendíngum.* 17. ár. Copenhagen, 1857.

Westergård-Nielsen, Christian. *Låneordene i det 16. århundredes trykte islandske literatur.* Bibliotheca arnamagnæana, vol. VI. Copenhagen, 1946.

CDU 803.959-54

Janez Orešnik

ON THE PHONOLOGICAL BOUNDARY BETWEEN CONSTITUENTS OF MODERN ICELANDIC COMPOUND WORDS

Summary.[1] If the word boundary is posited between constituents of Modern Icelandic compound words, a number of mutually unrelated phonological phenomena are accounted for without any extra machinery (say, in the structure of rules). However, I have not been able to prove that any Modern Icelandic phonological phenomena actually REQUIRE the word boundary between constituents of compound words. I could only demonstrate that certain phenomena require SOME boundary between constituents of compound words; if the boundary required in those cases is identified with the morpheme boundary, certain phonological rules of Modern Icelandic have to be complicated in ways which can be avoided when the said boundary is assumed to be a word boundary.

§ 1. The Modern Icelandic lexicon contains many compound words, such as *bók-menntir* 'literature', *til-einkaður* 'dedicated', *guð-fræði* 'theology'. From the phonological point of view these words behave differently from simplex words in some respects, notably as regards the quantity of their stressed vowels, the permitted consonant clusters, and their stress pattern. The differences could presumably be captured in several ways, none of which have so far been applied to the Icelandic situation, to the best of my knowledge. The method used in comparable situations in other languages is to posit, between constituents of compound words, a boundary of a kind that does not occur in simplex words. Applying this to Modern Icelandic, it should first be noticed that the examination of Icelandic phonology has so far recognized the need for not more than two phonological boundaries, the morpheme boundary (+) and the word boundary (# #). Until this limitation of the kinds

---

[1] My thanks are due to Miss Margaret G. Davis, who has improved the style of the paper. All errors are my own. The theoretical framework and the terminology of this paper are those of generative phonology as expounded by Chomsky and Halle 1968. Non-phonetic representations are bounded by the obliques, //, except in phonological derivations, where the obliques are omitted. Very often the reader will find italicized, i. e. orthographic representations within obliques. They are used to represent phonological units in those cases where I am unwilling to commit myself on the exact nature of the segments involved.

of Icelandic phonological boundaries is disproved, the boundary which can occur in simplex words is by definition the morpheme boundary, and the one never to be found in simplex words is the word boundary. Compound words can contain morpheme boundaries, and presumably contain at least one word boundary. To facilitate the exposition, the word boundary occurring between constituents of compound words will be designated with the ad hoc symbol §. For example, the compound word *bóka-safn* 'library', literally 'book collection', is phonologically (roughly) /*bóka§safn*/.

This kind of treatment, with which the initiated reader will be familiar from elsewhere (see, for instance, Chomsky and Halle 1968 for English) takes care of many mutually unrelated phonological phenomena which would otherwise have to be accounted for less generally. Here follows a sample of such phenomena.

(I) The phonological component of Modern Icelandic grammar contains a VOWEL SYNCOPE RULE:

(1)
$$
\begin{bmatrix} V \\ - \text{ stress} \\ - \text{ »tense«} \\ + \text{ 'elidible'} \end{bmatrix} \rightarrow \emptyset \; / \; \underline{\quad\quad} \begin{bmatrix} C \\ + \text{ coronal} \\ - \text{ tense} \end{bmatrix} + V
$$

i. e. an unstressed non-»tense« 'elidible' vowel is deleted if followed by a coronal lax consonant, the morpheme boundary, and a vowel, in that order. The rule is discussed and formulated in Orešnik 1972. The feature »TENSE« (within quotation marks) is a common property of the segments which are in Icelandic phonetics usually referred to as *breið sérhljóð* (Einarsson 1949:11), i. e. the diphthongs and the monophthongs *í*, *ú*, [y] (the last one as in *hugi*). The feature 'ELIDIBLE' is an ad hoc feature associated with all the vowels that actually undergo the vowel syncope rule (1). Thus the unstressed vowel of *mikill* 'great, large' is 'elidible', and that of *heimill* 'at free disposal' is 'inelidible' because of contrasts such as dat. pl. *miklum* vs. *heimilum*. The fact that the ad hoc feature 'elidible' is mentioned in (1) shows that the present formulation of the rule is provisional. The feature CORONAL refers to *l r n ð þ t d s*. TENSE, this time without quotation marks, is used in its accepted meaning.

Formulation (1) shows that the rule applies across a morpheme boundary (and in fact can apply only if a morpheme boundary immediately follows the vowel to be deleted). Example: *jökull* 'glacier' contains an 'elidible' *u*, cf. nom. pl. *jöklar* from /*jökul + ar*/. On the other hand, the rule never applies if the vowel to be deleted is immediately followed by a §-boundary and another vowel. Cf. *jökul-alda* 'moraine', from /*jökul§alda*/, not **jökl-alda*, which would be the expected normal result if the phonological representation were /*jökul + alda*/.

(II) Benediktsson 1969:394 has formulated, for Old Icelandic, a VOWEL TRUNCATION RULE which deletes unstressed vowels immediately followed by the morpheme boundary and another vowel. This rule still operates in

Janez Orešnik

Modern Icelandic, with the result that there are no segment clusters of un-stressed lax vowel plus vowel in simplex words, on the phonetic level. The rule applies, e. g., in the 1p. pl. pres. *köllum* from /*kalla* + *um*/, and in the 2p. pl. pres. *kallið* from /*kalla* + *ið*/, of *kalla* 'call'. (That the stem of *kalla* is phono-logically bisyllabic, /*kalla*/, follows from the singular present indicative forms *kalla(r)*, the imp. sg *kalla*, and from the dental stem *kallað-*.) On the other hand, the rule does not apply in compound words like *sögu-eyja* 'saga island', from /*sögu§eyja*/. If the phonological representation were /*sögu(+)eyja*/, we would expect **sögeyja* on the phonetic level.

(III) A *d* is usually inserted between an *n* and the immediately preceding *r*. Einarsson 1949:21. The insertion is performed by the D-INSERTION RULE. The rule can apply even if the *r* and the *n* are separated by a morpheme bound-ary. Cf. dat. pl. *förnum* of *farinn* 'gone', from /*far*+*in*+*um*/, where the vowel syncope rule first applies to yield /*far*+*n*+*um*/, whereupon the u-um-laut rule and the d-insertion rule produce *förnum*, pronounced with *d* before *n*. On the other hand, the d-insertion rule does not apply across a §-boundary. Cf. *stór-netla* '(plant) urtica dioeca', without *d* before *n*, from /*stór§netla*/. If the phonological representation were /*stór(+)netla*/, the expected phonetic representation would contain *d* before *n*.[2]

(IV) The consonantal segments which are realized as non-preaspirated stops in intervocalic position, are preaspirated if they immediately precede *n* within the word. Einarsson 1949:23. The sandhi rule which affects this change can apply even across a morpheme boundary. Cf. dat. pl. *sopnum*, with preaspirated p, from /*sop*+*in*+*um*/, of *sopinn* 'drunk'; dat. pl. *getnum*, with preaspirated *t*, from /*get*+*in*+*um*/, of *getinn* 'begotten'; dat. pl. *auknum*, with preaspirated *k*, from /*auk*+*in*+*um*/, of *aukinn* 'increased'. (In these examples, the vowel syncope rule (1) first brings the lax stop and the *n* into contact, whereupon the stop is preaspirated across the intervening morpheme bound-ary). On the other hand, the rule which preaspirates the stops in the above examples cannot operate across the §-boundary. Cf. *djúp-nökkvi* '(seal) han-

---

2 In order to diminish the number of the unknowns, I have here and elsewhere in this paper avoided those phonological rules concerning which I cannot prove that the presence of the morpheme boundary does not block their operation. Thus there is a change of *rl* to *rdl* (with subsequent loss of *r* in a number of cases), very similar to the change of *rn* to *rdn* (and further to *dn* in a number of cases) described sub III. I know of no reliable examples proving that *(r)dl* ever comes from phonological /*rl*/ if /*r*/ and /*l*/ are separated by a morpheme boundary. Examples like the contracted cases *ferl-*, pronounced with *rdl*, of *ferill* 'trace, path', show that the d-insertion rule must operate in the context r—l, but are not reliable instances of the substring /*r*+*l*/; the morpheme boundary after *fer-* is uncertain, for we lack
(a) any phonological evidence for such a boundary in *ferill* and similar words. In fact, I do not know of any phonological phenomena of Modern Icelandic that would REQUIRE the positing of morpheme boundaries whose decisive motivation would come from facts of word derivation. As will be seen below, the situation is different with regard to word composition.
(b) a theory which would tell us whether *fara* 'go, travel' and *ferill* (historically the latter is a derivative of the former) are sufficiently similar to each other seman-tically and phonologically for the word-formational relation between them to exist synchronically, and thus help motivate a morpheme boundary after *fer-* in *ferill*.

leyja abyssorum', with non-preaspirated *p*, from /*djúp*§*nökkvi*/; *mat-niđingur* 'one stingy with food', with non-preaspirated *t*, from /*mat*§*niđingur*/; *bak-naga* 'slander', with non-preaspirated *k*, from /*bak*§*naga*/. If the three examples were phonologically /*djúp*(+)*nöklcvi*/, /*mat*(+)*niđingur*/, and /*bak*(+)*naga*/, respectively, their *p*, *t*, and *k* would be preaspirated on the phonetic level. See also footnote 2.

(V) The phonological fricatives /v/ and /q/ (i. e. voiced velar fricative) become stops when immediately followed by *n* and a vowel. Einarsson 1949:13—14. The process is not blocked if a morpheme boundary intervenes between the sounds involved in the change. Cf. nom. pl. masc. *sofnir*, with *b* before *n*, from /*sof*+in+ir/, of the past part. *sofinn* 'slept'; nom. pl. fem. *dregnar*, with a velar stop before *n*, from /*dreg*+in+ar/, of the past part. *dreginn* 'drawn'. No such process applies across the §-boundary. Cf. *of-næmi* 'allergy', with [vn], from /*of*§*næmi*/; *hag-nýta* 'use', with [qn], from /*hag*§*nýta*/. If the phonological representation of the two compounds were /*of*(+)*næmi*/ and /*hag*(+)*nýta*/, respectively, we would expect to find [bn] and [gn] in them on the phonetic level.[3] See also footnote 2.

(VI) Whenever any number of segments from the set {*t, d, þ, đ*} immediately follow each other in a simplex word on the phonological level, and such a consonantal group is not accompanied by additional consonants, a sandhi rule applies to coalesce such a consonantal cluster into a long preaspirated *t* if at least one of the original segments is *t*, and into a long *d* otherwise. The following examples show that the coalescing rule can apply even across a morpheme boundary (Einarsson 1949:54, 82—83):

(2) (a) Preterite and past participle stem of regular weak verbs:
root + dental suffix ($\neq$ /t/)

hræđa 'frighten', pret. and past part. stem	*hrædd-*
mæta 'meet'	*mætt-*
brydda 'border, edge'	*brydd-*
hitta 'hit'	*hitt-*

(b) Nom./acc. sg. ntr. of strong adjectives: root + *t*

glađur 'glad', nom./acc. sg.	*glatt*
latur 'lazy'	*latt*
saddur 'satisfied'	*satt*
brattur 'steep'	*bratt*

---

[3] Phonetic [qn] exists in Modern Icelandic, cf. the contracted cases *brugđn-* [brYqn-] of the past part. *brugđinn* 'moved quickly'. Pending an examination of the Modern Icelandic internal sandhi rules I assume for the time being that the rule which changes /q/ into a stop before /n/ precedes the loss of /đ/ in the context q—n. The following derivation results, for the strong nominative plural feminine:

	brugđ+in+ar
vowel syncope rule	*brugđ*+n+ar
q → g / —n	non-applicable
đ → Ø / q—n	*brug*+n+ar
	[brYqnar]

Janez Orešnik

On the other hand, the coalescing rule does not apply across the §-boundary. Cf. *hvit-þinur* '(plant) abies alba', from */hvit§þinur/*, not from */hvit(+) þinur/*, which would yield preaspirated *tt* instead of *tþ*; *rit-deila* 'polemics (in the press, etc.)', from */rit§deila/*, not from */rit(+)deila/*, which would yield preaspirated *tt* instead of *td*; *rót-tækur* 'radical', from */rót§tækur/*, not from */rót(+)tækur/*, which would yield preaspirated *tt*; *blóð-þyrstur* 'bloodthirsty', from */blóð§þyrstur/*, not from */blóð(+) þyrstur/*, which would presumably yield *dd* instead of *ðþ*; *stað-deyfing* 'local anaesthesia', from */stað§deyfing/*, not from */stað(+)deyfing/*, which would yield *dd* instead of *ðd*. Etc.

(VII) The consonantal segments which are realized phonetically as the preaspirated labial stop *(pp)*, as the non-preaspirated labial stop *(p)*, as the preaspirated velar stop *(kk)*, and as the non-preaspirated velar stop *(k)* become fricatives [f] and [x], respectively, in the context V—t in simplex words. Einarsson 1949:17, 20, 29. The process is not stopped by an intervening morpheme boundary, as the following examples show:

(3) imperative singular with postposed personal pronoun:
   súptu 'sip', with [ft], from */súp+tu/*[4]
   taktu 'take', with [xt], from */tak+tu/*
   slepptu 'let go', with [ft], from */slepp+tu/*
   slökktu 'quench', with [xt], from */slökk+tu/*

On the other hand, this sandhi rule does not operate across the §-boundary. Cf. *skip-tapi* 'loss (of ship)', with [pt], from */skip§tapi/*; *upp-tekinn* 'occupied', with [ʰpt], from */upp§tekinn/*; *bak-tala* 'slander', with [kt], from */bak§tala/*; *stekk-tíð* 'eleventh month in the Icelandic calender', with [ʰkt], from */stekk§tíð/*. These contrast, in pronunciation, with the examples listed in (3). See also footnote 2.

(VIII) In Orešnik 1971 b I mentioned the Modern Icelandic PALATALIZATION RULE, which accounts for the fact that velar consonants are almost invariably palatalized if immediately followed by *i, í, e, æ*, or by diphthongs that begin with *i* or *e*. The palatalization rule is not blocked when it applies across a morpheme boundary, as shown by the weak nom. sg. masc. *hagi*, with palatalized */g/* and diphthongized root vowel, from */hag+i/*, of *hagur* 'skilful; elaborate'. On the other hand, the palatalization rule cannot apply across the §-boundary. Cf. *hag-yrðingur* 'rimester', from */hag§yrðingur/*, with non-fronted *g* before the §-boundary, and consequently without the diphthongization of the *a*.

(IX) Stressed vowels are phonetically long if immediately followed by just one lax consonant within the simplex word (or by certain consonant clusters, see Einarsson 1949:4; such clusters will be disregarded in this discussion). Otherwise stressed vowels are short. When the stressed vowel is separated by a morpheme boundary from the consonant which determines, or from (a part of) the consonants which determine, its quantity, this circumstance has

---

[4] The non-phonetic representations of (3) within the obliques are the not necessarily phonological representations to which the sandhi rule discussed sub VII applies.

no bearing upon the quantity of that vowel. Cf. *ást* 'love', with phonetically short *á* and no morpheme boundary anywhere in the word; the middle infinitive *ást* of *á* 'rest and graze horses', likewise with a phonetically short *á*, and with a morpheme boundary before *st*; strong nom./acc. sg. ntr. *fúst.* of *fús* 'willing', again with a phonetically short vowel, and with the morpheme boundary between *s* and *t*. On the other hand, if the stressed vowel and the immediately following *st* are separated by the §-boundary, the stressed vowel is phonetically long. Cf. *á-stæða* 'ground, reason', from /*á§stæða*/, with phonetically long *á*. If the phonological representation were /*á(+)stæða*/, the present rules, as formulated on the basis of the situation in simplex words, would produce, wrongly, phonetically short *á*.

§ 2. The discussion in I—IX has shown that the identification of the boundary between constituents of compound words with the word boundary takes care of many phonological phenomena — some of which have just been sketched — typical of compound words, without the need for any extra machinery. This of course speaks in favour of the said identification. However, it should be noted that the phenomena under discussion, in fact, as far as I know, Icelandic phonological phenomena in general, do not seem to REQUIRE this particular treatment. To see this, consider again the situations described in I—IX.

It suffices to emend the rules discussed sub I—VII with the stipulation that the first vowel after the segments to be affected by the rules in question be unstressed, and the operation of the rules is blocked in the relevant environments in compound words without further complications, as far as can be seen. The alteration of course presupposes that the stress is allocated to vowels before the operation of the rules discussed sub I—VII. This is the case anyway. One of the rules discussed, the vowel syncope rule, happens to be one of the earliest rules in the Modern Icelandic phonological component, and all the remaining rules discussed here follow it in the ordering.[5]

---

[5] The relative ordering of the vowel syncope rule and of the vowel truncation rule has not yet been determined, but both are certainly »early« rules, and even considered subparts of the same rule by one scholar (Benediktsson 1969:394).

The sandhi rules discussed sub VI and VII follow the vowel syncope rule: the latter creates some of the segment clusters to which those sandhi rules apply. Cf. the derivations of the lp. sg. pret. subj. *mætti* of *mæta* 'meet', and *sleppti* of *sleppa* 'let go':

	mæt+i+D+i	*slepp*+i+D+i
vowel syncope rule	*mæt*+D+i	*slepp*+D+i
sandhi rules	*mæ*[ʰt]+i	*sle*[ft]+i
	[maɪʰtI]	[slɛftI]

[D] is a cover symbol for a dental consonant from the set *t, ð, þ, ð*. For the justification of the representations [*mæt*+i+D+i] and [*slepp*+i+D+i] being trisyllabic, see Orešnik 1971 a.

For the arguments concerning the ordering of the remaining rules mentioned in the main text, with respect to the vowel syncope rule, see Orešnik 1972.

Janez Orešnik

It follows from formulation (1) that the stress must be determined — lexically and/or by a rule — by the time the vowel syncope rule applies, and consequently the distribution of the stresses can also be utilized when the remaining rules apply. The said alteration even abolishes the need for any kind of boundary between the constituents of compound words. On the other hand, the revision has two unpleasant consequences. First, the rules are now not only more complicated than they were before the reformulation, but also less general, because the adjustment, occasioned by the facts typical of compound words, does not have any positive effects outside compound words. Secondly, once the non-morpheme boundaries are barred from compound words, the stress can only be allotted lexically. To appreciate this point consider how the stress can be assumed to be placed if the constituents of compound words are allowed to be separated from each other by word boundaries.[6] There must be an early rule (operating before the vowel syncope rule, as explained above), which assigns [+ stress] to the first vowel after a word boundary. Given the phonological representation /jökul§alda/ of *jökul-alda* 'moraine', the rule would stress /ö/ and the constituent-initial /a/. Next there must be a rule which weakens certain stresses that are not word initial to different degrees, taking into consideration the syntactic structure of the compound in the process. For example, *skóla-bóka-safn*, literally 'school book collection', has one stress pattern when the word means 'collection of school books', and another when it means 'school library'. Now, if the only boundaries permitted in compound words are morpheme boundaries, and the syntactic structure of the compound words is not indicated,[7] this system of stress rules cannot produce the desired phonetic results. Consequently the stress must be allotted lexically in such a case.

However, while the modification of the rules sub I—VII can thus be seen to be somewhat disadvantageous, it is not unrealistic in the sense of not obeying the established constraints on the form of phonological components. It is in this sense that it can be asserted that the rules described sub I—VII do not require that there be non-morpheme boundaries in compound words. Moreover, those rules do not require any boundaries at all between the constituents of compound words.

A different situation obtains with the revision of the palatalization rule, discussed sub VIII. To prevent the fronting of *g* in *hag-yrðingur* 'rimester', it is not enough that the fronting vowel be stressed, for stressed vowels do front preceding velar consonants in simplex words. Cf. the singular present indicative forms *geng-*, *skef-*, *kem-*, etc., with fronted velars before the stressed *e*, as against their respective present stems *gang-*, *skaf-*, *kom-*, of the strong verbs

---

[6] What follows builds on the analogy of the relevant aspects of the English stress rules as expounded by Chomsky and Halle 1968.

[7] It is assumed here that strings such as]+[, where the square brackets indicate the syntactic structure, are impossible on the phonological level. Since this assumption makes it more difficult, rather than easier, for me to prove the existence of the word boundary between constituents of compound words, I accept it for the sake of argument without further discussion.

ganga 'go', *skafa* 'scrape', and *koma* 'come'; cf. also the preterite subjunctive forms *kæmi, skæfi, kefði, gysi, kynni*, etc., with fronted velars before stressed vowels, as against the respective preterite indicative stems *kom-/kóm-, skóf-, kafð-, gus-, kunn-,* of *koma* 'come', *skafa* 'scrape', *kefja* 'suffocate', *gjósa* 'gush', *kunna* 'know how to'. It is therefore necessary to reformulate the palatalization rule so that a stressed vowel does not palatalize a preceding velar if the two are separated by any kind of boundary. Thus the palatalization rule offers precious positive evidence that there must be SOME boundary between the constituents of compound words in Icelandic.

The same important result is achieved if the vowel quantity rule, discussed sub IX, is altered to accommodate the hypothesis that compound words do not contain any non-morpheme boundaries. Suppose that the vowel quantity rule lengthens vowels before a single lax consonant (the proviso, mentioned sub IX, about certain consonant clusters as allowing lengthening, is still to be kept in mind). In this case the vowel quantity rule would fail to lengthen the word-initial vowel of the compounds *í-stað* 'stirrup' and *ís-turn* 'ice tower', for their phonological representation would be /í+stað/ and /ís+turn/, respectively, the morpheme boundary would be disregarded (cf. *ást, á+st*, and *fús+t*, discussed sub IX above), and the rule blocked because of the cluster /st/ which follows the *í* to be lengthened. The desired phonetic output, with long *í*, would not be secured. And it does not help to stipulate that the vowel quantity rule is blocked if the next vowel in the compound word is stressed, for this stipulation would still fail to differentiate between, say, *á-stæða* 'reason, ground', with phonetically long *á*, and *ást-úð* 'lovable character, kindness', with phonetically short *á*. Obviously the rule must be formulated so that it counts the postvocalic consonants only as far as the first boundary, which is after *á* in *á-stæða*, and after *t* in *ást-úð*. This of course is tantamount to saying that the vowel quantity rule requires that there be a boundary between constituents of compound words, otherwise the correct phonetic results cannot be obtained without calling in hopelessly ad hoc machinery. — The same conclusion would have been arrived at if the vowel quantity rule were formulated, not as lengthening certain vowels (as has just been done above), but as shortening certain other vowels.[8]

Thus, while I still have not been able to present positive evidence for the word boundary between constituents of compound words, I hope to have succeeded in demonstrating that at least two Modern Icelandic phonological rules, viz. the palatalization rule and the vowel quantity rule, require that there be SOME boundary between the constituents of compound words.

If the boundary between the constituents of certain compound words which seems to be required by at least two phonological rules is to be more than an ad hoc device limited to just those compound words, some further motivation must be found for it. Such motivation could possibly be found in a theory

---

[8]The uninitiated reader should be warned that the facts presented here in the discussion of the vowel quantity rule by no means exhaust the problems connected with that rule. See, for instance, Bergsveinsson 1941:84—86, for the description of some additional relevant facts.

Janez Orešnik

which would identify at least (*n*—1) of the *n* constituents of any compound word with some word/stem to be found in the same lexicon. Thus, if the *jökul-* of *jökul-alda* 'moraine' is identified with the stem *jökul-* of the simplex word *jökull* 'glacier', the boundary between *jökul-* and *-alda* is motivated. Furthermore, the theory I have in mind would automatically extend this type of motivation beyond the examples which have originally stimulated the search for such motivation, to all compound words the (*n*—1) of whose *n* constituents can be identified with other words/stems in the lexicon. It can be foreseen that semantics will play an important part in such a theory, seeing that the link between, say, *jökull* 'glacier' and *jökul-alda* 'moraine' is primarily semantic. Until that theory is constructed, we must try to establish the existence and the nature of the boundary between constituents of compound words on purely phonological grounds. While the present paper may have established the EXISTENCE of a boundary between the constituents of at least some Modern Icelandic compound words, the NATURE of that boundary remains a field for further research.

REFERENCES

Benediktsson, Hreinn: »On the inflection of the ia-stems in Icelandic« in *Afmælis-rit Jóns Helgasonar* 30. júní 1969. Reykjavík, 1969.

Bergsveinsson, Sveinn. *Grundfragen der isländischen Satzphonetik.* Phonometrische Forschungen Reihe A, Band 2. Copenhagen and Berlin, 1941.

Chomsky, Noam, and Morris Halle. *The Sound Pattern of English.* New York, 1968.

Einarsson, Stefán. *Icelandic Grammar Texts Glossary.* Baltimore, 1949.

Orešnik, Janez. »On some weak preterite subjunctives of otherwise strong verbs in Modern Icelandic« in *Arkiv för nordisk filologi* 86:139—78. Lund, 1971. (Referred to as Orešnik 1971 a.)

Orešnik, Janez. »Morphophonemic notes on the Modern Icelandic imperative singular.« Forthcoming. (Referred to as Orešnik 1971 b.)

Orešnik, Janez. »On the epenthesis rule in Modern Icelandic.« Forthcoming. (Referred to as Orešnik 1972.)

POVZETEK

V duhu generativne fonologije se raziskuje vprašanje, ali je med sestavnimi deli novoislandskih sestavljenih besed kaka fonološka meja. Dveh pravil novoislandske slovnice — tistega o mehčanju zadnjenebnih soglasnikov in tistega o fonetični dolžini poudarjenih samoglasnikov — sploh ni mogoče pravilno izreči, če se na omenjenem mestu ne postulira obstoj kake meje, morfemske ali besedne ali katere druge. Odprto pa ostaja vprašanje o naravi te meje.

JANEZ OREŠNIK

On the Epenthesis Rule in Modern Icelandic

In Icelandic, "an epenthetic vowel, which eventually merged with unstressed *u*, developed before postconsonantal *r* followed by a consonant
or a juncture ... This change took place mainly in the fourteenth century,
though it no doubt began in the late thirteenth century" (Benediktsson
1969: 394): e.g. *armr* 'arm' > *armur*; *veðrs* > *veðurs*, genitive singular of
veðr 'weather'. It has been assumed in the literature on the subject that
the grammar of Modern Icelandic contains a phonological rule which is
basically a replica of this historical change. The only published formalized
version of the rule in question is Anderson's (1969a: 56):[1]

(1) $\emptyset \rightarrow u \, / \, C\underline{\qquad}r \begin{Bmatrix} C \\ \# \end{Bmatrix}$

This paper was prepared in Åbo, Finland, in the summer of 1971. My thanks are
due to the staff of Åbo akademis bibliotek for their frequent help. Miss Margaret
G. Davis has improved the style of the paper. All errors are my own. The theoretical
framework and the terminology of this work are those of generative phonology as
expounded in Chomsky and Halle 1968, except that no phonological representations
and no rule orderings will be posited here whose only or decisive motivation comes
from word-formational facts.

Non-phonetic representations are bounded by the obliques, //, except in phonological derivations, where the obliques are omitted. Very often the reader will find
italicized, i.e. orthographic, representations within obliques. They are used to
represent phonological units in those cases where I am unwilling to commit myself
on the exact nature of the phonological units involved.

I have discussed some aspects of Modern Icelandic phonology in two of my
earlier articles. Since a certain evolution of my ideas concerning Icelandic phonology
is reflected in those articles, the reader might wish to know the chronological order
in which they were written: Orešnik 1971a; 1971b; the present work.

[1] Rule (1) is practically identical with Benediktsson's formalized presentation of the
historical change described above.

It is the purpose of this paper to discuss the evidence for the existence of such an EPENTHESIS RULE in the phonological component of Modern Icelandic grammar (section 1), and to suggest a more precise version of this rule (section 2). Some relevant historical considerations are presented in section 3, followed by two appendices in section 4.

1. **Evidence for the existence of the epenthesis rule (1).** In this section I present the evidence which confirms the existence of the epenthesis rule (1) in the grammar of Modern Icelandic. A major part of the evidence is based on certain aspects of the behavior of the inflexional ending -r ~ -ur, see 1.1. The evidence offered by contrasts such as *lifur* vs. *lifrin* is discussed in 1.2.

1.1. In various forms of Modern Icelandic inflected words there appears an ending -r alternating with -ur (and with -Ø, but this last allomorph will be disregarded in what follows). The distribution is -r after a vowel, -ur after a consonant. For examples, see (2). The argumentation below proceeds in the following way. Choosing -ur, rather than -r, as the phonological representation of the endings under discussion would lead into difficulties which can be avoided if -r is taken as basic, and -ur derived from it; to derive -ur from -r, we need the epenthesis rule (1) in the grammar. Subsections 1.1.1.—1.1.4 contain different arguments for choosing -r as basic. They are followed by some concluding remarks in 1.1.5.

(2) -r vs. -ur:
    in the nominative singular of strong masculine nouns:
    dag-ur, stem *dag-* 'day', vs. *bæ-r*, stem *bæ-* 'farm';
    in the strong nominative singular masculine of adjectives:
    harð-ur, stem *harð-* 'hard', vs. *ný-r*, stem *ný-* 'new';
    in the second and third persons singular present indicative of verbs:
    tek-ur, stem *tak-* 'take', vs. *n æ-r(ð)*, stem *ná-* 'reach'.

1.1.1. (This subsection is based on Valfells 1967 and Anderson 1969a, b.) Masculine strong nouns such as *lækni-r* 'physician' argue for the phonological representation /lækni + r/, rather than /lækni + ur/, by arguing in the following way against the more general phonological representation /lækni + Vr/, where V means any vowel.[2] To produce

---

[2] According to Benediktsson (1969: 398) stems such as *lækni-* (as against those like *læknir-*) have repenetrated the colloquial language "in the wake of the introduction of compulsory education, at the beginning of this century".

lækni-r out of /*lækni* + Vr/, we would need a phonological rule deleting vowels *after* vowels. However, other case forms of the same word need a rule deleting vowels *before* vowels; cf. nom. pl. *lækn-ar*, from /*lækni* + ar/. If the phonological representation of the nom. sg. *lækni-r* were /*lækni* + ur/, we would have to say that two different vowel deletion rules operate in different forms of this word, whereby the forms in which these two rules would apply satisfy the structural descriptions of both rules. A vowel would be deleted after another vowel in the nominative singular, but before another vowel in some of the remaining forms of the paradigm, e.g. in the nominative plural. There is a parallel situation in the verb inflexion. If we, on the basis of forms such as 3p. sg. pres. ind. *kref-ur* of *krefja* 'request', derive the 3p. sg. pres. ind. *elska-r* of *elska* 'love' from /*elska* + ur/, we would again have to maintain that two different vowel deletion rules operate in different forms of verbs such as *elska*: a vowel is deleted after a vowel in *elska-r*, but before another vowel in the lp. pl. pres. *elsk-um* from /*elska* + um/. Since such awkward situations can be avoided by starting from the phonological representation /r/ of the ending in question, I prefer this representation. As a consequence, the phonological representations /*lækni* + r/ and /*elska* + r/ of the nom. sg. *lækni-r* and of the 3p. sg. pres. ind. *elska-r*, respectively, are as near as possible to their respective phonetic representations, and the undesired vowel-after-vowel deletion rule is then unnecessary.[3] A phonological rule deleting vowels before vowels, which we still need, has been formulated by Benediktsson (1969: 394); I will refer to this rule as the VOWEL TRUNCATION RULE.

1.1.2. Consider the declension of the neuter strong noun *lyf* 'drug, medicine', given in (3). Observe the alternation *j* ~ Ø after *f* in (3) (ignoring the dative singular, which offers more problems than can be

(3) nom./acc.	sg. *lyf*	pl. *lyf*
dat.	*lyfi*	*lyfjum*
gen.	*lyfs*	*lyfja*

---

[3] It is quite another matter that the phonological component of Modern Icelandic possibly contains a CONTRACTION RULE to produce forms such as dat. pl. *skóm*, of *skór* 'shoe', from /*skó* + um/. Such a rule would apply to sequences of stressed plus unstressed vowels, deleting the unstressed second vowel in case the similarity between the stressed and the unstressed vowels should be too great. Compare also the remarks on principle A in 4.1 below.

Janez Orešnik

solved in the present paper): *j* appears in forms in which it is followed
by a vowel; it is not realized before a consonant or before the word
boundary. This distribution is typical of the language, and has led to the
formulation of the following rule (Benediktsson 1969: 394):[4]

$$(4) \quad j \rightarrow \emptyset \ / \ \underline{\hspace{1cm}} \left\{ \begin{matrix} C \\ \# \end{matrix} \right\}$$

I.e. /j/ is deleted if immediately followed by a consonant or a word boundary. Assuming that the phonological representation of the stem of *lyf* is
/livj/, the J-DELETION RULE (4) deletes the /j/ in the appropriate
contexts.

Now consider the declension of the masculine noun *bylur* 'snowstorm',
and the present indicative forms of the weak verb *krefja* 'request' in (5).
Observe the alternation *j* ∼ ∅ in the forms of (5). If it is assumed that

(5) nom.	sg. *bylur*	pl. *byljir*		1. sg. *kref*	pl. *krefjum*
acc.	*byl*	*bylji*		2. *krefur*	*krefjið*
dat.	*byl*	*byljum*		3. *krefur*	*krefja*
gen.	*byls/byljar*	*bylja*			

the phonological representations of the stems involved in (5) end in /j/,
the forms of (5) obey the j-deletion rule (4), except for the nom. sg. *bylur*,
where we would expect **byljur*, and the 2.3.p. sg. pres. ind. *krefur*,
where we would expect **krefjur*. (Words in *-jur* are otherwise commonplace in the language: cf. nom./acc. pl. *hetjur* of *hetja* 'hero', with the
morpheme boundary before *u*, as in the non-existent **byljur*, **krefjur*.)
The actual representations *bylur* and *krefur* are accounted for in a non-ad
hoc way if the phonological representation of their ending is /r/, and the
j-deletion rule (4) precedes the epenthesis rule (1), so that the two derivations proceed as shown in (6). If the phonological representations of
bylur and *krefur* ended in *-ur*, the j-deletion rule (4) would have to be
further complicated by the statement that /j/ is deleted in certain forms,

---

[4] Benediktsson has formulated his rule for Old Icelandic, whereas formulation (4),
which is only a subpart of Benediktsson's rule, is meant to be valid for Modern
Icelandic. Formulation (4) cannot be accepted as final, for it does not account for
the present behavior of /j/ before /i/. Cf. dat. sg. *lyfi*, not **lyfji*, of *lyf* 'drug, medicine', as against the 2p. pl. pres. *krefjið*, not **krefið*, of *krefja* 'request'. Furthermore, there is a systematic set of exceptions to rule (4): action nouns derived from
verbal stems ending in /ja/, cf. *grenj*, derived from *grenja* (pret. *grenjað-*) 'wail,
scream'. Rule (4) would produce **gren*.

e.g. in the nominative singular masculine of nouns, even if the structural description of the rule is not satisfied; or we would have to postulate that the stem of *bylur*, for example, has two pre-phonological allomorphs,

(6)	*byl*j + r	*kref*j + r
j-deletion rule (4)	*byl* + r	*kref* + r
epenthesis rule (1)	*byl* + ur	*kref* + ur
	bylur	*krefur*

one with, and another without, final /j/. Since the phonological representation /r/ of the two endings involved helps us to avoid these undesired consequences, examples such as *bylur* and *krefur* constitute evidence in favor of this representation.

1.1.3. A parallel piece of evidence is offered by the behavior of *v* in Icelandic. This segment behaves in the same way as *j*, when preceded by a velar consonant. Consider the paradigms of *söngur* 'song' and *sökkva* 'sink' (intrans.) given in (7). If the nom. sg. *söngur* and the 2.3.p. sg. pres. ind.

(7) nom. sg. *söngur*	pl. *söngvar*	pres. ind. 1. sg. *sekk*	pl. *sökkvum*
acc. *söng*	*söngva*	2. *sekkur*	*sökkvið*
dat. *söng*	*söngvum*	3. *sekkur*	*sökkva*[5]
gen. *söngs*	*söngva*		

sekkur are disregarded, a rule almost parallel to the j-deletion rule (4) can be formulated:[6]

---

[5] The contrast *e* vs. *ö* observed in the paradigm of the present indicative of *sökkva* is due to the Modern Icelandic i-umlaut rule, and is independent of the presence vs. absence of *v* in those forms.

[6] Formulation (8) of the v-deletion rule cannot be considered final. I have here stated only a part of the rule which is relevant to the main argument. A complete v-deletion rule would not be limited to the *v*'s preceded by a velar consonant, but would correspond even more closely to the j-deletion rule (4). There are, however, difficulties with this extended version of the v-deletion rule which have so far proved unsurmountable. There is at least one case of preserved postvocalic *v* in final and preconsonantal position: *máfur* 'seagull' has gen. sg. *máfs*, acc. sg. *máf*. etc. Kress 1963: 65. After *r* there is a contrast between *mör* 'suet', from /*mörv*/, cf. gen. pl. *mörva*, and the lp. sg. pres. ind. *hverf* of *hverfa* 'disappear'. Etc. In my earlier work (Orešnik 1971a: 159) I have tacitly assumed an underlying distinction between /w/, which is deleted, and /v/, which is not. This solution is ad hoc: I am not aware of any evidence besides the contrasts such as *mör* vs. *hverf* for the phonological contrast /w/ vs. /v/; on the phonetic level there is no distinction between the sounds from either source.

$$(8)\ \text{v} \to \emptyset\ /\ \begin{bmatrix} \text{C} \\ +\ \text{high} \end{bmatrix} \underline{\quad} \begin{Bmatrix} \text{C} \\ \# \end{Bmatrix}$$

I.e. the segment /v/ is deleted between a [+ high], i.e. velar consonant and another consonant or the word boundary.

Söngur and *sekkur* (as against dat. pl. *söngvum* and lp. pl. pres. *sökkvum*, with *v* preserved before *u*[7]) are accounted for in a non-ad hoc manner if the phonological representation of their ending is /r/, and the V-DELE-TION RULE (8) is made to precede the epenthesis rule (1), see (9). If the phonological representation of the ending in question were /ur/, the

(9)		*söngv + r*	*sekkv + r*
v-deletion rule (8)		*söng + r*	*sekk + r*
epenthesis rule (1)		*söng + ur*	*sekk + ur*
		söngur	*sekkur*

v-deletion rule (8), or some other part of the grammar, would have to be complicated by the statement that *v* is deleted before certain morphs of the shape *-ur* as well. (*v* is certainly not deleted before every morph of the shape *-ur*, cf. nom./acc. pl. *völvur* of *völva* 'prophetess'.) Since positing /r/ helps us avoid this complication, examples such as *söngur* and *sekkur* are here offered as evidence in favor of the representation /r/ of the ending under discussion.

1.1.4. (This subsection is based on Valfells 1967 and Anderson 1969a, b.) If forms like *hattur* 'hat' are derived from /*hatt* + ur/, they must be made exceptions to the Modern Icelandic u-umlaut rule, because that rule must not apply in *hattur* even if its structural description is satisfied by the noun. Alternatively, the phonological ending could be /or/, that is, non-umlauting, and another rule could be called upon to change /or/ to the phonetic representation *-ur*. Both alternatives are ad hoc solutions. The former alternative makes an exception out of a very normal form. As to the latter alternative, we lack evidence for /or/ beyond the fact of non-umlauting. Starting from /*hatt* + r/, however, avoids the adhocness of these alternative solutions if we stipulate that the epenthesis rule (1) follows the u-umlaut rule in the sequence of rules, so that the derivation

---

[7] It is argued in 2.2 below that the *u* of *söngur* is of the same feature composition as the *u* of the dat. pl. *söngvum*. If those arguments are accepted, the contrast *söngur* (without *v*) vs. *söngvum* (with *v*) cannot be ascribed to any difference, on whatever level, between the *u* of *söngur*, and that of *söngvum*.

of *hattur* proceeds as shown in (10). No facts require the reverse ordering of these two rules.

(10)   *hatt* + r

    u-umlaut rule   —

    epenthesis rule (1)   *hatt* + ur

                            hattur

1.1.5. The phonetic ending -*ur* of the nominative singular masculine etc. comes from the phonological representation /r/ in s o m e cases, as exemplified above. To diminish the underlying inventory of the endings and the adhocness of the phonological representations, I will now take one further step by stipulating that a ll instances of the ending under discussion come from /r/. I thus abolish a possible ending /ur/ from the nominative singular of masculine strong nouns and adjectives, from the non-first persons singular present indicative of verbs, etc. (but not, e.g. from the nominative/accusative plural of feminine weak nouns such as *liljur*, of *lilja* 'lily', in which cases -*ur* does not alternate with -*r* and -Ø on the phonetic level). I have enhanced the generality of the solution adopted because of the examples like *bylur*, *söngur*, etc. by not limiting it to the forms which have forced me to adopt this solution. I have postulated the representation /r/ outside its original sphere because this leads to no complications beyond those necessary in connection with the examples for which I have adduced evidence that their ending is /r/.

1.2. Some evidence will now be adduced for the epenthesis rule (1) which is independent of the ending -*r* ~ -*ur* treated above. In the morphological paradigms of Icelandic words, the alternation *r* ~ *ur* is often to be found. Cf. *akur* 'acre' with *ur*, as against dat. sg. *akri* with just *r*. Examples like *akur*, however, cannot be used as evidence for the epenthesis rule (1), because *ur* is phonological here, as explained in 2.1, and the loss of *u* in *akri* etc. is due to the VOWEL SYNCOPE RULE. This rule is discussed and formulated in 4.1.

It is a different matter with another class of examples, that represented by the definite nom. sg. *lifrin* 'liver', vs. nom. sg. *lifur* without suffixed article; definite nom. sg. *hreiðrið* 'nest', vs. *hreiður*. It would seem that *hreiður*, for example, whose declension is given in (11), is bisyllabic, like *akur*, and that its dative singular and plural, and its genitive plural have lost their phonological *u* because this segment undergoes the vowel

8   Janez Orešnik   [8

(11) nom./acc. sg. *hreiður*   pl. *hreiður*
     dat.   *hreiðri*   *hreiðrum*
     gen.   *hreiðurs*   *hreiðra*

syncope rule (22): /*hreiður* + i/ becomes *hreiðri*. The forms with the
suffixed article seem to corroborate this assumption: cf. nom./acc. sg.
hreiðrið, nom./acc. pl. *hreiðrin*. Cf. also the definite nom./acc. pl. *sumrin*
of *sumar* 'summer', neuter noun, vs. nom./acc. pl. *sumur* without suffixed
article. The latter form is from the stem *sumar*- by u-umlaut, as is usual
with neuter nouns and adjectives, cf. nom./acc. pl. neuter *önnur* of *annar*
'other'. The unstressed *u* of pl. *sumur* is thus not due to the epenthesis
rule (1), and it seems that *sumur* must have a bisyllabic representation
before the vowel syncope rule (22) applies; consequently, the vowel
syncope rule does apply in the definite form to yield *sumrin*. However,
this attractive proposal can be shown to lead in the wrong direction:

(I) The unstressed vowel of *sumar* is undoubtedly 'elidible' (see 4.1
for a discussion of this term), as witnessed by forms like dat. sg. *sumri*,
gen. pl. *sumra*, and dat. pl. *sumrum*. So, if the vowel syncope rule (22)
can use the suffixed article as part of its environment when vowels of the
preceding nouns are deleted, why is the vowel of the definite nom./acc. sg.
sumarið not syncopated by the vowel syncope rule (22) to yield **sumrið*?
Moreover, there is a definite plural *sumurin* beside *sumrin*. Why is the
unstressed *u* of *sumurin* not syncopated?

(II) In general the suffixed article does not constitute (a part of) the
environment for the syncope of vowels in nouns to which the article is
affixed. Here are some relevant examples containing 'elidible' vowels:
höfuð 'head', dat. sg. *höfði*, definite nom./acc. sg. *höfuðið*, definite nom./
acc. pl. *höfuðin*; *hamar* 'hammer', dat. sg. *hamri*, definite acc. sg. *hamar-
inn*; *akur* 'acre', dat. sg. *akri*, definite acc. sg. *akurinn*.[8]

It follows that pl. *sumrin*, unlike *sumurin*, is unique and to be handled
by some mechanism for exceptions. *Sumrin* is used in the idiom *á sumrin*
'in summer' (parallel to *á veturna(r)* 'in winter'), and *sumurin* is the normal

---

[8] I quote the acc. sg. *hamarinn* and *akurinn*, rather than the homophonous nominative singular forms, in order to be on the safe side. For the sake of the argument it
could be assumed that the nominative singular forms of *hamar* and *akur* are derived
from /*hamar* + r/ and /*akur* + r/, respectively, in which case the lack of syncope
in the definite nominative singulars of these nouns would be ascribable to the double
r after the vowel to be deleted. It is not possible to apply such an argument to the
accusative singular forms of these nouns.

form elsewhere. This distribution of the two plurals corroborates the exceptional character of *sumrin*.[9]

It also follows that forms like *lifrin* and *hreiðrið* cannot be derived from bisyllabic phonological representations of the nouns in question: there would not be any non-ad hoc way of getting rid of the unstressed vowel, seeing that the vowel syncope rule (22) cannot be used to this effect. Instead, monosyllabic phonological representations of these nouns must be posited. The bisyllabic shape of *lifur* and *hreiður* is thus due to the epenthesis rule (1), for which rule the said forms therefore constitute positive evidence.

2. Refined formulation of the epenthesis rule (1). In 2.1 the environment of the epenthesis rule (1) is discussed, followed by a remark on the structural change effected by this rule, in 2.2.

2.1. The environment of the epenthesis rule (1). It has been established in section 1 that the phonological representation of the nom. sg. *hattur* 'hat' is /hatt + r/, and that the unstressed vowel of the phonetic representation of this noun is due to the epenthesis rule (1). Similarly, the phonological representation of the corresponding definite form, *hatturinn*, must be /hatt + r/ followed by the suffixed article. Since the representation of the suffixed article begins with a vowel, one would think that the epenthesis rule (1) would be blocked, and the result **hattrinn*. However, in reality the suffixed article is preceded by a word boundary, as shown in 4.2 below, and the epenthesis rule (1) therefore applies, yielding the correct *hatturinn*. Yet the present formulation of the epenthesis rule (1) is not quite adequate, for it applies in *lifrin* as well, yielding **lifurin*. The relevant difference between *hatturinn* and *lifrin* is this: in the former, *r* is an ending, in the latter it is a part of the stem. I therefore reformulate the epenthesis rule (1) as (12):

(12) $\emptyset \rightarrow u \;/\; C\underline{\hspace{1cm}} + r \begin{Bmatrix} C \\ \# \end{Bmatrix}$

I.e. a /u/ is developed between a consonant and an *r* which is preceded by

---

[9] The existence of the definite nom./acc. pl. *sumrin* of *sumar* has been recognized in the grammatical literature, see Blöndal 1920—24 s.v. *sumar* and Kress 1963: 101. Incidentally, Blöndal s.v. *vetur* registers *á vetrin* beside *á veturna(r)*. Since I have no other data on pl. *vetrin* at hand, I prefer not to comment on this, likewise somewhat exceptional, form.

a morpheme boundary, and followed either by a consonant or a word boundary.

Some illustrations will now be presented. (13) offers the derivations of the definite nom. sg. *hatturinn* of *hattur* 'hat'; of the definite acc. sg. *hamarinn* of *hamar* 'hammer'; of the definite nom. sg. *brúðurin* of *brúður* 'bride' (stem *brúð-*, cf. gen. sg. *brúðar*); of the definite nom. sg. *lifrin* of *lifur* 'liver'; of nom. sg. *lifur*.[10] Examination of these derivations shows

	hatt + r # # inn	hamar # # inn	brúð + r # # in	lifr # # in	lifr
el syncope (22)	—	—	—	—	—
ithesis (12)	hatt + ur # # inn	—	brúð + ur # # in	—	—
itic boundary (25)	hatt + ur + inn	hamar + inn	brúð + ur + in	lifr + in	—
	hatturinn	hamarinn	brúðurin	lifrin	*lifr

that I still have not accounted for *lifur*. The rules I have suggested so far cannot produce the bisyllabic phonetic representation of this word and, say, of the nom./acc. neuter *hreiður* (cf. the definite forms, sg. *hreiðrið* and pl. *hreiðrin*), of the gen. sg. *hreiðurs*, etc. To account for the numerous forms of this type, we still need the original epenthesis rule (1), here repeated as (14):

$$(14)\ \varnothing \to \mathrm{u} \ / \ \mathrm{C}\underline{\hspace{1cm}}\mathrm{r}\begin{cases} \mathrm{C} & \text{(a)} \\ \# & \text{(b)} \end{cases}$$

Rule (14) is like rule (12), except that the morpheme boundary is not mentioned explicitly in (14). Case (a) accounts for words like gen. sg. *hreiðurs* from /hreiðr + s/; case (b) produces the nom./acc. *hreiður* from /hreiðr/, and the nom. sg. *lifur* from /lifr/. Notice that rules (12) and (14) cannot be collapsed: substituting (14) for (12) in the derivations of (13) would lead to the undesirable *lifurin* beside *brúðurin*. That is why the epenthesis rule (14) must operate at a time when the representation /lifr # # in/ no longer satisfies the structural description of the epenthesis rule (14), i.e. after the replacement of the word boundary by the morpheme boundary in this word, along the lines discussed in 4.2.4.

We are thus left with a somewhat unusual situation: two phonological rules, (12) and (14), effect the same structural change in environments that differ only in one explicitly mentioning the morpheme boundary,

---

[10] The enclitic boundary rule mentioned in (13) and (15) is discussed in 4.2.4. It rewrites the word boundary between the noun and the suffixed article as the morpheme boundary.

and the other not mentioning it. What my analysis shows is that the phonological component of a grammar can contain rules R_1 and R_2, in such a way that they are not adjacent in the ordering, R_1 precedes R_2, and R_1 is a subpart of R_2.[11] More cases like this will have to be studied before it can be decided whether this state of affairs is accidental, or reveals aspects of the structure of phonological components and of the behavior of rules.

Finally, consider the strong masculine noun *akur* 'acre'. The phonological representation of the stem of *akur* ends in *r*, cf. gen. sg. *akurs*, and is bisyllabic, /akur/. The vowel syncope rule (22) is responsible for the deletion of *u* in the dat. sg. *akri*, dat. pl. *ökrum*, etc. (Thus, the /u/ of *akur* must be marked as 'elidible'.) The stem of *akur* could not be phonologically monosyllabic, /akr/, in my analysis, because /akr/ would lead to the ungrammatical definite acc. sg. *akrinn, parallel to *lifrin*, whereas the correct form is *akurinn*.

By way of illustration, the derivations of the following noun forms are presented in (15): acc. sg. *akur* and *akurinn* 'acre'; nom. sg. *lifur* and *lifrin* 'liver'. The derivations of the latter two are also given in (13) above.

2.2. A remark on the structural change effected by the epenthesis rules (12) and (14). I will now discuss the question whether the vocalic segment produced by the epenthesis rules (12) and (14) need,

(15)	*akur*	*akur ǂ ǂ inn*	*lifr*	*lifr ǂ ǂ in*
u-umlaut	—	—	—	—
vowel syncope (22)	—	—	—	—
epenthesis (12)	—	—	—	—
enclitic boundary (25)	—	*akur + inn*	—	*lifr + in*
epenthesis (14)	—	—	*lifur*	—
	akur	*akurinn*	*lifur*	*lifrin*

[11] In the epenthesis rule (12), one of the environments, C__+ rC, could be omitted, for I am not aware of any derivations in which it is used: no Icelandic ending or suffix begins with /rC/. (An ending which possibly begins with /rC/ is *-rð* of the phonetically monosyllabic second person singular present forms like *ferð* of *fara* 'go, travel', *nærð* of *ná* 'reach', etc. This ending, however, never occurs in forms which have undergone either epenthesis rule.) The environment is nevertheless stated, so that the striking similarity of the epenthesis rules (12) and (14) is preserved.

Those readers less initiated in generative phonology might wish to know in what sense (12) is a subpart of (14). According to the currently used notational conventions (Chomsky and Halle 1968: 67), (14) is an abbreviation for a number of subrules, including (12), and in this sense (12) is notationally a subpart of (14).

at any point in any given derivation in which these rules apply, have
a different shape than the segments which are on the phonetic level
indistinguishable from the segments produced by the epenthesis rules
(12) and (14). There are, for example, nom. sg. *hattur* 'hat', where the *u*
is due to the epenthesis rule (12), and the nom. pl. *sögur*, of *saga* 'saga',
where the *u* had been put into the phonological representation of this
form by the mechanism which expands lexical into phonological representations. Supposing that *sögur* ends in /ur/ on the phonological level,
is it permitted to let the epenthesis rule (12) produce /u/ in *hattur*, or
should it produce a segment with a different feature composition, whereby
this segment is later changed in such a way that it is phonetically indistinguishable from the *u* in *sögur*? The crucial test would seem to be the behavior of these *u*'s with respect to u-umlaut: we see in fact that the *u* of
sögur umlauts the preceding *a* of *saga*, whereas the *u* of *hattur* does not
umlaut the stem vowel of this word. However, it has already been suggested in 1.1.4 that the u-umlaut rule precedes the epenthesis rule (12),
so that no conflict can arise from the assumption that the segments in
question are totally alike: the *u* of *hattur* is simply not yet there when
the *u* of *sögur* umlauts the stressed *a* of this word. Thus the pair *hattur*,
sögur does not require the segment produced by the epenthesis rule (12)
to be different from the *u* of *sögur* at any point in the respective derivations.

More important is the pair, nom. sg. *akur* vs. nom. pl. *sögur*. While the
u umlauts in *sögur*, it does not in *akur*. As suggested in section 2.1, the
phonological representation of the stem of *akur* is /akur/. This, however,
raises the following question. If the *u* of *akur* is present in the phonological
representation of the stem *akur*-, it must be there when the u-umlaut rule
applies. Why is the stem vowel not umlauted, to yield *ökur*? It is known
that the u-umlaut rule applies in two kinds of environments (Valfells
1967; Anderson 1969a, b): before a *u* realized on the phonetic level
(PHONOLOGICAL U-UMLAUT), and under certain morphological
conditions, whether *u* is present or not (MORPHOLOGICAL U-UM-
LAUT). By way of example, consider a few case forms of *harður* 'hard'.
In the nom. sg. masc. *harður* the stem vowel *a* is followed by a *u*, yet the *a*
is not umlauted; this is so because *harður* is from /harð + r/, and the
development is like that in *hattur* as discussed in 1.1.4. The dat. pl.
hörðum, on the other hand, is a case of the phonological u-umlaut, the
phonological representation being /harð + um/. By contrast, the *ö* of the
nom. sg. fem. *hörð* is a case of the morphological u-umlaut. Etc. The *a*
of *akur*, if umlauted, would be a case of the phonological u-umlaut. Now,

an examination of the environments of the phonological u-umlaut shows that the phonological u-umlaut applies only before *u*'s preceded by a morpheme boundary in Modern Icelandic.[12] If the phonological u-umlaut rule is so formulated, it accounts for the lack of umlauting in *akur* (there is no morpheme boundary before the *u* of the stem *akur-*). Thus the pair *akur, sögur* does not require any difference, at any point in the respective derivations, between the *u* of *akur* and that of *sögur*.

A third relevant contrast is nom. sg. *hattur* 'hat' vs. nom. sg. *höttur* 'hood, cap'. In both, the stem is /*hatt*/, as proved, for the latter noun, by its gen. sg. *hattar*, its dat. sg. *hetti* (with i-umlaut of the stem vowel), etc. According to our analysis, both nouns have the same phonological representation of their respective nominative singulars: /*hatt* + r/, the only difference between them being that the /*hatt*/ of *höttur*, unlike that of *hattur*, is lexically assigned to the *u*-stems. The umlaut in *höttur* cannot be due to the *u* of the form, for the u-umlaut is found also in the nominative singular of those *u*-stems in which no *u* follows the stem; cf. nom. sg. *björn* 'bear', *u*-stem, gen. sg. *bjarnar*. It follows that the umlaut in *höttur*, as in *björn*, must be due to the morphological u-umlaut. Thus these forms have no bearing on the main problem discussed in this section.

In short, I have so far found no evidence against the assumption that the *u* produced by the epenthesis rule (12) is in any way different from *u*'s of phonological representations as regards the feature composition of these segments. Since there is no difference between these segments on the phonetic level either, this was a desired result.

The discussion of this section has been limited to the epenthesis rule (12). As far as the epenthesis rule (14) is concerned, I know of no arguments with any bearing on the main issue of this section. I therefore assume that the conclusion reached here concerning the structural change effected by the epenthesis rule (12) can be extended to the epenthesis rule (14).

---

[12] There is an exception to this generalization. The singular oblique cases of *faðir* 'father' are *föður* (genitive also *föðurs*). The word is exceptional if there is no morpheme boundary before the *u* of *föður*: the /a/ of the hypothetical phonological representation /*faður*/ would not be umlauted because the /u/ is not preceded by a morpheme boundary (cf. *akur*). The /a/ of the alternative hypothetical phonological representation /*faðr*/ would not be umlauted because the epenthetic vowel could here be only produced by the epenthesis rule (14), which, however, follows the u-umlaut rule. This exceptional word could be treated in several ways. A solution that at present seems to me most attractive is to treat the stems *faðir-, föður-*, and pl. *feð(u)r-* as suppletive formations. *Faðir* is one of the most common words in the language, and it is such words that tolerate suppletiveness in their paradigms.

3. Remarks on the history of the contrast *akurinn* vs. *lifrin* and *hreiðrið*. I will now discuss some of the problems associated with the epenthesis rule from the historical point of view. As is well known, there was a time, prior to the late thirteenth century, when the grammar of Icelandic did not contain the epenthesis rule. At that time there were representations like the following in the language: *hattr, hattrinn, akr, akrinn, lifr, lifrin, hreiðr, hreiðrit*, etc. In the next phase the epenthesis rule appeared in the form and with the ordering relations of the present day epenthesis rule (14). This must have led to representations like *hattur, hattrinn, akur, akrinn, lifur, lifrin, hreiður, hreiðrið*, etc. A third stage was reached when

(a) the epenthesis rule (12) had become established in the grammar; *hattrinn* was replaced by *hatturinn*;

(b) the monosyllabic stems like /akr/ had become bisyllabic, /akur/; *akrinn* was replaced by *akurinn*.

This third stage, and thus the present situation, had been realized by the beginning of the fifteenth century, as witnessed by the following seven forms in the Icelandic charters written before 1440 (quoted from Karlsson 1963): ueturi*n* (no. 138, line 6, dated 1409), fiordungur*in* (ibidem, line 8), vet*v*rin*n* (no. 150, line 6, dated 1415), arfurin*n* (no. 193, line 6, dated 1424), dômvrin*n* (no. 202, line 13, dated 1426), *p*artvrin*n* (no. 241, line 11, dated 1433), uetturen (no. 245, line 4, dated 1433). (Nos. 202 and 241 are in the same scribal hand, that of Ólafur Loptsson.) All these forms occur in Northern charters; the lack of equally old non-Northern examples is presumably due to the circumstance that only relatively few non-Northern charters have been preserved from the time before 1440, see Karlsson 1963: XVIII-XX.

The "events" leading to the present state of affairs, in the subject under discussion, can be described as (I) processes that changed *hattrinn* to *hatturinn*, and resulted in the incorporation of the epenthesis rule (12) into the grammar; (II) processes that changed *akrinn* to *akurinn*. At present I feel unable to contribute towards the clarification of the processes sub I. Only processes sub II will therefore be discussed in the remainder of this section.

It is obvious that the change of *akrinn* to *akurinn* has nothing to do with the advent of the epenthesis rule (12) into the grammar: rule (12) does not participate in the derivations of *akur* and *akurinn*. My above descriptive analysis of *akurinn*, *lifrin*, and *hreiðrið* accounts for the differences between the three on the level of lexical representations, where there is /akur/, but /lifr/ and /hreiðr/. Since we know that before the introduction of the epenthesis rule (14) into the grammar *akr* was

/akr/ on the lexical level, my descriptive analysis of the present day situation forces us to see in the change from *akrinn* to *akurinn* a consequence of the introduction of /u/ into the lexical representation of *akur*. This LEXICALIZATION of *u* could take place only after the incorporation of the epenthesis rule (14) into the grammar: before that event, there were no *u*'s in the stem of *akur* either on the phonological or on the phonetic level. The *u* which is lexicalized in these cases is an epenthetic *u* in origin.

Why was the lexicalization of the epenthetic *u* limited to the masculine stems? There is no answer to this question in my descriptive analysis. This implies that the limitation of the lexicalization under discussion to masculine stems is accidental from the standpoint of Modern Icelandic grammar, and, therefore, has an historical explanation only.

This observation leads to two further questions: (a) If the contrast *akurinn* vs. *lifrin* and *hreiðrið* has been descriptively unmotivated since at least the fifteenth century, what are the consequences that this state of affairs must have had? (b) What is the historical explanation of the contrast *akurinn* vs. *lifrin* and *hreiðrið*? I will now try to answer these two questions.

The unmotivated character of the contrast *akurinn* vs. *lifrin* and *hreiðrið* has led to the lexicalizations of the epenthetic *u* not obeying the merely historically motivated division into masculine vs. non-masculine stems. Cases have been reported, from post-Reformation centuries, of sporadic lexicalizations of the epenthetic *u* in neuter nouns whose stems end in *r*, and rare and spurious cases of the lack of lexicalization of the epenthetic *u* in masculine stems ending in *r*. On the other hand, I am not aware of any certain case of comparable vacillation in feminine nouns.

A short list of cases showing the lexicalization of the epenthetic *u* in neuter nouns will now be given. Bandle (1956, passim) enumerates examples which show that, on the whole, the distribution of the epenthetic *u* in the sixteenth century *Guðbrandsbiblía* obeys the same rules as in Modern Icelandic. There are, however, sporadic examples of lexicalized epenthetic *u* in neuter nouns (p. 157): *Blomstured* (also *Blomstrid*, pl. *Blomstren*), *Dryckiar offurit* (also *Dryckiaroffred*), pl. *Myrkuren* (also sg. *Myrkrid*, pl. *Myrkren*), pl. *Vnduren*. In all, eight instances of the lexicalized epenthetic vowel are quoted. The seventeenth century writer Guðmundur Andrésson writes what Benediktsson (1948: 30) renders as *myrkurinn* (pl.); the example appears in a biblical quotation (Job 24, 15) and may thus have been copied from an older source. Jón Guðmundsson lærði has once pl. *dægurinn*; the form is preserved in a manuscript from the seventeenth, and in another from the eighteenth century (Helgason 1948: 125, 131). In the eighteenth century, Jón Ólafsson úr Grunnavík writes pl. *blómsturinn* (Helgason in Holberg 1948: 303).

Much rarer are the registered cases of missing lexicalization of the epenthetic *u* in masculine noun stems ending in *r*, so rare, in fact, that their genuineness can be doubted. Cf. Helgason 1948: 125 (once sg. *vetrenn*).

What is the historical explanation of the fact that the lexicalization of the epenthetic *u* was so complete in masculine stems ending in *r*, and only sporadic in non-masculine stems of the same type? Benediktsson (1969: 395—96) has described the lexicalization of the epenthetic *u* in masculines (*akr-* > *akur-*) in the following way: "The /masculine/ stems in -C_nr- have been transferred to the class of stems in -V*r*- (that is, have been changed to -VC_nVr-), not only taking the same morpheme variant (Ø) in the nom. sg., but also being subject to the same deletion rule before vocalic endings." Benediktsson then shows how the stems ending in /VC_nVr/ were able to attract yet another class of nouns, that represented by *hellir* 'cave', where the change is from *helli-* (gen. sg. *helli-s*) to *hellir-* (gen. sg. *hellir-s*) through the lexicalization of *r*.

The model for the change of the lexical representation /*akr*/ to /*akur*/ was thus supplied by the many non-derived masculine stems ending in /VC_nVr/, which had existed in Icelandic from classical or even earlier times (*hamar*, *Alexander*, etc.). Developing further this plausible idea of Benediktsson's, I submit that the same kind of change occurred only sporadically in non-masculine stems in /Cr/ because of the relative lack of model-serving non-masculine non-derived stems of the type /... VC_nVr/.

In feminines, unambiguous non-derived noun stems in /VC_nVr/ have always been represented by the kinship terms *móðir* 'mother', *dóttir* 'daughter', and *systir* 'sister' only.[13] These nouns are ill suited as models

---

[13] In this context, there is some justification for mentioning the feminine nouns whose nominative singular case forms end in -*ur* (*brúður* 'bride', etc.). There has been a tendency, at least since the sixteenth century, to extend the nominative -*ur* into the oblique singular cases of these nouns, and to make the singular paradigms of these nouns indeclinable. See Þórólfsson 1925: 82—83. As a case in point, consider *brúður*. Its inherited stem is *brúð-*, cf. gen. sg. *brúðar*. Beside *brúð-* there is also a stem *brúður-*, limited to the singular, indeclinable, and anathemized by the normative grammar. The latter form has existed in the language at least since the sixteenth century: the *Guðbrandsbiblía* has a gen. sg. *Brwdurinnar* beside the ambiguous nom. sg. *Brwdurenn* (Bandle 1956: 106, 225). Árnason 1961—64 (here quoted from Árnason 1874: 340—41) has one instance of the dat. sg. *brúðurinni*, and one instance of the acc. sg. *brúðurina*, beside the ambiguous nom. sg. *brúðurin*; the

for analogical levelling because they form a compact set semantically (and thus would tend to influence semantically similar nouns only), and because they are morphologically quite irregular. This may explain the lack of examples like *lifurin for the regular lifrin.

In neuters, the non-ambiguous non-derived noun stems in /VC$_n$Vr/ have always been represented by sumar 'summer' only.

The assumption that stems of the sporadic type /blómstur/ owe their origin to the existence of sumar, would lead to the following problem. If the lexicalization of the epenthetic u in stems ending in /Cr/ depends on the existence of noun stems ending in /VC$_n$Vr/, the quantity of such lexicalizations, in any given group of nouns, would depend on the quantity of model-serving stems. Now observe the correlation stated in (16). It does not make sense that sumar alone would be able to accomplish more in neuters than would móðir, systir, and dóttir in feminines. In view of this I think that it is more correct to assume that the sporadic forms like blómsturið are mostly due to the influence of the masculine stems, with which the neuter nouns share more morphological features (many of their case endings are alike) than with the feminine nouns.[14]

(16)

gender	no. of model-serving stems	no. of lexicalizations
masc.	many	many (practically no exceptions)
fem.	3	no registered cases
ntr.	1	a few registered cases

---

forms occur in a folk-tale. Nineteenth and twentieth century grammatical literature mentions the indeclinable brúður-; cf. Cleasby—Vigfusson 1874: xviii; Blöndal 1920—24 s.v. brúður; Guðmundsson 1922: 63. Since the plural stem is always brúð-, the natural analysis of the indeclinable singular brúður is into brúð- plus ending -ur. Thus the indeclinable sg. brúður has a monosyllabic stem, and cannot be added to móðir, dóttir, and systir as a model for the change of lifrin to *lifurin. The same is true of the other nouns of the type brúður.

[14] The lexicalization and the de-lexicalization of unstressed vowels has in general been a frequent phenomenon in the history of Icelandic. A case in point is the history of nokkur 'some', whose stem was nokkur-, with 'inelidible' u, in the thirteenth century (dat. pl. nokkurum, gen. pl. nokkurra); mostly nokkr- in the sixteenth century (dat. pl. nokkrum, gen. pl. nokkra beside the older and rarer nokkurra); mostly nokkur-, this time with 'elidible' u, nowadays (dat. pl. nokkrum, gen. pl. nokkurra beside the older and rarer nokkra). See Benediktsson 1961—62: 17 ff. Incidentally, the example shows that the insertion or deletion of an unstressed vowel in the lexical representation of a stem can be accompanied by a change in the

As to the plural of *sumar*, I am inclined to think that the regular *blómstur* nouns have influenced it. *Sumrin* may have either its origin in, or at least its decisive support from, the equation:

(17)   nom./acc. pl. *blómstur* : definite *blómstrin* = nom./acc. pl. *sumur* : X
       where X = *sumrin*

4. **Appendices.** To facilitate the reading of the main text, two longish excurses have been removed from it into this section: one on the vowel syncope rule (4.1), and the other on the nature of the phonological boundary between the suffixed article and the noun to which the article is affixed (4.2).

4.1. **Appendix A: The vowel syncope rule.** The grammar of Modern Icelandic contains a phonological rule, the vowel syncope rule, which has been formulated as follows by Benediktsson (1969: 394):

$$(18) \quad V \rightarrow \emptyset \ / \ VC_n \underline{\quad} \begin{Bmatrix} l \\ r \\ n \end{Bmatrix} + V$$

I.e. a vowel preceded by another syllable is deleted if followed by either *l*, or *r*, or *n*, the morpheme boundary, and another vowel. The rule accounts for alternations such as *hamar-* ~ *hamr-* in the declension of *hamar* 'hammer', cf. dat. sg. *hamri*, etc.

'elidibility' of that vowel. This last factor can be seen at work by itself in the masculine *ia*-stems, e.g. *hellir* 'cave': after it had become established both in the singular and plural by the end of the sixteenth century, the stem *hellir-* contained an 'inelidible' *i* (dat. sg. *hellir*, dat. pl. *hellirum*); from the mid seventeenth century onwards, it has been optionally 'elidible' (dat. sg. *hellri*, dat. pl. *hellrum*). See Benediktsson 1969, section 5. Even nouns like *akur* can occasionally change their 'elidible' *u* to 'inelidible'. A case in point is the masculine noun *nykur* 'water sprite', stem /nikur/, cf. gen. sg. *nykurs*, whose plural forms are given as nom. *nikurar*, etc., and the dat. sg. as *nikur*, by the eighteenth century grammarian Jón Magnússon, see Þórólfsson 1925: 76. The definite dat. pl. *myrkurunum* of the neuter noun *myrkur* 'darkness', which appears once in the *Guðbrandsbiblía* beside the regular definite dat. pl. *Myrkrunum* (Bandle 1956: 157), could be a form of the same kind as *nikurar*.

The reasons for the changes subsumed under the term (de)lexicalization above may be different from case to case, and have to be determined with painstaking research along the lines indicated in Benediktsson's work referred to in this footnote.

Formulation (18) is not quite correct, for the following reasons: (I) That the vowel to be deleted is unstressed, is indicated in formulation (18) by the aid of VC$_n$ which precedes the segment to be deleted, in the structural description of the rule. This is correct on the whole, seeing that Icelandic words are stressed on their first syllables. The formulation fails, however, in the case of the suffixed article -*in*-, in which rule (18) operates although the *i* to be deleted is not preceded by VC$_n$ within the same word. (It is argued in 4.2 that the suffixed article is separated from "its" noun by the word boundary, and that the vowel syncope rule, which is responsible for the deletion of *i* in -*in*-, applies before the deletion of the word boundary between the noun and the suffixed article.) Cf. the paradigm of -*in*- given in (19). The suffixed article sometimes contains, and sometimes does not contain, the stem vowel *i* on the phonetic level. The distribution of *i* is governed by two principles. Principle A: The segment *i* tends to be lacking if the preceding noun form ends in a vowel; this accounts for acc. sg. *lilju-na* of *lilja* 'lily' vs. *kinn-ina* of *kinn* 'cheek', both feminine.

(19)			masc.	fem.	ntr.
sg.	nom.	masc.	*staður-inn*	fem. *kinn-in*	ntr. *barn-ið*
	acc.		*stað-inn*	*kinn-ina*	*barn-ið*
	dat.		*stað-num*	*kinn-inni*	(*barni-nu*)
	gen.		*staðar-ins*	*kinnar-innar*	*barns-ins*
pl.	nom.		*staðir-nir*	*kinnar-nar*	*börn-in*
	acc.		*feður-na*	*kinnar-nar*	*börn-in*
	dat.		(*stöðu-num*)	(*kinnu-num*)	(*börnu-num*)
	gen.		(*staða-nna*)	(*kinna-nna*)	(*barna-nna*)

Principle B: The *i* of the stem is absent from the case forms in which it is followed by a short *n* and another vowel; cf. nom. sg. *staður-inn* of *staður* 'place' vs. dat. sg. *stað-num*. Of no importance for principle B are the genitive and dative plural, and the dative singular neuter, because the noun forms to which the article is affixed in these cases always end in a vowel, and lack the *i* of the article anyway, in accordance with principle A. (That is why the forms of the article in (19) are, whenever possible, preceded by noun forms which end in a consonant.)

Principle B is in fact a special case of the vowel syncope rule: the stem vowel *i* obeys this rule because it is unstressed. Yet the formulation given in (18) cannot accomodate this case; I will therefore reformulate it as (20):

$$(20) \quad \begin{bmatrix} V \\ -\text{stress} \end{bmatrix} \rightarrow \emptyset \; / \underline{\hspace{1cm}} \begin{Bmatrix} l \\ r \\ n \end{Bmatrix} + V$$

I.e. an unstressed vowel is deleted if followed by either *l*, or *r*, or *n*, the morpheme boundary, and another vowel.[15]

(II) It is not the case that unstressed vowels can only be deleted if followed by *l*, or *r*, or *n*. They can also be deleted when followed by *ð* or *s*: *höfuð* 'head', dat. sg. *höfði*; *ýmist* 'various, diverse', neuter, dat. sg. *ýmsu*. It follows that all the dental consonants can occupy the position in question and be deleted. (The dental consonants *t*, *d*, and *þ* appear very rarely in positions that satisfy the structural description of the vowel syncope rule.) Furthermore, the vowel to be deleted is never what is in Icelandic phonetics usually called "tense", i.e. a diphthong or one of the following vowels: *i*, *ú*, [y], the last one as in *hugi*. Einarsson 1949: 11. (Since this use of the term TENSE is somewhat unusual, I bound it here with quotation marks.) The limitation of the vowel syncope to non-"tense" vowels accounts for cases like dat. sg. *Nikulási*, not **Nikulsi*, of *Nikulás* 'Nicholas'. (The syncopation of *u*, to yield **Niklás-*, is prohibited by the morpheme boundary in Benediktsson's rule (18): there is no reason to assume the analysis /Nikul+ás/.) Moreover, the single consonant which immediately follows the vowel to be deleted must not be tense (this time the phonological term TENSE is used in its accepted meaning), i.e. aspirated/preaspirated and/or long. This accounts for the lack of syncope in the postconsonantal gen. sg. fem. *-innar* and the dat. sg. fem. *-inni* (and in the gen. pl. *-inna*, although principle A intervenes here, seeing that the preceding noun always ends in a vowel) of the suffixed article.

---

[15] The above remarks on the shape of the suffixed article do not exhaust the complex of problems associated with this difficult area of Icelandic morphology. For example, we would expect the suffixed article to undergo the vowel syncope rule in the accusative singular feminine (*-ina* > *-na*), yet we find *-na* only when principle A requires this shape (cf. *lilju-na*), whereas principle B fails to change acc. sg. *nál-ina* of *nál* 'needle' to **nál-na*. The type of forms represented by *nál-ina* actually contradict principle B. However, since the suffixed article is one of the most common lexico-morphological units of the language, an irregularity, even a weak form of suppletiveness, here and there in its paradigm should come as no surprise. Thus I have to stipulate that the accusative singular feminine of the suffixed article is an exception to the vowel syncope rule (22). This stipulation does not deny the fact that the vowel syncope rule applies in some of the forms of the suffixed article, and this fact suffices as argumentation for reformulation (20) of the vowel syncope rule.

Cf. gen. sg. *víkur-innar* of *vík* 'bay, inlet', dat. sg. *vík-inni*. That the *nn* is here phonologically long (more generally speaking, tense), though it is not long on the phonetic level, follows from cases like the definite dat. sg. *á-nni*, gen. pl. *á-nna*, both with [n:], of *á* 'river'. In *víkur-innar*, *vík-inni*, and in gen. pl. *víka-nna* the phonetic length, indicated in the orthography (*nn*), is lacking, because the consonant is here, unlike that in *á-nni*, *á-nna*, preceded by an unstressed vowel.—I therefore formulate (21):

$$(21) \quad \begin{bmatrix} V \\ -\text{stress} \\ -\text{``tense''} \end{bmatrix} \rightarrow \emptyset \ / \underline{\hspace{1cm}} \begin{bmatrix} C \\ +\text{coronal} \\ -\text{tense} \end{bmatrix} + V$$

I.e. an unstressed non-"tense" vowel is deleted if followed by only one lax (= non-tense) dental (= coronal, see Chomsky and Halle 1968: 177, 304) consonant which is in turn followed by the morpheme boundary and a vowel.

(III) Even if a vowel satisfies the structural description of (21), it is not invariably deleted, as many relevant examples without vowel syncope show. Cf. *mikill* 'great, large', *heimill* 'at free disposal', vs. dat. pl. *miklum*, *heimilum*. We will say, following Orešnik 1971a: 159, that the unstressed *i* is 'ELIDIBLE' in *mikill*, and not 'elidible' in *heimill*. All attempts to define the class of 'elidible' vowels beyond what is suggested in rule (21) have failed so far. I therefore conclude the discussion of the vowel syncope rule by formulating the still unsatisfactory rule (22):

$$(22) \quad \begin{bmatrix} V \\ -\text{stress} \\ -\text{``tense''} \\ +\text{'elidible'} \end{bmatrix} \rightarrow \emptyset \ / \underline{\hspace{1cm}} \begin{bmatrix} C \\ +\text{coronal} \\ -\text{tense} \end{bmatrix} + V$$

I.e. an unstressed non-"tense" 'elidible' vowel is deleted if followed by a lax dental consonant, a morpheme boundary, and a vowel, in that order.

4.2. Appendix B: The nature of the boundary between a noun and the article affixed to it. I will refer to the boundary which intervenes between a noun and the article affixed to the noun as an AMPERSAND BOUNDARY. It will now be argued that the ampersand boundary is in reality a word boundary which behaves in a peculiar way because the suffixed article is inherently without stress. The argumentation will proceed as follows. In 4.2.1 it is suggested that the ampersand boundary is stronger than the morpheme boundary, and in 4.2.2 that it is weaker than the word boundary. In 4.2.3 an observation concerning the ordering of the phonological rules which play a role in the determination of the nature of the ampersand boundary is stated and substantiated. In 4.2.4 it is suggested that, in spite of the relative weakness of the ampersand boundary with respect to the word boundary, the ampersand boundary is identical with the word boundary; the enclitic boundary rule is formulated, and some consequences of the identification of the ampersand boundary with the word boundary are discussed.

4.2.1. Some evidence for the assertion that the ampersand boundary does not behave in the same way as the morpheme boundary will now be presented:

(I) The vowel syncope rule (22) can apply across the morpheme boundary, cf. dat. sg. *hamri* of *hamar* 'hammer', from /hamar+i/. By contrast, the rule cannot apply across the ampersand boundary (see section 1.2), cf. acc. sg. *hamarinn*, not **hamrinn*, from /hamar&inn/ (where & = the ampersand boundary).

(II) The /j/'s and /v/'s which are deleted by the j-deletion rule (4) and the v-deletion rule (8), respectively, before a consonant or before a word boundary, are not deleted before a morpheme boundary. Cf. gen. pl. *bylja* of *bylur*, and *söngva* of *söngur*, from /bylj+a/ and /söngv+a/, where /j/ and /v/ are followed by a morpheme boundary, yet they are not deleted. On the other hand, they are deleted before the suffixed article, i.e. before the ampersand boundary, even if the article begins with a vowel. Cf. acc. sg. /bylj&inn/ and /söngv&inn/, which end as *bylinn* and *sönginn*, not as **byljinn* and **söngvinn*.

(III) The u-umlaut rule can apply across a morpheme boundary, cf. dat. pl. *stöðum* of *staður* 'place', from /stað+um/. By contrast, the rule cannot apply across the ampersand boundary, cf. the definite dat. sg. *staðnum*, not **stöðnum*, of the same noun, from /stað&num/.[16]

---

[16] It might be useful to point out that the *u* of *staðnum* is structurally the same *u* as in the strong dat. sg. masc. *hörðum* of *harður* 'hard', from /harð + um/, where it causes the u-umlaut: the *u* pertains to the adjectival dative singular ending *-um*, and is thus preceded by a morpheme boundary. In section 4.1 it is assumed that the dative singular masculine of the suffixed article, *-num*, comes from /in + um/ by the vowel syncope rule (22). As the u-umlaut rule cannot apply across an /i/ (Anderson 1969a: 58), the lack of the u-umlaut in *staðnum* could possibly be explained by the presence of /i/ in the phonological representation of the article form. However, as pointed out by Anderson, the vowel syncope rule (22) applies before the u-umlaut rule, as shown by examples such as strong dat. sg. masc.

(IV) In section 1.1.1 I mentioned a vowel truncation rule which deletes unstressed vowels before another vowel. From the examples adduced there it can be seen that the vowel truncation rule can delete a vowel across a morpheme boundary. On the other hand, the rule cannot operate across the ampersand boundary, as a comparison of the paradigms of the definite singular declensions of *staður* 'place' and *tími* 'hour' shows, see (23). If the vowel truncation rule applied in the case forms of the

(23)	sg. nom.	*staður-inn*	*tími-nn*	from	*/tími&inn/*
	acc.	*stað-inn*	*tíma-nn*		*/tíma&inn/*
	dat.	*stað-num*	*tíma-num*		*/tíma&inum/*
	gen.	*staðar-ins*	*tíma-ns*		*/tíma&ins/*

definite *tími*, we would expect nom. *tíminn*, acc. **tíminn*, dat. **tímnum* or *tímanum* (depending on the relative ordering of the vowel truncation rule and of the vowel syncope rule), gen. **tímins*. The actual shapes of the definite singular forms of *tími* outside the dative are due to the operation of principle A discussed in 4.1.

Paragraphs I—IV suggest that the ampersand boundary is not identical with the morpheme boundary. As the latter is by definition the weakest boundary available in phonology, it follows that the ampersand boundary is stronger than the morpheme boundary.

4.2.2. The following phenomena show that the ampersand boundary does not behave in quite the same way as the word boundary:

(I) The phonetic length of stressed vowels depends on the number and quality of the consonants which immediately follow such vowels. Thus, the stressed vowel is phonetically long in the nom. sg. masc. *staðinn*, past participle of *standa* 'stand', where it is followed by just one lax consonant, and phonetically short in the dative plural of the same word, *stöðnum*, where it is followed by two consonants. The sounds of the suffixed article also participate in the determination of the phonetic length of the stressed vowels. In the definite acc. sg. *staðinn* of *staður* 'place' the *a* is phonetically long, in the definite dat. sg. *staðnum* of the same word it is short. The normal state of affairs before a word boundary is shown by the acc. sg. *stað*: the vowel is phonetically long. Thus, the ampersand boundary, like the morpheme boundary, is ignored when the phonetic quantity of

---

förnum of *farinn* 'gone', from */far + in + um/* by the vowel syncope rule. This shows that the /i/ of the phonological representation of the article case form is no obstacle to the umlauting of *a* in *staðnum*.

stressed vowels is determined, whereas the word boundary cannot be so ignored. These statements concern words pronounced in isolation, i.e. followed by a phonetic pause. Notice in passing that the ampersand boundary cannot be realized as a phonetic pause.

(II) Velar consonants are almost invariably palatalized if immediately followed by vowels like *i*, *i*, *e*, *æ*, within the word. In cases where the palatal feature of the velar consonant is not present in the phonological representations, whereas it is present in the corresponding phonetic representations, the fronting of the velar is due to a PALATALIZATION RULE (Orešnik 1971b). A case in point is the noun *bak* 'back'. Its *k* is not fronted in the phonological representation of the stem, as follows from the gen. pl. *baka* and similar case forms; a phonological /k'/ would remain on the phonetic level before a vowel, so we would get **bakja* (cf. *askja* 'box', from /ask'a/). The *k* of *bak* is fronted in the dat. sg. *baki*, by the palatalization rule. The *k* is also fronted in the definite case forms *bakið* and *bakin*, although the fronting *i* is here separated from the fronted *k* by the ampersand boundary. Again, the morpheme and the ampersand boundaries do not hinder the palatalization, whereas the fronting cannot take place across a word boundary in connected speech. Cf. *það sprakk eitt dekkið* 'one of the tires punctured', not [spra^{h}k$_J$].

(III) Only very rarely does the liquid *r* immediately precede *n*; a *d* is usually inserted between the two, and the *r* may even be deleted before the *dn*. The rule which performs the d-insertion—it will be referred to ad hoc as the D-INSERTION RULE—can be seen at work in the dat. pl. *förnum*, with *d*, of *farinn* 'gone', stem *farin-*. It can be seen in passing that the d-insertion rule is ordered after the vowel syncope rule (22), which brings the *r* and *n* into contact in *förnum*, and that the d-insertion rule can apply across a morpheme boundary. That it can also apply across an ampersand boundary follows from the definite nom. pl. *hestar-nir*, with *d*, of *hestur* 'horse', and *ærnar*, with *d*, of *ær* 'ewe'. On the other hand, no d-insertion is observed between an *r* and an *n* if the word boundary intervenes: *fer núna* 'goes now' is not pronounced with a *d* before the word initial *n*.

(IV) Phonological lax stops *p*, *t*, *k* become tense (preaspirated) if immediately followed by an *n* within the word. An underlying /v/ becomes the lax stop *b* in the same environment. An underlying *g* is lost between *n*'s. Both the fricative and the plosive /g/ appear as the stop *g* before *n*, unless the *g* is also preceded by *n*. Examples: nom. pl. masc. *opnir*, with preaspirated *p*, of *opinn* 'open', from /opin+ir/ (the example also shows that the preaspirating rule, as well as the other rules implied in the statements just made, must follow the vowel syncope rule (22)); nom. pl. masc. *étnir*, with preaspirated *t*, of *étinn* 'eaten', from /ét+in+ir/; nom. pl. masc. *teknir*, with preaspirated *k*, of *tekinn* 'taken', from /tek+in+ir/; nom. pl. masc. *gefnir*, with *b*, of *gefinn* 'given', from /gef+in+ir/; nom. pl. masc. *sungnir*, with velar *n* before dental *n* and without *g*, of *sunginn* 'sung', from /sung+in+ir/; nom. pl. masc. *dregnir*, with plosive *g*, of *dreginn* 'drawn', from /dreg+in+ir/. All these examples, with the exception of *opnir*, show that the morpheme boundary does not stop the processes described. On the other hand, the word boundary does stop them: *p, t, k* are not preaspirated in *hljóp núna* 'ran now', *skaut núna* 'shot now', and *tók núna* 'took now'. Phonological /v/ does not become *b* in *gaf núna* 'gave now'. Phonological /g/ does not disappear in *söng núna* 'sang now'. The fricative *g* can be realized at the end of a word even if the next word begins with *n*, cf. *dreg núna* '(I) pull now'. The ampersand boundary is like the morpheme boundary, and unlike the word boundary in the above respects. Cf. definite dat. sg. *skápnum*, with preaspirated *p*, of *skápur* 'cupboard', from /skáp&in+um/; definite dat. sg. *bátnum*, with preaspirated *t*, of *bátur* 'boat', from /bát&in+um/; definite dat. sg. *kærleiknum*, with preaspirated medial *k*, of *kærleikur* 'love', from /kærleik-&in+um/; definite dat. sg. *þjófnum*, with *b*, of *þjófur* 'thief', from /þjóf&in+um/; definite dat. sg. *hringnum*, with velar *n* before dental *n* and without *g*, of *hringur* 'ring', from /hring&in+um/; definite dat. sg. *vegnum*, with plosive *g*, of *vegur* 'way', from /veq&in+um/, where q=fricative g.

Paragraphs I—IV suggest that the ampersand boundary is weaker than the word boundary: the former permits the operation of more phonological processes across itself than does the latter.

4.2.3. Observation (24) concerning the ordering of the phonological rules involved in the determination of the nature of the ampersand boundary will now be stated:

(24)   All the phonological rules whose application is stopped by the ampersand boundary precede the rules which can apply across that boundary, in the sequence of the phonological rules.

I will now substantiate this claim by discussing some of the rule orderings involved. It has been shown that the following rules cannot ignore the ampersand boundary: the vowel syncope rule (22), the vowel truncation rule, the u-umlaut rule, the j-deletion rule (4), the v-deletion rule (8), and the epenthesis rule (12). On the other hand, it has been shown that the following rules can operate across the ampersand boundary: the palatalization rule, the vowel quantity rule, the d-insertion rule, and the sandhi rules discussed sub IV in 4.2.2. From among all the theoretically possible pairs of these rules those will now be singled out in which one member of the pair pertains to the former, and the other member to the latter set of rules. I will establish the relative orderings in some of these pairs. (An exhaustive investigation of these orderings is beyond the present state of our knowledge about the phonological component of Modern Icelandic.)

(a) The vowel syncope rule (22) precedes the vowel quantity rule mentioned sub I in 4.2.2. This ordering follows from examples like nom. sg. masc. *staðinn* vs. dat. pl. *stöðnum*, past participle of *standa* 'stand'. The nominative contains a phonetically long root vowel, the dative a short one. This difference in quantity depends on the quality and number of consonants which immediately follow the respective root vowels. Prior to the operation of the vowel syncope rule (22), *stöðnum* is /stað+in+um/. If the vowel quantity rule applied at that stage, the root vowel would end as phonetically long in *stöðnum*, just as it does in *staðinn*. Since this is not the case, it must be assumed that the vowel syncope rule (22) first brings the *ð* and *n* together by deleting the intervening *i*, and then the vowel quantity rule applies.

(b) The vowel syncope rule (22) precedes the d-insertion rule, as shown sub III in 4.2.2.

(c) The vowel syncope rule (22) precedes the sandhi rules mentioned sub IV in 4.2.2, as shown there.

(d) The vowel truncation rule, which deletes unstressed vowels before vowels, precedes the palatalization rule mentioned sub II in 4.2.2. This ordering is required by examples such as 1p. sg. pres. subj. *lagi* of *laga* 'repair', a *kalla* verb. The phonological representation of this form is /laga+i/, cf. the singular present indicative stem *laga-* and the dental stem *lagað-*. If the palatalization rule applied when the unstressed *a* is still present in the representation, we would expect the velar consonant of the form not to be palatalized on the phonetic level. However, it is palatalized: [laɪ:jɪ]. Therefore the unstressed *a* must be deleted by the vowel truncation rule before the application of the palatalization rule, so that the velar consonant and the *i* are brought into contact in time for the palatalization rule to front the velar consonant.

(e) The j-deletion rule (4) precedes the d-insertion rule mentioned sub III in 4.2.2. Cf. the definite dat. sg. *byrnum*, with *d*, of *byr* 'wind for sailing', from /byrj&in+um/. (That the stem of this noun is /byrj/ follows from case forms like gen. sg. *byrjar*, gen. pl. *byrja*, and dat. pl. *byrjum*.) If the d-insertion rule preceded the j-deletion rule (4), the former could not apply to /byrj&n+um/ after the vowel syncope rule (22): it would be blocked by the presence of the /j/. Since the phonetic representation of *byrnum* with *d* before *n* witnesses that the d-insertion rule has applied in *byrnum*, it is assumed that the ordering is, the j-deletion rule (4) before the d-insertion rule.

(f) The j-deletion rule (4) precedes at least two of the sandhi rules described sub IV in 4.2.2. Cases in point are, the definite dat. sg. *bandvefnum*, with *bn*, of *bandvefur* 'connective tissue', from /bandvefj+in+um/ (as to the postulated /j/ of the stem, cf. gen. pl. *vefja* and dat. pl. *vefjum*); the definite dat. sg. *þytnum*, with preaspirated *t*, of *þytur* 'rushing sound (of wind)', from /þytj&in+um/ (for /j/, cf. gen. pl. *þytja*, dat. pl. *þytjum*). The argument for the suggested ordering runs parallel to that in (e) above.

(g) The j-deletion rule (4) precedes the vowel quantity rule mentioned sub I in 4.2.2. Cf. nom. sg. fem. *mið*, with a phonetically long vowel, of *miður* 'in the middle', from /miðj/ by the j-deletion rule (4), as against acc. sg. masc. *miðjan*, with a phonetically short stressed vowel. If the vowel quantity rule applied before the j-deletion rule (4), we would expect the same phonetic quantity of the stressed vowel both in *mið* and *miðjan*, for prior to the application of the j-deletion rule (4) the *i* is followed by /ðj/ in both forms. The difference in the quantity of the stressed vowels is accounted for if it is assumed that the j-deletion rule (4) precedes the vowel quantity rule.

(h) The v-deletion rule (8) precedes the palatalization rule discussed sub II in 4.2.2. Cf. the definite acc. sg. *sönginn*, with palatalized *g*, of *söngur* 'song', from /söngv&inn/ (for /v/, see 1.1.3). The argumentation for the suggested ordering runs parallel to that in (e) above.

(i) The v-deletion rule (8) precedes the d-insertion rule described sub III in 4.2.2. Cf. the definite dat. sg. *mörnum*, with *d*, of *mör* 'suet', from /mörv&in+um/ (for the /v/, cf. gen. pl. *mörva*). The argument for the suggested ordering runs parallel to that in (e) above.

(j) The v-deletion rule (8) precedes at least one sandhi rule described sub IV in 4.2.2. Cf. the definite dat. sg. *söngnum*, with velar *n* before dental *n* and without *g*, of *söngur* 'song', from /söngv&in+um/ (for the /v/, see 1.1.3). The argument for the suggested ordering runs parallel to that in (e) above.

(k) The v-deletion rule (8) precedes the vowel quantity rule mentioned sub I in 4.2.2. Cf. acc. sg. *mör*, with a phonetically long vowel, of *mör* 'suet', from /mörv/ (cf. (i) above), as against the genitive plural of the same word, mörva, with a phonetically short vowel. If the vowel quantity were adjusted prior to the application of the v-deletion rule (8), we would expect the same vowel quantity in both mör and mörva on the phonetic level, seeing that both are followed by /rv/ at that stage. Since the vowel quantity in mör is different from that in mörva, I conclude that the v-deletion rule (8) applies before the vowel quantity rule, thus causing a change in the postvocalic consonantism, and consequently in the vowel quantity.

(l) The epenthesis rule (12) precedes the vowel quantity rule mentioned sub I in 4.2.2. Cf. svalur 'cool', with a phonetically long stressed vowel, as against gen. sg. masc. svals, with a phonetically short vowel. This difference in vowel quantity is due to the a being followed by only one consonant in the former case, and by two in the latter. The nom. sg. masc. svalur is from /sval+r/ by the epenthesis rule (12). If the vowel quantity rule applied before the operation of the epenthesis rule (12), we would expect the same vowel quantity in svalur and svals on the phonetic level. (For the phonetic quantity of vowels before lr, cf. gen. pl. svalra, with phonetically short a in the stem.) Since this expectation is not realized, I assume that the epenthesis rule (12) first changes the environment for the vowel quantity rule by separating the l from the r in the nom. svalur, so that a is followed only by one consonant in svalur, and by two in svals, when the vowel quantity rule applies and causes the differentiation of the vowel quantity in the two case forms.

(m) Since I could not find any similar argument to substantiate the claim that the u-umlaut rule precedes any of the rules which operate across the ampersand boundary, indirect evidence will be considered. The u-umlaut rule precedes the epenthesis rule (12); this is suggested in 1.1.4 above. Since we know that the epenthesis rule (12) precedes the vowel quantity rule (see (l) above), it follows that the u-umlaut rule also precedes the vowel quantity rule.

This concludes the survey of the rule orderings. While more orderings remain to be ascertained, I have so far found no counterexamples to observation (24) stated at the beginning of this subsection, and will below assume that that observation is correct.

4.2.4. In 4.2.1 and 4.2.2 it was seen that the ampersand boundary is different both from the morpheme boundary and from the word boundary. In 4.2.3 I added observation (24), a statement which is undoubtedly relevant to the determination of the nature of the ampersand boundary.

So far, however, that observation stands as something accidental, and unintegrated into the grammar in the sense that it does not follow from anything else.

In order to make observation (24) follow from something else, the idea that Icelandic phonology operates with three boundaries will here be rejected in favor of the assumption that the ampersand boundary is identical with the word boundary; the latter is replaced by the morpheme boundary before the suffixed article at some point in the derivation of the forms containing the suffixed article.[17] I posit phonological representations such as /hatt+r# #inn/ for *hatturinn*, /söngv# #inn/ for *sönginn*, etc., where one # denotes the word boundary with which the respective noun ends, and another # denotes the word boundary with which the suffixed article begins.

I will now formulate the ENCLITIC BOUNDARY RULE, i.e. the rule which rewrites any number of word boundaries as a morpheme boundary before the suffixed article. The rule will be temporarily formulated as assimilating the value of a boundary feature to the value of the feature [enclitic] of the next lexical item:

(25) $[] \rightarrow [\alpha \text{ word boundary}] / \left[\dfrac{}{-\text{segment}}\right]_1 [\phi \text{ enclitic}] \quad \alpha = + \text{ or} -$ [18]

I.e. any number of subsequent word boundaries remains if immediately followed by a non-enclitic word, and are rewritten as a morpheme boundary if immediately followed by an enclitic word. Assuming that Icelandic distinguishes between two boundaries only (viz. the word boundary and the morpheme boundary), a change of [+word boundary] to [—word boundary] means a change from the word boundary to the morpheme boundary.[19] I assume, until the contrary is proved, that the enclitic boundary rule (25) applies to enclitic words in general. (An enclitic is a

---

[17] In most of the present work the term WORD BOUNDARY refers to the symbol # #, which is to be found between any two words on the phonological level. In the main text between the footnotes 17 and 19, however, a more technical usage has to be resorted to, viz. that in which the term refers to only one #.

[18] But only +, or only —, in the same application of the rule.

[19] The formulation (25) and the subsequent statements are to be understood in the light of the proposal (Chomsky and Halle 1968: 364—71) that boundaries are feature complexes. In Icelandic the word boundary is presumably [— segment, + word boundary]; the morpheme boundary would then be [— segment, — word boundary], under the assumption that these are the only phonologically relevant boundaries in Icelandic. Rule (25) actually rewrites # # as + +; a general convention, irrelevant in the present context, replaces + + by only one +.

word which is inherently unstressed, and is part of the preceding word on the phonetic level.)

I assume that the suffixed article of Modern Icelandic is an inherently unstressed word, so that the enclitic boundary rule (25) replaces the word boundary before it by a morpheme boundary. I further stipulate that the enclitic boundary rule (25) follows the rules which cannot ignore the ampersand boundary. If the assumption and the stipulation just stated are granted, observation (24) on the ordering of phonological rules is incorporated into the phonological component of Modern Icelandic.

I thus posit the following ordering of the phonological rules of Modern Icelandic (here the rules of (a) precede (b), and (b) precedes the rules sub (c)):

(26)   (a) the vowel syncope rule (22), the vowel truncation rule, the u-umlaut rule, the j-deletion rule (4), the v-deletion rule (8), the epenthesis rule (12), and some other rules
       (b) the enclitic boundary rule (25)
       (c) the palatalization rule, the vowel quantity rule, the d-insertion rule, the sandhi rules described sub IV in 4.2.2, and some other rules, including the epenthesis rule (14).

It was observed above in 4.2.2 that the ampersand boundary is weaker than the word boundary. We now know what this means: the ampersand boundary is deleted at a point in the derivation at which other word boundaries are not (yet) deleted.

The suffixed article consists of a stem (-in-) followed by adjectival case endings. (If this analysis into morphs were not granted, all the case forms of the suffixed article would have to be considered unanalyzable endings, that is, suppletive forms.) Such structures are most naturally classified as words in Modern Icelandic, and thus are bounded with # on the phonological level. Here my identification of the ampersand boundary with the word boundary agrees well with the most natural classification of the suffixed article as a word.

The environments of at least three phonological rules must mention both the word boundary and the ampersand boundary: the epenthesis rule (12), the j-deletion rule (4), and the v-deletion rule (8). This has been shown elsewhere in this paper. Thus there are at least three rules that mention (27). If the ampersand boundary is interpreted as identical with

$$(27)\quad \left\{\begin{matrix} \text{\# \#} \\ \text{\&} \end{matrix}\right\} \qquad (28)\quad \left\{\begin{matrix} \text{\# \#} \\ \text{\# \#} \end{matrix}\right\} \qquad (29)\quad \text{\#}$$

a word boundary, (27) can be replaced by (28) and reduced to (29), in the formulation of rules (4), (8), and (12). The reduction implied in (29) has been incorporated into these rules above. Since it is the interpretation of the ampersand boundary as # # that makes this simplification possible, the latter argues for the said identification.

References

Anderson, Stephen. "An outline of the phonology of Modern Icelandic vowels" in *Foundations of Language* 5: 53—72. Dordrecht, 1969. (Referred to as Anderson 1969a.)

Anderson, Stephen. *West Scandinavian Vowel Systems and the Ordering of Phonological Rules.* M.I.T. doctoral dissertation. Cambridge, Mass., 1969. (Referred to as Anderson 1969b.)

Árnason, Jón. *Íslenzkar þjóðsögur og æfintýri.* Vol. I—II. Leipzig, 1862—64. The second edition of the second volume, 1874.

Bandle, Oskar. *Die Sprache der Guðbrandsbiblía.* Bibliotheca arnamagnæana, vol. XVII. Copenhagen, 1956.

Benediktsson, Hreinn. "Óákv. forn. nokkur, nokkuð" in *Íslenzk tunga* 3: 7—38. Reykjavík, 1961—62.

Benediktsson, Hreinn. "On the inflection of the ia-stems in Icelandic" in *Afmælisrit Jóns Helgasonar* 30. júní 1969. Reykjavík, 1969.

[Benediktsson.] Andrésson, Guðmundur. *Deilurit.* Edited by Jakob Benediktsson. Íslenzk rit síðari alda gefin út af Hinu íslenzka fræðafélagi í Kaupmannahöfn, vol. 2. Copenhagen, 1948.

Blöndal, Sigfús. *Íslenzk-dönsk orðabók.* Reykjavík, 1920—24.

Chomsky, Noam, and Morris Halle. *The Sound Pattern of English.* New York, 1968.

[Cleasby—Vigfusson.] *An Icelandic-English Dictionary.* Initiated by Richard Cleasby. Subsequently revised, enlarged and completed by Gudbrand Vigfusson. Oxford, 1874.

Einarsson, Stefán. *Icelandic Grammar Texts Glossary.* Baltimore, 1949.

Guðmundsson, Valtýr. *Islandsk Grammatik. Islandsk Nutidssprog.* Copenhagen, 1922.

Helgason, Jón, ed. *Ármanns rímur eftir Jón Guðmundsson lærða (1637) og Ármanns þáttur eftir Jón Þorláksson.* Íslenzk rit síðari alda gefin út af Hinu íslenzka fræðafélagi í Kaupmannahöfn, vol. 1. Copenhagen, 1948.

Holberg, Ludvig. *Nikulás Klím.* Translated into Icelandic by Jón Ólafsson úr Grunnavík (1745). Edited by Jón Helgason. Íslenzk rit síðari alda gefin út af Hinu íslenzka fræðafélagi í Kaupmannahöfn, vol. 3. Copenhagen, 1948.

Karlsson, Stefán, ed. *Islandske originaldiplomer indtil 1450. Text.* Editiones arnamagnæanæ, series A, vol. 7. Copenhagen, 1963.

Kress, Bruno. *Laut- und Formenlehre des Isländischen.* Halle/Saale, 1963.

Orešnik, Janez. "On some weak preterite subjunctives of otherwise strong verbs in Modern Icelandic" in *Arkiv för nordisk filologi* 86: 139—178. Lund, 1971. (Referred to as Orešnik 1971a.)

Orešnik, Janez. "Morphophonemic notes on the Modern Icelandic imperative singular." Forthcoming. (Referred to as Orešnik 1971b.)

Þórólfsson, Björn Karel. *Um íslenzkar orðmyndir á 14. og 15. öld og breytingar þeirra úr fornmálinu.* Reykjavík, 1925.

Valfells, Sigrid. *"Umlaut"-Alternations in Modern Icelandic.* Harvard doctoral dissertation. Cambridge, Mass., 1967.

University of Ljubljana
      Jugoslavija

CDU 803.959 — 54

Janez Orešnik
Ljubljana

FOUR MODERN ICELANDIC DEVOICING RULES

Summary.[1] Modern Icelandic generative phonology contains devoicing rules responsible for the partially devoiced character of the final segments of words like *dag*, for the voicelessness of the stem final segments in words like *dag-s*, *rusl(-s)*, and for the voicelessness of the segments followed by *t* in words like *sval-t*, *skamm-t* (the latter in southern pronunciation only). — One detail worth emphasizing: if the rules presented here are correctly formulated, the feature [voiced] is not distinctive in the Modern Icelandic phonological segments /b d g/.

1.1. The phonological component of Modern Icelandic grammar contains the following CONTINUANT DEVOICING rule:

$$(1) \; | \;] \rightarrow [- \text{ voiced}] \; / \; [+ \text{ syllabic}] \begin{bmatrix} \overline{\phantom{- \text{tense}}} \\ - \text{ tense} \\ + \text{ continuant} \\ \begin{Bmatrix} - \text{ coronal} \\ - \text{ anterior} \end{Bmatrix} \end{bmatrix} + [- \text{ voiced}]$$

I.e. any non-coronal or non-anterior lax continuant is devoiced if immediately preceded by a syllabic segment and immediately followed by the morpheme boundary and a voiceless phonological segment. — At the point in the derivation when the Continuant Devoicing rule (1) applies, LAX (= non-TENSE) segments are simply short. The features VOICED, CONTINUANT, ANTERIOR, and CORONAL are to be understood in the sense of Chomsky and Halle 1968, see especially table (1) on pp. 176—77. For SYLLABIC, see *ibidem*, table (67) on p. 354; vowels are the only syllabic segments of Modern Icelandic. — It follows from the list given here sub (2), and from the formulation of the Continuant

---

[1] My thanks are due to Miss Margaret G. Davis, who has improved the style of the paper. All errors are my own. The theoretical framework and the terminology of this paper are those of generative phonology as expounded by Chomsky and Halle 1968. Non-phonetic representations are bounded by the obliques, //, except in phonological derivations, where the obliques are omitted.

(2) Lax voiced continuant phonological segments of Modern Icelandic:[2]

    (a) coronal: /đ r l/   (c) anterior: /v đ l/

    (b) non-coronal: /v q/   (d) non-anterior: /q r/

Devoicing rule (1) that the rule applies, in certain environments, to the Icelandic segments v q r/, changing them to /f x r/, respectively.[3] The reason for the very general formulation to the right of the plus will become evident below, in section 1.3. I am setting up rule (1) to account for the consonantal alternations in Modern Icelandic simplex words of the type exemplified in (3 a, b). That the application of the rule must be limited to short /v r q/. can be seen from the examples given in (3 c-e).

(3)	voiced stem final C	voiceless stem final C
(a) *haf* 'sea'	gen. pl. *haf-a*	gen. sg. *haf-s*
vor 'spring'	gen. pl. *vor-a*	gen. sg. *vor-s*
dagur 'day'	gen. pl. *dag-a*	gen. sg. *dag-s*
(b) *ákafur* 'violent'	nom. sg. m. *ákaf-ur*	gen. sg. m. *ákaf-s*
		nom. sg. ntr. *ákaf-t*
akur 'acre'	dat. sg. *akr-i*	gen. sg. *akur-s*
audugur 'wealthy'	nom. sg. m. *audug-ur*	gen. sg. m. *audug-s*
		nom. sg. ntr. *audug-t*
(c) *bad* 'bath'	gen. sg. *bad-s*	
tal 'talk'	gen. sg. *tal-s*	
	gen. pl. *tal-a*	
heimur 'world'	gen. sg. *heim-s*	
	gen. pl. *heim-a*	
venja 'accustom'	1p. sg. pres. ind. med. *ven-st*	
	1p. sg. pres. subj. *ven-j-i*	
hringur 'ring'	gen. sg. *hring-s*	
	gen. pl. *hring-a*	
(d) *höfud* 'head'	gen. sg. *höfud-s*	
	gen. pl. *höfd-a*	
gamall 'old'	gen. sg. m. *gamal-s*	
atóm 'atom'	gen. sg. *atóm-s*	
alinn 'fed'	gen. sg. m. *alin-s*	
víkingur 'viking'	gen. sg. *víking-s*	
(e) *kjarr* 'thicket'	gen. sg. *kjarr-s*	
	dat. sg. *kjarr-i*	
ball 'dance'	gen. sg. *ball-s*	
	dat. sg. *ball-i*	
gramm 'gram'	gen. sg. *gramm-s*	
	dat. sg. *gramm-i*	
madur 'man'	gen. sg. *mann-s*	
	dat. sg. *mann-i*	

Janez Orešnik

The morpheme boundary posited in the structural description of the Continuant Devoicing rule (1) reflects the fact that the only segments which cause loss of voice in simplex words under rule (1) are /s/ and /t/, i.e. the only voiceless segments which can occur immediately to the right of the morpheme boundary in simplex words. (Words such as *sterkur* 'strong', with voiceless *r* in all their case forms, contain a phonological voiceless /r/.) However, I am not aware of any compelling reason for the morpheme boundary to be obligatorily present in the structural description of the Continuant Devoicing rule (1).

It is here stipulated that any segment to be devoiced by the Continuant Devoicing rule (1) be immediately preceded by a vowel. This reflects the fact that rightmost voiced consonants in consonantal groups are not devoiced by that rule. For examples of consonantal strings which do not undergo rule (1), see (4 a), in which Einarsson's (1945) transcriptions are presented. (On the basis of the situation in compound words, cf. section 1.3, Bérkov-Böðvarsson 1962 can be assumed to concur.) A

(4) Einarsson's transcriptions s.vv.:

    (a) *horf* 'direction'   gen. sg. *horf-s* [-rvs]
        starf 'work'   *starf-s* [-rvs]
        gólf 'floor'   *gólf-s* [-l(v)s]
        kálfur 'calf'   *kálf-s* [-l(v)s]
    (b) *torf* 'sod'   *torf-s* [-rfs]
        úlfur 'wolf'   *úlf-s* [-lfs]

similar situation obtains in compound words, see section 1.3 below. On the other hand, Blöndal 1920-24 devoices the rightmost segments in all consonantal strings if they satisfy the structural description of the Continuant Devoicing rule (1), ignoring the [+ syllabic] segment of the structural description of the rule. Thus, the genitive singular forms analogous to those quoted in (4 a) are all transcribed with [f] instead of [v]; see, for instance, Blöndal's *arf-s*, s.v. *arfur*, and similarly in compound words, cf. section 1.3 below. Einarsson has such transcriptions only seldom; for examples, see (4 b). I interpret this situation as indicating that Icelandic has reformulated its Continuant Devoicing rule (1) since Blöndal's time, limiting its domain to consonants immediately preceded by a vowel. (Einarsson's forms given sub (4 b) above are thus sporadic remnants of the older pronunciation.) I assume that the change can be ascribed to the interaction of the Continuant Devoicing rule (1) and of the Cluster Devoicing rule (10), on which see section 2 below,

---

[2] Note that nasals are non-continuant in the distinctive feature system of Chomsky and Halle 1968. Here and elsewhere in this paper the symbol q denotes a voiced velar continuant.

[3] Boldface indicates voicelessness.

but I am not able to describe the mechanism which has putatively caused the change. The matter deserves separate treatment.

On the other hand, Blöndal 1920-24, Einarsson 1945, and Bérkov-Böðvarsson 1962 unanimously indicate, in their respective transcriptions, the devoicing of two consonants immediately preceding the morpheme boundary whenever the consonant immediately following the morpheme boundary is /t/ (/CC + t/, where both devoiced consonants pertain to the set {/v r q'/}): e.g. nom./acc. sg. ntr. *þarf-t*, with voiceless *r* and *f*, of *þarfur* 'useful'. Moreover, the devoicing is indicated in the *l* of /lC + t/. where /C/ pertains to the set {/v r q/}, although so far no phonological rule is known which would devoice the *l* in such an environment; see the discussion of *sjálf-t* in footnote 13. However, in no single case is the transcription with voiceless *r/l* and *f* the only one given; it is always accompanied by a transcription not containing the [f] intervening between the liquid and the *t*. Thus there is [þart], which is a normal form easily derived by aid of the Continuant Devoicing rule (1) after the deletion of /v/. I evaluate the situation just described as follows. The forms pronounced without [f] are normal; those pronounced with [f] and voiceless *l* are artificial. If this evaluation should prove wrong, my Continuant Devoicing rule (1) will have to undergo a major revision.

1.2. In some cases the correct phonetic representations seem to depend on the assumption that the Continuant Devoicing rule (1) is preceded by some other phonological rule in the ordering. Two such cases will now be mentioned briefly sub (I-II).

(I) The genitive singular of the noun *bragd* 'trick' is *bragd-s*, often pronounced [braxs]. Unless we are willing to see an exception in the latter form, its phonological representation must be /braqð + s/. (The velar cannot be voiceless, as it is on the phonetic level in the genitive singular, because it would then have to be voiceless in the phonological representation of the nom. sg. *bragd* as well, with the result that the Cluster Devoicing rule, discussed below, in section 2, would — wrongly — devoice the stem final *d* of this form.) To achieve the phonetic representation [braxs], a rule deleting *d* between *g* and *s* has to be posited. and the derivation must be assumed to proceed as follows:

(5)
$ð \rightarrow \emptyset / q\text{---}s$
Continuant Devoicing rule (1)

braqð + s
braq + s
brax + s
[braxs]

Thus the ð-deletion rule must precede the Continuant Devoicing rule (1).

(II) The nom./acc. sg. ntr. of *margur* 'many' is *marg-t* [mart], with voiceless *r* and without *g*. Unless *marg-t* is allotted the status of an exception, for which there seems to be no need. its *r* cannot be under-

Janez Orešnik

lyingly voiceless in the framework of the present paper, for this would require the r to be voiceless in the phonological representation of, say, nom. sg. masc. *margur*; this, however, would lead to a wrong result on the phonetic level, for no rule has been posited which could voice the r in *margur*. Consequently the phonological representation of *margt* is 'marg + t/, with voiced r. The derivation of *margt* proceeds as follows:

(6)   marg + t
  $g \rightarrow \emptyset / r—t$ mar + t
  Continuant Devoicing rule (1)   mar + t
                                         [mart]

Since /g/ is not distinctively voiceless (cf. section 1.3), the Continuant Devoicing rule would not be able to devoice the r of *margt* if /g/ were still present in the representation when the Continuant Devoicing rule applied. Therefore it is necessary to postulate the ordering, the g-deletion rule first, the Continuant Devoicing rule next. (The argument of this paragraph is valid only for the northern form *margt*; in the homophonous and synonymous southern *margt*, the T-Devoicing rule, discussed below, in section 4, may be responsible for the devoicing of the r.)

1.3. The Continuant Devoicing rule (1) applies in compound words as well.[4] See the illustrations in (7 a). That the rule applies only when the left constituent of the compound word ends in /v/, or /r/, or /q/, follows from the fact that other sounds than these are not devoiced in

---

[4] Within the framework described here, a voiced /v/ must be posited in, say, *haf* 'sea' on the phonological level. Not so in the compound words like *haf-sild* '(kind of) herring'; here a phonological /f/ is not out of the question. True enough, a phonological boundary has to be posited between constituents of compound words in Modern Icelandic (Orešnik 1971 and footnote 15 below), and the only conceivable natural motivation of this boundary is achieved if at least (n—1) of the n constituents of any compound word are identified with some simplex in the lexicon. However, this identification need not be exhaustive. As is well known, simplexes can assume special forms when incorporated into compound words as their constituents (Bloomfield 1933: 225, 229). Thus it is conceivable that beside the stem /hav/ there is a compounding variant stem /haf/, and that the latter is used in *haf-sild*. Similarly, *adför* 'attack' when pronounced with [þ] (as it sometimes is, see Böðvarsson 1963 s.v. *d*), and *adferd* 'method' when pronounced with [þ] (as it sometimes is, see Gudfinnsson 1946: 71), are not necessarily counterexamples to the Continuant Devoicing rule (1), because they can be assumed EITHER to contain a compounding stem *ap-* in the speech of those speakers who use the pronunciations just indicated, OR to have become simplex words through the loss of the boundary between the two constituents. (There may be even other possibilities.) Such examples could be easily multiplied.

Still, it is a fact that the compound-internal sandhi obeys the Continuant Devoicing rule, in that it does not allow segment clusters which are destroyed by the Continuant Devoicing rule in simplex words. I interpret this situation as an argument for the view that in the majority of cases the identity of the left constituents of compound words with some simplex words of the lexicon is exhaustive in the sense intended here.

the said position, see (7 b). It can be seen in (7 a) that the segments which cause devoicing are not limited to /s/ and /t/, as in simplex words. It must also be noted that the lax constituent initial *b, d, g,* although phonetically voiceless in the speech of most speakers, do not act as devoicing segments, see (7 c), and consequently cannot be voiceless phonologically. The implications of this situation for the phonological theory are as yet unclear to me.

(7) (a) The final segment of the left constituent is phonetically voiceless:

af-komandi 'descendant'
for-seti 'president'
lög-frædingur 'lawyer'. and many other examples

(b) The final segment of the left constituent is phonetically voiced:

sam-kennd 'sympathy'
grammófón-plata 'record'
bíl-slys 'automobile accident'
vid-koma 'touch', and many other examples

(c) The final segment of the left constituent is phonetically voiced although the constituent initial *b, d, g* are phonetically voiceless:

haf-gola 'sea breeze'	*sam-band* 'connection'
sér-deilis 'especially'	*ein-göngu* 'exclusively'
dag-bók 'diary'	*til-bod* 'offer'
	vid-bót 'addition'

As far as the devoicing of strings of voiced consonantal segments is concerned, the situation in left constituents of compound words is parallel to that obtaining in simplex words, cf. section 1.1 above. Blöndal's transcriptions are as predicted by the Continuant Devoicing rule (1) if the [+ syllabic] segment of the structural description of the rule is ignored; e.g. *torf-þak* 'sod roof' is transcribed with [rf]. Einarsson's transcriptions only seldom follow Blöndal's; *torf-þak* is transcribed with [rf] in Einarsson as well, whereas many other words, e.g. *starf-semi* 'activity', contain [rv]. The transcriptions in Bérkov-Böðvarsson do not indicate devoicing in comparable situations at all; even *torf-þak* is transcribed with [rv].

In one respect, however, the compound words do not follow the simplexes: in the behaviour of constituent final strings such as /rv/ before constituent initial /t/. While the nom./acc. sg. ntr. *djarf-t,* of *djarfur* 'daring', is transcribed with [r(f)t] in the three handbooks consulted, the compound *djarf-tækur* 'daring' is transcribed with voiced *r* in Blöndal and Bérkov-Böðvarsson. (There is no suitable example of the kind in Einarsson.) This supports my claim that the transcriptions with [rft] of words such as *djarft* are spurious.

Janez Orešnik

1.4. To some extent, the Continuant Devoicing rule (1) also applies to any word final segment not separated from the immediately following word by a phonetic pause. I base this statement on two relatively large published samples of transcribed connected speech, Malone 1923 and Bergsveinsson 1941, which I have investigated. The statistical results of this investigation are summarized in table (8).[5] It can be seen there that /r/ obeys the Continuant Devoicing rule (1) in word final position when no phonetic pause immediately follows it, and the next word begins with a distinctively voiceless sound (not *b, d,* or *g*!). The data on /v q/ are statistically insignificant, and caution is indicated because of the fact that there is no instance of total devoicing of /q/ in the two sources, whereas there are at least solitary examples of partially devoiced or even voiced /q/. On the other hand, the sentence *ég sagdi* 'I said' is to be found transcribed in the handbooks, always either with voiceless word final [x], or without any consonant at all in the left word (see, for instance, Einarsson 1945: 23 and Bérkov-Bödvarsson 1962: 962).

(8) The sounds mentioned in the present table occur in word final position, are immediately followed by a distinctively voiceless word initial sound, and no phonetic pause intervenes between the two.

	Number of examples in	
(a) /r v q/:	Malone 1923	Bergsveinsson 1941
voiceless [r]	31	18
partially devoiced [r]	1	1
voiced [r]	1	1 (long *r*)
[f]	0	1
partially devoiced [v]	0	0
[v]	0	0
[x]	0	0
partially devoiced [q]	2	0
[q]	1	1
(b) other sounds:		
voiced sound	18	13
partially devoiced sound	2	10
voiceless sound	0	0

[5] Malone 1923 is a little difficult to interpret. Line *d* of his transcription is essential in the respect under consideration: if the column under the segment observed contains figures 2 or 3 in line *d*, the segment is voiced; if the column contains figures 8 or 9 in the same place, the segment is voiceless; a dot instead of a figure means that the segment has the same specification of the feature [voiced] as the immediately preceding segment; a closing parenthesis between two symbols in line *d* means that the segment to the left of the parenthesis is partially assimilated in voice to the segment immediately to the right of the parenthesis.

The statistics on Bergsveinsson 1941 are based on his narrow transcription, i.e. on line c of his texts I and II.

In more than a few cases included in table (8) the critical segments are partially devoiced although we would expect them to be voiceless, or voiced. Since the acoustic difference between voiced/voiceless and partially (de)voiced sounds is difficult to hear, especially in quick speech, such examples are here not considered counterexamples to the Continuant Devoicing rule (1).

An experimental field investigation of the devoicing in inter-word sandhi remains a desideratum.

2.1. The Continuant Devoicing rule (1) cannot account for the consonantal alternations exemplified in (9), where # denotes a phonetic

(9)	voiced stem final C	voiceless stem final C
ʋopn 'weapon'	dat. sg. *ʋopn-i*	nom. sg. *ʋopn#*
		gen. sg. *ʋopn-s*
rusl 'rubbish'	dat. sg. *rusl-i*	nom. sg. *rusl#*
		gen. sg. *rusl-s*
gutl 'dabbling'	dat. sg. *gutl-i*	nom. sg. *gutl#*
		gen. sg. *gutl-s*
tagl 'tail'	dat. sg. *tagl-i*	nom. sg. *tagl#*
		gen. sg. *tagl-s*
pukr 'secret dealing'	dat. sg. *pukr-i*	nom. sg. *pukr#*[6]
fálm 'fumbling'	gen. sg. *fálm-s*	
	dat. sg. *fálm-i*	
uml 'mumbling'	gen. sg. *uml-s*	
	dat. sg. *uml-i*	
klifr 'climbing'	nom. sg. *klifr#*[7]	
	dat. sg. *klifr-i*	

Dialect pronunciation with stop before *d*:

sagdur 'said'	nom. sg. m. *sagd-ur*	nom. sg. f. *sögd#*
hafdur 'had'	nom. sg. m. *hafd-ur*	nom. sg. f. *höfd#*

pause. Rule (1) cannot devoice the stem final segments in the forms of the rightmost column of (9), because the segments to be affected are either word-final or non-continuants and/or anterior AND coronal. To account for these voice alternations, I posit the following CLUSTER DEVOICING rule (10):

(10) [− syllabic] → [− voiced] / not [+ voiced] − $\left\{ \begin{matrix} + \ [- \text{voiced}] \\ \# \end{matrix} \right\}$ (a)
(b)

---

[6] The *r* of the nom. sg. *pukr* is totally voiceless, not only partially devoiced My source of *pukr*, without epenthetic *u*, is Gudfinnsson 1946: 144.

[7] The *r* of the nom. sg. *klifr* is partially devoiced when followed by a phonetic pause. It is, however, not voiceless, as it should be if the Cluster Devoicing rule were not blocked by the presence of voiced [v] in the word. My sources for *klifr*, without epenthetic *u*, are Blöndal 1920-24. Bérkov-Böðvarsson 1962, Böðvarsson 1963, etc.

Janez Orešnik

I. e. any non-syllabic segment is voiceless if immediately preceded by a segment that is not voiced, and immediately followed by the word boundary, or by the morpheme boundary AND a voiceless segment, in that order. — By "a segment that is not voiced" I mean any phonologically voiceless segment or any segment which is neither voiced nor voiceless at the time of the application of rule (10).[8] /b d g/ are segments of the latter type.

By way of illustration consider a few forms of *rusl* 'rubbish': the phonological representation of the stem is /rusl/, with voiced /l/. The voiced stem final segment is preserved before desinences beginning with a vowel, e.g. dat. sg. *rusl-i*. Since /l/ is preceded by a voiceless /s/, rule (10) applies in the nom. sg. *rusl,* where /l/ is word final, and in the gen. sg. *rusl-s,* where it is followed by the morpheme boundary and the voiceless desinence /s/, and changes /l/ into the phonetically voiceless [l]. No such processes apply in, say, *uml* 'mumbling', for /l/ is here preceded by a voiced /m/.

The following segments are devoiced by the Cluster Devoicing rule (10): /m n r l/ and — in dialect — /đ/. For examples, see (9).

In all the examples known to me in which case (a) of rule (10) applies, the devoiced segment is immediately followed by the morpheme boundary. For this reason the morpheme boundary has been posited in (10 a). However, I am not aware of any compelling reason for it to be there.

Case (b) of the Cluster Devoicing rule (10) could be a part of the Word Final Devoicing rule (15), discussed below, in section 3. It would be natural to say that voiced non-syllabic segments are totally devoiced if preceded by a segment that is not voiced, and only partially devoiced otherwise, in the environment of the Word Final Devoicing rule (15). I am not able to choose between these alternatives. Below I tacitly assume, for purely practical reasons, that the Cluster Devoicing rule (10) is correctly formulated.

2.2. In some cases the correct phonetic representations seem to depend on the assumption that the Cluster Devoicing rule (10) is preceded by some other phonological rule in the ordering. Two such cases will now be briefly mentioned sub (I-II).

(I) If the phonological representation of the stem of *fjall* 'mountain' is /fjadl/, and if the alternation [dl ~ l] of the nom./acc. sg. *fjall* vs. gen. sg. *fjall-s* [fjals] is due to a d-deletion rule which deletes the /d/ in the segment group /dls/ whenever the three segments involved pertain to

---

[8] No systematic status can be claimed for the ad hoc features NOT |+ VOICED| used in the formulation of the Cluster Devoicing rule (10), and |PARTIALLY VOICED| used in the formulation of the Word Final Devoicing rule (15), until more is known about the distinctive features of Modern Icelandic consonantal segments.

the same simplex word (contrast *fjall-safn* 'gathering of sheep in mountains', with [dls]), then this rule must apply before the Cluster Devoicing rule (10), or else the phonetic result would be a wrong genitive singular form, [fjals], with voiceless *l*, for the derivation of the form would proceed as follows:

(11)   fjadl + s
        Cluster Devoicing rule (10)   fjadl + s
        d-deletion rule   fjal + s
                                        *[fjals]

(II) The nouns *fugl* 'bird' and *tagl* 'tail' treat their consonant group *gl* alike in all their respective case-forms except in the genitive singular, where *fugl-s* contains a spirantal *g* and a voiced *l*, whereas the *g* of *tagl-s* is a full stop, and its *l* is voiceless. One way to account for this difference in pronunciation is to posit different segment clusters in the phonological representations of the two nouns: /fuql/ vs. /tagl/. A phonological rule (presumably the same rule which also changes /v q/ into stops before *n*, see Orešnik 1972) changes /q/ to /g/ before /l/ whenever the latter is not followed by a true consonant. (The stipulation that the consonant be "true" is presumably necessary, for a following /r/ probably does not block the creation of the stop.) This leaves *fugl-s* intact. with [q], but creates /gl/ in the remaining forms of the word. If this treatment of the difference in pronunciation between *fugl-s* and *tagl-s* is correct, the rule which changes /ql/ to /gl/ must precede the Cluster Devoicing rule (10), and the derivation of the case-form *fugl* proceed as follows:

(12)   fuql
        ql → gl   fugl
        Cluster Devoicing rule (10)   fugl
                                        [fʏgl]

If the relative ordering of the two rules were the opposite, the Cluster Devoicing rule (10) would not have a chance to apply to /fuql/, seeing that the conditions for the application of the rule are not met by the latter representation: /q/ is distinctively voiced. This would leave us with no means of devoicing the /l/.[9]

---

[9] To account for the difference in pronunciation between *fugl-s* and *tagl-s*. two different lexical representations were posited in each case. The same treatment is necessary to account for the two pronunciations of *bragd* 'trick': the southern pronunciation is [braqd], with partially devoiced stem final sound before realized phonetic pause, the northern is [brakþ] in the same environment; the case-forms in which the stem is followed by a vowel contain [qd] in the South, and [gd] in the North. The phonetically correct results are guaranteed if the lexical representation of the southern stem is /braqd/, and that of the northern stem /bragd/. The Cluster Devoicing rule (10) then applies in the northern nominative/accusative forms and devoices the word final /d/ into /p/.

Janez Orešnik

2.3. As far as I can see, the situation in compound words is such as predicted by the Cluster Devoicing rule (10). I am basing this claim on the transcriptions in Einarsson 1945 and Bérkov-Böðvarsson 1962. See (13). Blöndal 1920—24, however, italicizes the final segment of the left constituent in the types of compound words exemplified by *tungl-koma* and *jafn-gamall* in (13); according to Ófeigsson in Blöndal 1920—24: XX.

(13) environment of   final segment X of the left constituent

segment X	voiceless	voiced
voiceless_voiceless	*vopn-fimi* 'skill at arms'	
voiceless_voiced		*vopn-laus* 'unarmed'
voiced_voiceless		*tungl-koma* 'new moon'[10]
voiceless_/b d g/	*vopn-bitinn* 'wounded w. arms'	
/b d g/_voiceless	*jafn-fætis* 'on equal standing'	
/b d g/_/b d g/	*jafn-gamall* 'of the same age'	
voiced_voiced		*tungl-myrkvi* 'lunar eclipse'
voiced_/b d g/		*tungl-braut* 'lunar orbit'
/b d g/_voiced		*jafn-lyndi* 'even temper'

this means that the segments in question are sometimes pronounced voiced, and sometimes voiceless, but it is not clear whether they can vacillate in the speech of the same person, or of the same community, or anything else. The Cluster Devoicing rule (10) cannot account for this vacillation, and will have to be reformulated if the transcriptions of Blöndal 1920—24 turn out to be nearer to reality than the more recent data on which this section is based.

2.4. The handbooks offer hardly any information on the behaviour of the consonantal clusters enumerated in the left column of (13) in connected speech. The Cluster Devoicing rule (10) predicts pronunciations such as those indicated in (14), where each pair of words is supposed to pertain to the same breath group. My own impressionistic observations of spoken Icelandic confirm the data presented in (14). However, a special investigation of this matter is a desideratum.

A similar treatment helps to account for the two pronunciations of *blíðka* 'soften': the southern with [þg], and the northern with [ðk]. /þ/ and /ð/, respectively, are posited in the lexical representation of the stem, and no devoicing rules apply in the derivations of the two pronunciation variants. Such simple treatment would not do in the case of the past participles *hafður* pronounced with [b], of *hafa* 'have', and *sagður* pronounced with non-continuant *g*, of *segja* 'say'. Here underlying /hav + ð/ and /saq + ð/ must be posited, cf. the present-stem members of the respective verbal paradigms. A special northern rule changes /vð/ to /bð/, and /qð/ to /gð/, in the appropriate contexts.

[10] The pronunciation of *tungl-* which I have in mind here and in (14) does not contain [g].

(14) environment of   final segment X of the left word is

    segment X   voiceless   voiced

    voiceless‿voiceless   *ʋopn fékk*

    voiceless‿voiced   *ʋopn lét*

    voiced‿voiceless   *tungl kom*

    voiceless‿/b d g/   *ʋopn beit*

    /b d g/‿voiceless   *jafn straumur*

    /b d g/‿/b d g/   *jafn baggi*

    voiced‿voiced   *tungl ʋex*

    voiced‿/b d g/   *tungl gekk*

    /b d g/‿voiced   *jafn líka*

3. In Modern Icelandic phonology there is also a WORD FINAL DEVOICING rule:

(15)
$$
\begin{bmatrix}
-\text{syllabic} \\
+\text{voiced} \\
-\text{tense}
\end{bmatrix}
\rightarrow \text{partially voiced} \; / \_ \#
$$

I.e. any lax voiced non-syllabic segment is partially devoiced if immediately followed by a word boundary. (See also footnote 8.) [+ voiced] must be mentioned in the structural description of the rule, otherwise distinctively voiceless segments, e.g. /s/, would be turned into partially voiced sounds by this rule. At the time that the Word Final Devoicing rule (15) applies, lax non-syllabic segments are simply short. Examples

(16)   stem final consonant
               voiced   partially devoiced

(a) *bad* 'bath'   dat. sg. *bad-i*   nom. sg. *bad#*
   hefd 'title'   gen. sg. *hefd-ar*   nom. sg. *hefd#*[11]
   dagur 'day'   nom. sg. *dag-ur*   acc. sg. *dag#*
   emj 'cry'   dat. sg. *emj-i*   nom. sg. *emj#*
   öl 'ale, beer'   gen. sg. *öl-s*   nom. sg. *öl#*
   horf 'direction'   dat. sg. *horf-i*   nom. sg. *horf#*
   akur 'acre'   dat. sg. *akr-i*   nom. sg. *akur#*
   gamall 'old'   dat. pl. *göml-um*   nom. sg. f. *gömul#*
   höfud 'head'   dat. sg. *höfd-i*   nom. sg. *höfud#*
   gaman 'fun'   gen. sg. *gaman-s*   nom. sg. *gaman#*
   talkúm 'talcum'   gen. sg. *talkúm-s*   nom. sg. *talkúm#*
(b) *skammur* 'short'   nom. sg. f. *skömm#*
   unna 'love'   lp. sg. pres. ind. *ann#*
   kjarr 'thicket'   nom. sg. *kjarr#*
   ball 'dance'   nom. sg. *ball#*

---

[11] The pronunciation of *hefd* which I have in mind here contains [v] before the dental.

Janez Orešnik

like *hefd, emj* and *horf* of (16) show that rule (15) must be limited to the word final position: voiced non-final non-syllabics in contact with word final segments are not partially devoiced by rule (15).

The Word Final Devoicing rule (15) accounts for the consonantal alternations of the type exemplified in (16 a), where the simbol # denotes a phonetically realized pause. Examples showing that the rule must be restricted to short non-syllabic segments are given in (16 b).

Einarsson 1945: 5, 25 asserts that the consonants in the endings *-inn* and *-um* retain some length and are voiced, at least in careful speech. These data are disputed. As regards unstressed *-inn*, they are stated similarly in Einarsson 1927: 38. 79, in Gudfinnsson 1946: 68 (where the author describes the length of [n] in the said ending as vacillating between voiced long [n] and partially devoiced short [n]), by implication also in Kress 1963, e.g. p. 57, as pointed out by Benediktsson 1963: 112. On the other hand, Benediktsson *l.c.* believes that no such vacillation exists, except perhaps in an affected lecture style of pronunciation. As to the unstressed ending *-um*, the length of its *m* is asserted by Einarsson 1927: 38, 79 and by Kress 1963: 33. Benediktsson 1965: 112 can be construed as denying the existence of any special length of *m* in *-um*. Whatever the truth about this quantity problem, the Word Final Devoicing rule (15) predicts that word final *m* and *n* will be voiced when long, and partially devoiced when short.

On the phonetic level, the effects of the Word Final Devoicing rule (15) can only be observed at the absolute end of breath groups, i.e. at phonetically realized pauses (Einarsson 1945: 24). Although the environment of rule (15) mentions the word boundary, and although the latter is present in the phonological representations of nouns with suffixed article (Orešnik 1972, app. B), and assumedly present in the phonological representations of compound words (cf. footnote 15), the Word Final Devoicing rule (15) never seems to leave any traces behind in nouns with suffixed articles or in compound words. We return to this fact in section 4.3 below.

4.1. The Continuant Devoicing rule (1), the Cluster Devoicing rule (10), and the Word Final Devoicing rule (15) apply with equal force in all Modern Icelandic dialects, as far as I know. This is not the case with the T-DEVOICING rule to which we now pass. The T-Devoicing rule must be stated separately for southern and northern dialect areas:[12]

(17) [—syllabic] → [— voiced] / _t in southern pronunciation

I.e. in southern pronunciation any non-syllabic segment is devoiced if immediately followed by /t/. Rule (17) accounts for consonantal alternations like those exemplified in (19).

---

[12] The terms SOUTHERN and NORTHERN are approximate labels. For a stricter geographical delimitation of the two pronunciations, see Gudfinnsson 1964: 17—43.

The northern counterpart of rule (17) is as follows:

(18) [+ lateral] → [− voiced] / _t in northern pronunciation

I.e. in northern pronunciation any /l/ is devoiced if immediately followed by /t/. Rule (18) accounts for the consonantal alternations exemplified sub (19 a). There are no comparable alternations in the words given sub (19 b), in northern pronunciation, hence the need for the more restricted northern T-Devoicing rule (18). The southern version (17) is thus seen to be more general, and presumably easier for language-learning children to learn and remember, than the northern rule (18). This may be one of the factors contributing to the spread of (17) at the expense of (18).

(19)	consonant before the hyphen	
	voiced	voiceless
(a) *svalur* 'cool'	nom. sg. m. *sval-ur*	nom. sg. ntr. *sval-t*
(b) *skemma* 'damage'	inf. *skemm-a*	supine *skemm-t*
vanur 'used to'	nom. sg. m. *van-ur*	nom. sg. ntr. *van-t*
hringja 'ring'	inf. *hringj-a*	supine *hring-t*

Almost all the forms in which the T-Devoicing rule (17/18) HAS to apply seem to involve /t/ preceded by a morpheme boundary at the point in the derivation when the T-Devoicing rule (17/18) applies. (Words like *vanta* 'lack', with voiceless *n* in all the forms of the word in southern pronunciation, do not argue against the presence of the morpheme boundary in the structural description of the T-Devoicing rule (17/18), for the voiceless *n* can be present in the phonological representation of the word, and is thus not necessarily due to the T-Devoicing rule (17/18).) I know only four exceptions: in the singular preterite indicative of the strong verbs *halda* 'hold', *gjalda* 'pay', *svelta* 'be hungry', and *velta* 'fall', voiced and voiceless *l* alternate with each other, as shown

(20) (a) voiceless *l*: 1p. and 3p. sg. pret. ind. active *hélt, galt, svalt, valt*

    (b) voiced *l*: 2p. sg. pret. ind. active and the whole sg. pret. ind. middle: *hélzt, galzt, svalzt, valzt*

in (20). No morpheme boundary can be posited before *t* in the forms sub (20 a). Nor can it be plausibly argued that the forms are suppletive formations, with their voiceless *l* not due to the operation of the T-Devoicing rule (17/18), but present in the underlying representations of these forms, for one suppletive form would then be necessary in the first and third persons singular preterite indicative active, and another in all the remaining forms of the singular preterite indicative, including the middle voice. It seems to me much more plausible that the voicelessness

Janez Orešnik

of the *l* in the forms of (20 a) is due to the T-Devoicing rule (17/18).[13] To accommodate the forms sub (20), the morpheme boundary is not posited in the structural description of the T-Devoicing rule (17/18).

4.2. Unlike the Continuant Devoicing rule (1) and the Cluster Devoicing rule (10), the T-Devoicing rule (17/18) does not operate across the boundary between the constituents of compound words, or across the boundary between words.[14] In fact, the morpheme boundary is the only boundary which does not block the T-Devoicing rule (17/18). For crucial examples in which the T-Devoicing rule (17/18) does not apply, see (21).

4.3. One reason why no attempt has been made here to collapse the T-Devoicing rule (17/18) with the Continuant Devoicing rule (1) and/or the Cluster Devoicing rule (10) is that the T-Devoicing rule (17/18) is, unlike the other rules just mentioned, a dialect dependent rule. Another argument against the collapsing is that the T-Devoicing rule precedes the Compound Boundary rule, whereas the Continuant Devoicing rule (1) and the Cluster Devoicing rule (10) follow the said boundary rule in the ordering. This matter will now be briefly discussed.

---

[13] The alternation between voiced and voiceless *l* is also observed in the imperative singular of the verbs under discussion: the active form *haltu* contains a voiceless *l*, the middle form *halztu* a voiced *l*. However, the T-Devoicing rule (17/18) can account for this alternation even if its structural description contained an obligatory morpheme boundary, for the phonological representations of these forms are /hald + tu/ and /hald + st + tu/, where the morpheme boundary before /tu/ may be a rewritten stronger boudary, in which case the rewriting rule operates before the T-Devoicing rule.

The supines such as *siglt* of *sigla* 'sail' may also be relevant with respect to the morpheme boundary in the structural description of the T-Devoicing rule (and, incidentally, even with respect to the structural descriptions of some other devoicing rules). However, these supines require separate treatment because of the many problems associated with their derivation (metathesis, etc.).

Forms such as nom./acc. sg. ntr. *sjálf-t*, of *sjálfur* 'self', are partly enigmatic. One of the pronunciations of *sjálft* is [-lt], with voiceless *l* and without *f*; this pronunciation is easily accounted for by the T-Devoicing rule (17/18) if the deletion of the phonological segment between *l* and *t* precedes the application of the T-Devoicing rule; cf. footnote 18 ad finem. Another pronunciation of *sjálft* contains [-lft], with voiceless *l*. This *l* cannot be devoiced by any of the rules posited here. I evaluate the [-lft]-forms as artificial.

Gudfinnsson 1964: 17—43, especially 30 ff., reports some dialect pronunciations of *sjálft*. Normally his informants, school children, did not pronounce the *f* at all, and they either devoiced the *l* in accordance with the T-Devoicing rule in such forms (this was the normal situation), or did not devoice the *l*; in the latter case the T-Devoicing rule was only optional in their mental grammars, or they (more seldom) lacked it altogether. In rare but interesting cases the *f* was pronounced as [v]: [-lvt], *o.c.* pp. 33, 35; this pronunciation is predicted by my above devoicing rules for the dialect areas in which the northern variant of the T-Devoicing rule is in use. The Continuant Devoicing

(21) (a) The final consonant of the left constituent is voiced:

til-tala 'proportion'	*gamal-tungla* 'barren old sheep
sam-tal 'conversation'	*atóm-tákn* 'symbol of chemical element'
ein-tala 'singular'	*saman-tekning* 'compilation'
vid-tal 'talk'	*höfud-tilgangur* 'chief goal'

(b) The final consonant of the left word is voiced:

bíl tel	*bidil tel*
tóm tel	*atóm tel*
ein tel	*saman tel*
aud tel	*höfud tel*

(Each pair of words sub (b) pertains to the same breath group.)

On the phonological level words, simplex or compound, are bounded with word boundaries. There are also boundaries between the constituents of compound words, although the precise nature of these boundaries has not yet been determined for Modern Icelandic; most likely they are word boundaries, and this assumption is accepted in the present paper.[15] On the phonetic level, word boundaries are realized as phonetic

---

rule (1) is blocked because the /v/ is not preceded by a vowel; the T-Devoicing rule (18), which only affects /l/, cannot operate because of the intervening /v/. Gudfinnsson reports cases of [-lvt] from the Northern districts only: from Eyjafjardarsýsla (including Akureyri) and Sudur-þingeyjarsýsla. (The voiced pronunciation of the middle segment in [-lvt] cannot have been influenced by the spellings in the text which the investigator asked the children to read during the interviews; the text in question, as published by Gudfinnsson 1946: 145—46, contains the forms *ljúft* and *líft*, which could have led to spelling pronunciations with [-vt] as well, but the author reports none.)

To facilitate the exposition, I now state the pronunciations of *sjálft* predicted by my devoicing rules:

	South	North
with [f] or [v]	[-lft]	[-lvt]
without [f] or [v]	[-lt]	[-lt]

The [-lft]-form is adduced in Kress 1963: 42; Kress has [telft] *teflt*, the supine of *tefla* 'play chess'.

Incidentally, the cases of the absent T-Devoicing rule, mentioned above, involve the northern variant (18). Diachronically, these are cases of rule loss, presumably due to the very narrow domain of the rule. It should be recalled that in contact with the southern variant (17) the northern rule (18) is giving way; this must be another facet of the same phenomenon.

[14] One apparent exception to this claim is *mál-tíd* 'meal', which is sometimes pronounced with a voiceless *l*, see Blöndal 1920-24 s. v., Gudfinnsson 1946: 71, and Bérkov-Bödvarsson 1962 s.v. This word can be accounted for in the same way as *adför* and *adferd*, see footnote 4 above.

[15] That there must be a boundary between constituents of compound words, is proved in Orešnik 1971, where, however, the nature of that boundary was not strictly determined, although is was shown that several phonological

Janez Orešnik

pauses. (Phonetic pauses delimit breath groups.) Since the number of the word boundaries on the phonological level largely exceeds the number of phonetic pauses, the phonological component of Modern Icelandic (in fact, of every language) must contain a mechanism which cancels some of the phonological word boundaries during derivation. I imagine, maybe prematurely, that such a mechanism consists of rules interspersed among other phonological rules, deleting certain word boundaries or replacing them by weaker boundaries, most likely by morpheme boundaries. It is assumed here that the Modern Icelandic phonological component contains a mechanism whose duty is to replace word boundaries with morpheme boundaries, so that at the end of derivations only those word boundaries are preserved which correspond to phonetic pauses. The rules of this mechanism — let us call them BOUNDARY RULES — apply at different stages in derivations. One of the earliest boundary rules affects the word boundary between a noun and a suffixed definite article (Orešnik 1972).[16] A later boundary rule — let us call it the COMPOUND WORD BOUNDARY rule — replaces the word boundary between the immediate constituents of compound words with the morpheme boundary. A still later boundary rule — let us call it the INTER WORD BOUNDARY rule — replaces certain word boundaries between words with morpheme boundaries, and thus creates what are to be realized phonetically as breath groups.

We already know that, while the T-Devoicing rule (17/18) can operate across a morpheme boundary, it cannot operate across any other boundaries. On the other hand, case (a) of the Cluster Devoicing rule (10) operates freely across the word boundary between constituents of compound words, and most probably also across the inter-word word

---

phenomena of Modern Icelandic can be handled more satisfactorily if the said boundary is assumed to be a word boundary, than without that assumption. To the arguments of *o.c.* in favour of the word boundary between the constituents of compound words it can be added that one should think the boundary between a noun and a suffixed article to be weaker than the boundary between constituents of compound words. As the boundary between a noun and a suffixed article has been identified with a word boundary (in Orešnik 1972), it is likely that the boundary between constituents of compound words is at least as strong as a word boundary; and since the phonological theory does not provide any stronger boundary than the word boundary, the boundary between constituents of compound words is likely to be identical with the word boundary.

[16] Through my negligence a minus sign has been omitted in the formalized version of the Enclitic Boundary rule as printed in Orešnik 1972: 29. The formulation is therefore repeated here:

$$[\ ] \rightarrow [\alpha \text{ word boundary}] / \left[\overline{\ -\text{segment}\ } \right]_1 [-\alpha \text{ enclitic}]$$

I.e. any number of subsequent word boundaries remains if immediately followed by a non-enclitic word, and are rewritten as a morpheme boundary if immediately followed by an enclitic word.

boundary within breath groups. Case (b) of the Cluster Devoicing rule (10) and the Word Final Devoicing rule (15) operate only at the word boundary at the end of a breath group. The Continuant Devoicing rule (1) can operate across a morpheme boundary and across the word boundary between constituents of compound words, whereas it is unclear whether it can apply across the inter-word word boundary.

A natural way to account for this situation is to assume that the devoicing rules (1), (10), (15), and (17/18) are interspersed among the boundary rules in such a way that the state of affairs just described follows as a consequence of the relative rule orderings posited. The orderings which accomplish just this are stated in (22), q.v. The generally

(22)   T-Devoicing rule (17/18)
         Compound Word Boundary rule
         Inter Word Boundary rule
         {Cluster Devoicing rule (10)   }
         {Word Final Devoicing rule (15) }
         Breath group boundary → phonetic pause[17]

accepted conventions concerning rule orderings ensure the desired results. For instance, no word boundary is mentioned in the T-Devoicing rule (17/18), and the rule applies before the word boundaries between constituents of compound words have been rewritten as morpheme boundaries; this automatically ensures that the T-Devoicing rule (17/18) applies only in simplex words and in those constituents of compound words which are not themselves compound words. No word boundary is mentioned in the structural description of case (a) of the Cluster Devoicing rule (10). This means that the rule cannot operate across those word boundaries present in the representations at the time when rule (10) applies. Since, however, the word boundary between constituents of compound words and the inter-word word boundary had been rewritten as the morpheme boundary by the time rule (10) applies, the rule can operate freely in simplex as well as in compound words, and between words within breath groups. On the other hand, a word boundary is mentioned in case (b) of the Cluster Devoicing rule (10) and in the Word Final Devoicing rule (15). As the Compound Word Boundary rule and the Inter Word Boundary rule have applied by the time that rule (10) applies, the structural description of its case (b) is only met at the breath-group final word boundaries. Similarly, at the time that the Word Final Devoicing rule (15) applies, all the word boundaries within breath groups, except those bounding the breath groups, have been rewritten

---

[17] The relative ordering of the rules within the braces is at present unclear to me. The Continuant Devoicing rule (1), not mentioned in (22), certainly follows the Compound Word Boundary rule. Its ordering with respect to later boundary rules is at present unclear to me.

Janez Orešnik

as morpheme boundaries; consequently no effects of rule (15) can be observed in compound words or in words not followed by a phonetic pause.[18]

REFERENCES

Benediktsson, Hreinn. Review of Kress 1963. *íslenzk tunga* 6: 109—17. Reykjavík, 1965.

Bergsveinsson, Sveinn. *Grundfragen der isländischen Satzphonetik.* Phonometrische Forschungen, Reihe A. Band 2. Copenhagen and Berlin. 1941.

Bérkov, Valerij P., and Árni Böðvarsson. *íslenzk-rússnesk orðabók.* Moscow, 1962.

Blöndal, Sigfús. *íslenzk-dönsk orðabók.* Reykjavík. 1920-24.

Bloomfield, Leonard. *Language.* New York, 1933.

---

[18] As the relation of the devoicing rules to the Enclitic Boundary rule mentioned above is not relevant to the problem under discussion, the matter has been relegated to this footnote. The T-Devoicing rule (17/18) FOLLOWS the Enclitic Boundary rule; hence, the Continuant Devoicing rule (1) and the Cluster Devoicing rule (10) follow it as well. For evidence that the T-Devoicing rule follows the Enclitic Boundary rule in the ordering, consider the derivation of the supine *rignt* of *rigna* 'rain'. The derivation of the definite dat. sg. *hring-num* of *hringur* 'ring' is added for comparison; the word boundary and the morph /in/ are justified in Orešnik 1972, app. A. B:

	rign + D + t	hriNg ## in + um
Vowel Syncope rule	—	hriNg ## n + um
metathesis	ring + D + t	—
nasal assimilation	riNg + D + t	—
Enclitic Boundary rule	—	hriNg + n + um
b, d, g→ ∅ / _D. n	riN + t (2 applications)	hriN + n + um
T-Devoicing rule	riN + t (southern only)	—

(The /D/ in the phonological representation of *rignt* is phonologically a cover symbol for a dental consonant, and morphologically the dental suffix. Its presence in the phonological representation of the supine is not proved; however, the point made here remains valid even if the true phonological representation of *rignt* is just /rign + t/. /N/ represents the velar nasal.) The last three lines of the derivation are relevant to the point under consideration. The relative ordering of the Enclitic Boundary rule and of b. d. g → ∅ / _D depends crucially on the question as to whether the deletion of g in *rignt* is performed by the same rule as the deletion of g in the definite dat. sg. *hringnum*. It is assumed here that this is the case. It is claimed in Orešnik 1972 that the loss of g in *hringnum* follows the Enclitic Boundary rule. Hence. g → ∅ / _D follows the Enclitic Boundary rule as well. Since the T-Devoicing rule (17/18) can only apply to the nasal of *rignt* after the deletion of g, the T-Devoicing rule must follow b, d, g→∅ / _D. Hence, a fortiori, the T-Devoicing rule must follow the Enclitic Boundary rule. Consequently the Continuant Devoicing rule (1) and the Cluster Devoicing rule (10) also follow the Enclitic Boundary rule.

Incidentally, the derivation of *rignt* shows that the present formulation of the T-Devoicing rule presupposes that a number of other phonological rules precede it in the ordering and thus create the conditions for its operation: the metathesis rule; nasal assimilation; b, d, g→∅ / _D. Other rules which must precede the T-Devoicing rule include the loss of /v/ between /l/ and dental, cf. nom./acc. sg. ntr. *hál(f)t* of *hálfur* 'half'.

Böðvarsson, Árni, ed. *Íslenzk orðabók handa skólum og almenningi*. Reykjavík, 1963.

Chomsky, Noam, and Morris Halle. *The Sound Pattern of English*. New York, 1968.

Einarsson, Stefán. *Beiträge zur Phonetik der isländischen Sprache*. Oslo. 1927.

Einarsson, Stefán. *Icelandic Grammar. Texts. Glossary*. Baltimore, 1945. — I have used the slightly revised fifth printing of 1967.

Guðfinnsson, Björn, *Mállýzkur*. Vol. I. Reykjavík. 1946.

Guðfinnsson, Björn. *Um íslenzkan framburð. Mállýzkur II*. Edited and prepared for the press by Ólafur M. Ólafsson and Óskar Ó. Halldórsson. Studia islandica vol. 23. Reykjavík, 1964.

Kress, Bruno. *Laut- und Formenlehre des Isländischen*. Halle/Saale, 1963.

Malone, Kemp. *The Phonology of Modern Icelandic*. Menasha, Wisconsin, 1923.

Orešnik, Janez. "On the phonological boundary between constituents of Modern Icelandic compound words." *Linguistica* 11: 51—59. Ljubljana, 1971.

Orešnik, Janez. "On the epenthesis rule in Modern Icelandic." *Arkiv för nordisk filologi* 87: 1—32. Lund, 1972.

Povzetek

ŠTIRI NOVOISLANDSKA RAZZVENITVENA PRAVILA

Novoislandska generativna fonologija vsebuje štiri razzvenitvena pravila. ki povzročajo delno razzvenitev končnih glasov v besedah kot *dag*, popolno razzvenitev končnih glasov osnove v besedah kot *dag-s, rusl(-s)* in popolno razzvenitev glasov pred *t* v besedah kot *sval-t, skamm-t* (v zadnji samo v južnem izgovoru). — Od nadrobnosti je vredno omeniti: če so tu predložena pravila izrečena pravilno, fonološka oznaka [zveneč] ni razločevalna (distinktivna) v islandskih fonoloških enotah /b d g/.

JANEZ OREŠNIK

MODERN ICELANDIC U-UMLAUT FROM THE DESCRIPTIVE POINT OF VIEW

Survey. Par.1: The present study investigates the so-called u-umlaut alternations /a⁀ö/ and /a⁀ʏ/, and is arbitrarily limited to u-umlaut alternations within morphological paradigms.

Par. 2: It is necessary to distinguish between u-umlaut in monosyllabic and u-umlaut in polysyllabic stems. Monosyllabic stems display only the alternation /a⁀ö/, e.g. *barn⁀börn*. Polysyllabic stems manifest two types of u-umlaut, Final and Initial umlaut. A stem shows Final umlaut if the alternation /a⁀ö/ occurs in the last syllable of the stem only, e.g. *almanak⁀almanök*. This type of u-umlaut is normal and productive in polysyllabic stems. A stem manifests Initial umlaut if it undergoes the alternation /a⁀ö/ in its stressed syllable and-or the alternation /a⁀ʏ/ in its unstressed syllable(s), e.g. *gamall⁀gömul*. There are astonishingly few reliable examples of Initial umlaut, and a few classes of ambiguous examples. Beside Final and Initial umlauts there is a special marginal type illustrated by *hafald⁀höföld*. A few lexical items, such as *hérað*, display more than one type of u-umlaut, e.g. *héruð⁀héröð*.

Par. 3 describes the phonological properties of the environments in which u-umlaut shows up. Stems which manifest u-umlaut are often followed by *u*-initial desinences, e.g. *göml-um*, but just as often such stems are not followed by anything, e.g. *gömul*, or by endings which do not begin with *u*, e.g. *börn-in*. Par. 4 enumerates the morphological environments in which u-umlaut takes place in nouns, adjectives and verbs. Par. 5 enumerates the inflexional classes of words in which the basic vowel of the u-umlaut alternation is more likely /ö/ than /a/. Par. 6 studies the u-umlaut alternation /au⁀öi/, which occurs before palatal or velar nasal (e.g. *langur⁀löngum*), and the behaviour of the diphthong /ai/ with respect to the u-umlaut.[1]

[1] My thanks are due to Miss Margaret G. Davis, who has corrected my English,

152   GRIPLA

1. The label U-UMLAUT belongs to historical grammar. However, in this descriptive study it will be used as a convenient name for the vowel alternations /a—ö/ and /a—Y/ which are found in many morphological paradigms of Modern Icelandic, and which have mostly arisen through the prehistorical process of u-umlaut. An example is *gamall* 'old' versus nom. sg. f. and nom./acc. pl. n. *gömul*. From the descriptive point of view the limitation of the scope of the present paper to just these alternations, in morphological paradigms only, is arbitrary. What remains outside are other vocalic alternations and

(a) Inflected words displaying no u-umlaut alternations in their morphological paradigms. If such inflected words contain, for instance, non-alternating /ö/, as in (1a), q.v., that segment is here assumed to have been lexicalized.

(b) Uninflected words. In this context there is of course no point in keeping the /ö/'s and /Y/'s which are due to pre-historical u-umlaut apart from the /ö/'s and /Y/'s of other origin. Thus in (1b), q.v., the /ö/ of *mjög* is from older ǫ, the latter from *a* by u-umlaut, according to the most probable conception of breaking before *u*, see Nielsen 1957: 38–42. *Sjö* is from older *sjau*.

(1) (a) Inflected words: *mör* 'suet'
              Böðvar masculine given name
              fölur 'pale'
       (b) Uninflected words: *mjög* 'very'
              sjö 'seven'
       (c) Uninflected constituents of compound words:
              böggla-afgreiðsla 'parcel post delivery'
              dökk-grænn 'dark green'
              fjöl- 'multi-, poly-'
              sögu-staður 'historical place'
       (d) Derivational paradigms:
              fara 'go, travel'   vs. *förull* 'rambling'
              saga 'history'   *sögulegur* 'historical'

and to Baldur Jónsson and Stefán Karlsson, who have read an earlier version of the paper and suggested improvements. All errors are my own.

baggi 'pack'   *böggull* 'parcel'
kanna 'explore'   *könnuður* 'explorer'

(c) Uninflected constituents of compound words. Admittedly a word like *sögustaður* of (1c), q.v., can be related to *saga* on the level of descriptive word formation, as it unquestionably is in historical word formation, but I doubt that the phonological representation of the compound begins with /saqɣ/ or /saq + ɣ/, so that /ö/ were due to the synchronic u-umlaut rule.

(d) Derived lexical items displaying the alternation /a—ö/ and-or /a—ɣ/ in their derivational paradigms. For instance, *förull* of (1d), q.v., is related to *fara* in historical word formation, and may be so related in descriptive word formation as well. But I doubt that the phonological representation of its stem is /far + ɣl/ and its /ö/ due to the synchronic u-umlaut rule.

2. Kinds of u-umlaut. It is practical to treat umlaut in monosyllabic stems and in polysyllabic stems in separate paragraphs. In polysyllabic stems I distinguish between Final and Initial u-umlaut.

2.1. U-umlaut in monosyllabic stems. The only u-umlaut alternation found in monosyllabic stems is of course /a—ö/, never /a—ɣ/; see (2a). Those stems having a monosyllabic and a non-monosyllabic shape on the phonetic level, behave as true monosyllabic stems as far as their monosyllabic allomorphs are concerned; see (2b).

(2) (a) Stems which are always monosyllabic
        barn 'child', nom./acc. pl. *börn*, dat. pl. *börn-um*
        gata 'street', oblique sg. *göt-u*, nom./acc. pl. *göt-ur*, dat. pl.
        göt-um
        hvass 'sharp', nom. sg. f. and nom./acc. pl. n. *hvöss*, dat. pl.
        hvöss-um, etc.
    (b) Stems having mono- and polysyllabic allomorphs
        farinn 'gone', several weak cases *förn-u*
        akur 'field', dat. pl. *ökr-um*
        hamar 'hammer', dat. pl. *hömr-um*
        annar 'other, second', dat. sg. n. *öðru*, cf. nom. pl. m. *aðrir*

154 GRIPLA

2.2. Final u-umlaut. Final umlaut is only possible in polysyllabic stems. A polysyllabic stem is here said to undergo Final umlaut if it displays the alternation /a—ö/ in the last syllable of the stem; the remaining syllables of the stem do not undergo any u-umlaut.For examples see (3).

Which polysyllabic stems undergo Final umlaut? Excepting stems undergoing Initial umlaut and some irregular formations (see par. 2.3 and 2.4 below), Modern Icelandic polysyllabic stems undergo Final umlaut generally—if their rightmost vowel is susceptible to the u-umlaut alternation: contrast *japönsk* of *iapanskur* 'Japanese' and *falleg* of *fallegur* 'beautiful'. Final u-umlaut seems to represent the normal and productive kind of u-umlaut in Modern Icelandic polysyllabic stems: naturalized polysyllabic stems susceptible to u-umlaut display Final umlaut.

(3) Illustrations of Final umlaut, including naturalized stems
    almanak 'calender': nom./acc. pl. *almanök*, dat. pl. *almanök-um*
    albanskur 'Albanian': *albönsk(-um)*
    apaldur 'apple-tree': *apöldr-um*
    akarn 'acorn': *akörn(-um)*
    rambaldi 'bell beam': *rambö!d-um*
    bikar 'drinking cup': *bikör-um*
    heilagur 'holy': *heilög(-um)*
    folald 'young foal': *folöld(-um)*
    spekúlant 'speculator, gambler': *spekúlönt-um*
    gímald 'vast opening': *gímöld(-um)*
    organ 'organ': *orgön(-um)*
    karat 'carat': *karöt(-um)*
    blýantur 'pencil': *blýönt-um*
    kórall 'coral': *köröll-um*
    Albani 'Albanian': *Albön-um*
    skandali 'scandal': *skandöl-um*
    Skandínavi 'Scandinavian': *Skandínöv-um*
    atlas 'atlas': *atlös-um*
    kvaðrat 'square': *kvaðröt(-um)*
    Ameríkani 'American': *Ameríkön-um*
    dínarður 'dinner': *dínörð-um*
    kartafla 'potato': *kartöfl-um*
    bastarður 'bastard': *bastörð-um*

Arabi 'Arab' sb.: *Aröb-um*
dívan 'couch': *dívön-um*
fosfat 'phosphate': *fosföt(-um)*
salat 'salad': *salöt(-um)*
serenaða, serenata 'serenade': *serenöð-u, serenöt-u*
smaragður 'emerald': *smarögð-um*
spítali 'hospital': *spítöl-um*
standarður 'standard, flag': *standörð-um*
túlípani 'tulip': *túlípön-um*
klóak 'drain, sewer': *klóök(-um)*

2.3. Initial u-umlaut. A polysyllabic stem is here said to undergo Initial u-umlaut if it displays the alternation /a—ö/ in the syllable under primary stress, and-or the alternation /a—Y/ in one or more remaining syllables. For examples see (4).

(4) (a) /a—ö/ under primary stress, /a—Y/ elsewhere
           annar 'other, second', nom. sg. f. *önnur*
           gamall 'old'   *gömul*
     (b) Only /a—Y/ in at least one unstressed syllable, no u-umlaut
          alternation in the stressed syllable
           sumar 'summer', nom./acc. pl. *sumur*
           hundrað 'hundred'   *hundruð*
     (c) Only /a—ö/ in the stressed syllable, no u-umlaut alternation
          in the unstressed syllable(s)
           fagur 'fair', nom. sg. f. *fögur*
           mastur 'mast', nom./acc. pl. *möstur*[2]

Which stems undergo Initial umlaut? There are astonishingly few reasonably unambiguous examples of stems undergoing Initial umlaut, and no other type of umlaut. A hopefully exhaustive list of such cases is given sub (5), q.v. (For cases such as pl. *héruð—héröð* see par. 2.5.) All told, Initial umlaut seems to be limited to a few old and-or much used, often idiosyncratic, preponderantly native lexical items. (*Markaður* and *mastur* are pre-Reformation loanwords. The archaic *atall*, now usually *ötul-* in all its case forms, with lexicalized u-umlaut, cannot

---

[2] Here belongs also the substandard lp. pl. pres. *öthugum* and pret. pl. *öthuguð-* (normal forms *athugum, athuguð-*) of *athuga* 'examine'.

156   GRIPLA

(5) A list of stems undergoing Initial umlaut
   (a) Nouns
        markaður 'market', dat. pl. *mörkuð-um*
        faðir 'father', oblique sg. *föður*
        mastur 'mast', nom./acc. pl. *möstur*
        sumar 'summer', nom./acc. pl. *sumur*
        hundrað 'hundred', nom./acc. pl. *hundruð*
   (b) Adjectives
        gamall 'old', nom. sg. f. *gömul*
        annar 'other, second', nom. sg. f. *önnur*
        atall 'energetic', nom. sg. f. *ötul*
        einsamall 'alone', nom. sg. f. *einsömul*
        allursaman 'all together', nom. sg. f. *öllsömun*
        the type *fagur* 'fair', nom. sg. f. *fögur*
   (c) Verbs: no unambiguous examples

be characterized as much used or idiosyncratic.) *Faðir* belongs to an
idiosyncratic inflexional type (cf. the plural stem *feð(u)r-*) and is also
the only Modern Icelandic stem displaying u-umlaut before an *u* not
immediately preceded by a morpheme boundary; cf. par. 3 below.
Sumar has double definite nominative/accusative plural, *sumrin* and
sumurin. *Gamall* has suppletive comparison, comparative *eldri*, superlative *elztur*. *Annar* has unique inflection, cf. its stems *annar-* (*önnur-*)
and *aðr-* (*öðr-*). *Einsamall* and *allursaman* manifest unique allomorphic
variation. For instance, their respective nominative singular feminine
case forms are *ein-sömul -sömun* and *öll-sömul -sömun*. *Saman* occurs
inflected only in the compounds *einsamall* and *allursaman*, and only in
a few case forms at that: nom. sg. f. and nom./acc. pl. n. *ein- öll-
sömun*, nom./acc. sg. n. *alltsaman(t)*, cf. Blöndal 1920–24 s.v. *allur*
and p. 1008 s.v. *allur*; Böðvarsson 1963 s.v. *allursaman*. *Fagur* (with
epenthetic *u* and stem final *r*) displays allomorphic variation in comparison (e.g. comparative *fegri, fegurri, fagrari*,[3] superlative *fegurstur,
fagrastur*) and sometimes even in the morphological paradigm (gen. sg.
f. *fagurrar*, rarer *fagrar*, dat. sg. f. *fagurri*, rarer *fagri*, gen. pl. *fagurra*,
rarer *fagra*).—The irregularity of *mastur, sumar, gamall, -samall*, and

[3] The last mentioned form is not adduced in the handbooks, but the OHÍ has it
registered.

the *fagur* type is enhanced by the circumstance that they display the alternation vowel—Ø in the unaccented syllable.

The less certain instances of Initial umlaut are nouns in *-naður*, *-uður*, *-ari*, *-un*, *-an*; adjectives in *-aður* and *-astur*; verbal forms such as pret. pl. *kölluð-* of *kalla* 'call'.

The nouns in *-naður* are all masculine and derived. Being preponderantly abstract in meaning, they occur mostly in the singular only. A list of those that are used in the plural as well, together with their dative plural, their only case displaying reflexes of u-umlaut, is given sub (6), q.v. If these lexical items are analyzed as containing an *-að*-final stem (e.g. *fatnað-*) followed by the case markers, their respective dative plural forms are instances of Initial umlaut. On the other hand, in all the nouns of the list, monosyllabic base stems can be easily recognized before the suffix *-naður*, cf. the lexical items in the rightmost column of (6). It is therefore possible that the true analysis is the stem *fat-* plus *-nað-/-nuð-*-initial case markers. In that event the case marker of the

(6) Examples of nouns in *-naður* which are also used in the plural

verknaður 'work',	dat. pl. *verknuðum*,	cf. *verk(a)* 'work'
skilnaður 'divorce'	*skilnuðum*	*skilja* 'separate'
-fatnaður 'clothes'	*-fötnuðum*	*föt* pl. 'clothes'
-klæðnaður 'clothes'	*-klæðnuðum*	*klæði* 'clothes'

dative plural can be *-nuðum,* with lexicalized *u* in the penultimate syllable, and the dative plural stem *föt-* is a case of umlaut in monosyllabic stems. A consequence of this analysis would be that the *fatnaður* type would constitute its own declension class characterized by its own set of case desinences. A third alternative analysis takes to account the fact that *-að-* is one of the commonest suffixes in Icelandic. It is possible that *fatnaður* is analyzed as *fatn-* plus *-að-/-uð-*-initial case markers. The dative plural marker could then be *-uðum,* with lexicalized *u* in the penultimate syllable, and the dative plural stem *fötn-* a case of u-umlaut in monosyllabic stems. Again, the *fatnaður* type would constitute its own declension class. For the declension of *fatnaður* under this analysis, see (7). The same analysis could also be assumed for *markaður* 'market', adduced above in (5a), under the presupposition that its *-að-* was identified with the common suffix *-að-*, and-or its *mark-* with the stem *mark-* in *mörk* 'weight/value unit *mark*' or 'open space' (folk etymology). In

(7) nom. sg. *fatn* + aðʏr   pl. *fatn* + aðɪr
     acc.   *fatn* + að   *fatn* + aðɪ
     dat.   *fatn* + aðɪ   *fatn* + ʏðʏm
     gen.   *fatn* + aðar   *fatn* + aða

this case *markaður* ceases to be a case of Initial umlaut. I would here mention the possibility that the -að- of *hundrað* has also been identified with the common suffix -að-, in which case the nom./acc. pl. *hundruð* and the dat. pl. *hundruðum* need not contain /a/ changed to /ʏ/ by the synchronic rule of u-umlaut, but the case desinences / + ʏð/ and / + ʏðʏm/, respectively, in which event the noun is removed from the sphere of Initial umlaut.—A set of further analyses is generated by the possibility that there is more than one morphological cut in every form, e.g. /*fat* + nað + ʏr/. As these analyses all operate with either Initial umlaut or with umlaut in monosyllabic stems, not with any third kind of u-umlaut, they are not treated in detail here. Last but not least, it is conceivable that not all speakers of Icelandic analyze the lexical items à la *fatnaður* in the same way, but some choose (unconsciously of course) one, and some another alternative analysis. In particular, it is possible that for some speakers *fötnuðum* is a case of Initial umlaut, for others a case of umlaut in monosyllabic stems. The fact that there are so many descriptive alternatives is the reason why I characterize the *fatnaður* type, and the remaining types of words to be discussed presently, as unreliable instances of Initial umlaut.

The nouns in -*uður*. Most nouns in -*uður* are masculine, derived, and do not display synchronic u-umlaut in their inflexion at all. If they contain /ö/ in their root syllable beside *u* in -*uð*-, those /ö/ and /ʏ/ are lexicalized; examples: *frömuður* 'pioneer', *hugsuður* 'thinker', etc. On the other hand, a few nouns in -*uður* display Initial umlaut outside their genitives of both numbers, e.g. *söfnuður* 'congregation', gen. sg. *safnaðar*, pl. *safnaða*. (Halldórsson 1950:99 adduces gen. pl. *safnaða*

(8) Examples of nouns in -*uður*, gen. -*aða(r)*
     söfnuður 'congregation',   cf. *safna* 'collect'
     fögnuður 'joy'   *fagna* 'rejoice'
     jöfnuður 'equity'   *jafna* 'make even'
     söknuður 'sorrow'   *sakna* 'miss'
     mánuður 'month'   —

and *söfnuða*.) For a list of non-archaic stems in *-uður* showing u-umlaut see (8). If the only or main morphological cut in these nouns is after *uð*, the forms manifest Initial umlaut. On the other hand, the stems of these examples, excepting *mánuður*, are readily identified with the respective stems of the lexical items in the rightmost column of (8). Therefore the nouns sub (8) are perhaps analyzed by at least some Icelanders as stem + *-uð-/-að*-initial desinences. In that case it can be said that in the genitive plural the ending / + aða/ alternates with / + Yða/, the latter accompanied by u-umlaut, *söfnuða*.

There is a further set of non-phonetic representations utilizing /ö/ as the basic root vowel, /Y/ as the basic vowel of *uð*, and changing them to /a/ in the genitives; this is also Initial umlaut (in the direction /ö, Y/ → /a/) according to my definition of u-umlaut. Alternatively, the root could be /*söfn*/, changed to /*safn*/ in the genitives, whereas / + aða(r)/ would be lexicalized desinences; this would be umlaut (again in the direction /ö/ → /a/) in monosyllabic stems. That the basic shape of the root is /*söfn*/, rather than /*safn*/, is made probable by the following: All case forms but the genitives contain /ö/ on the systematic phonetic level; the maximally unmarked case, nominative (of both numbers), contains /ö/. An example of such an analysis will be found sub (9), q.v.

(9) nom. sg. *söfn* + YðYr   pl. *söfn* + Yðɪr
    acc.   *söfn* + Yð   *söfn* + Yðɪ
    dat.   *söfn* + Yðɪ   *söfn* + YðYm
    gen.   *söfn* + aðar → *safn* + aðar   *söfn* + aða → *safn* + aða

Under all the analyses operating with non-umlauting (lexicalized) desinence-initial /að/ and /Yð/, for instance under the analysis of (9), the nouns like those in (8) form their own declension class. Their stems are monosyllabic, and thus fall outside the scope of Initial umlaut.

The *-uður* of the non-derived noun *mánuður* has probably been identified with the *-uður* of the *-uður* nouns, so that whatever analysis is correct for, say, *söfnuður*, is correct also for *mánuður*. The identification in question may have been facilitated by folk-etymologizing the noun as containing the stem *mán-* of *máni* 'moon'.

The masculine nouns in *-ari*. They form an open set and mostly denote performers of action or occupation. For examples see (10).

(10) Examples of nouns in -*ari*

bakari 'baker',	dat. pl. *bökurum,*	cf. *baka* 'bake'
fiðlari 'fiddler'	*fiðlurum*	*fiðla* 'violin'
kennari 'teacher'	*kennurum*	*kenna* 'teach'
dómari 'judge'	*dómurum*	*dómur* 'judgement'
kjallari 'cellar'	*kjöllurum*	—

The u-umlaut alternation shows up in the dative plural, see the central column of (10), and represents Initial umlaut if the main morphological cut is just before -*um*; the dative plural is then morphologically /*bakar* +ʏm/. However, since so many Icelandic nouns end in -*ari*, and-or because of their synchronic word-derivational ties with their respective bases such as those in the rightmost column of (10), it is possible that at least some Icelanders analyze *bakari* etc. as /*bak*+aʀɪ/ etc., making the stem monosyllabic and thus not subject to Initial umlaut. For an example of this analysis see (11). Under this analysis the nouns in -*ari*

(11)　nom. sg. *bak*+aʀɪ　　pl. *bak*+arar
　　　acc.　　*bak*+ara　　　*bak*+ara
　　　dat.　　*bak*+ara　　　*bak*+ʏʀʏm
　　　gen.　　*bak*+ara　　　*bak*+ara

form their own declension class, different from the declension of other masculine weak nouns.

Speaking against Initial umlaut in the morphological paradigm of the *ari*-nouns are lexical items such as *kristall-ari* 'crystallizer', whose dative plural is *kristöllurum*, not *kristullurum*, which makes sense if the main morphological cut is after *ll*, /*kristall*+ʏʀʏm/; in that event it can be argued that *kristöllurum* displays the expected Final umlaut. However, this argument is weak, because examples such as *kristöllurum* are few in number and the type of their umlaut could be due to the influence of their word-derivational bases, cf. the verb *kristalla* 'crystallize', whose third person plural preterite is *kristölluðu*. Or it could be argued that *kristöllurum* is simply an exceptional form.

The non-derived *kjallari* 'cellar' (and *meistari* 'master', *marmari* 'marble', *keisari* 'emperor', etc.) has joined the derived nouns in -*ari* just as *mánuður* has joined those in -*uður*.

The deverbative feminine nouns in -*un*, mostly nomina actionis, form an open set as well. For examples see (12). Their association with the lexical items in the rightmost column of (12) is strong. Initial umlaut is realized in the whole singular and in the dative plural: *pöntun*, gen. sg. *pöntun-ar*, dat. pl. *pöntun-um*. Many of these nouns, being abstract, are

(12) Examples of those feminine nouns in -*un* used both in the singular and plural

pöntun 'commercial order',	*panta* 'order' vb.
kvörtun 'complaint'	*kvarta* 'complain'
fölsun 'forgery'	*falsa* 'forge'
töpun 'loss'	*tapa* 'lose'
verzlun 'store'	*verzla* 'do business'
einkunn 'school mark'[4]	—

used in the singular only, in which case they do not display any u-umlaut alternation, but exhibit lexicalized /ö/ and-or /ʏ/.

However, it is doubtful whether the nouns sub (12) are genuine instances of Initial umlaut. They can be analyzed so that -*un*- and -*an*- pertain to the endings, see (13). There is even a weak argument in

(13) nom. sg. *pant* + ʏn   pl. *pant* + anɪr

    acc.   *pant* + ʏn   *pant* + anɪr

    dat.   *pant* + ʏn   *pant* + ʏnʏm

    gen.   *pant* + ʏnar   *pant* + ana

favour of the cut being before *un/an*: The noun in -*un* made from the verb *kristalla* 'crystallize' is *kristöllun*, not *kristullun*. This speaks against the *pöntun* nouns undergoing Initial umlaut, and for their undergoing Final umlaut and for the main morphological cut being before -*un*. However, the argument is nonconclusive, in that it could be argued that nouns like *kristöllun* are simply exceptional, or due to analogy with their respective word-derivational bases. (The base verb *kristalla* has *kristölluðu* as its third person plural preterite.) If the ana-

---

[4] The feminine noun *einkunn*, originally a compound, is now pronounced as a simplex (velar *n* before *k*, short *n* at the end), and has developed a new plural *einkanir* beside *einkunnir* (Böðvarsson 1963 s.v. *einkanir*). The pl. *einkanir* means 'school marks'. Its origin is due to proportional analogy: *seinkun* 'delay': *seinkanir* = *einkunn*: X, where X = *einkanir*. The paradigm *einkunn*, *einkanir* belongs with *pöntun*, *pantanir*.

lysis exemplified under (13) is correct, the *pöntun* nouns form their own declensional class.

A further alternative analysis of *pöntun* takes into account the possibility that /ö/, not /a/, is the basic root vowel in the morphological paradigm of the *pöntun* nouns, at least in the singular. In the plural, a morphological rule would change /ö/ to /a/, and another rule would change /a/ back to /ö/ in the dative plural; e.g. nom. sg./*pönt* + ʏn/, nom. pl. /*pant* + anɪr/, dat. pl. /*pant* + ʏnʏm/ → /*pönt* + ʏnʏm/. There is a complication here, in that those *pöntun* nouns derived from verbal stems whose vowel is /ö/, do not change that /ö/ into /a/ in the plural. Example: *af-höföun* 'decapitation', nom. pl. *af-höföanir*, not *-hafðanir*. Since nouns like *-höföun* are rare, it could be postulated that they are exceptions from the plural /ö/ → /a/ rule. Alternatively, there may exist a language universal saying that derivatives must not display more variation in their morphological paradigms than their respective word-derivational bases. Thus, since *-höföun* is derived from *afhöföa* 'decapitate' (and the latter from *af* + *höfuð* 'head'), in whose morphological paradigm /ö/ does not alternate with anything else, even *-höföun* cannot display /ö/ → /a/. A third solution is outlined in par. 5.

Beside the feminine deverbative nouns in *-un* there are quite a few nouns in *-an*, also mostly nomina actionis. (In older times the nouns in *-an* were an open set. Most have now become *un*-nouns.) For examples (some repeated here from Kress 1963:85) see (14). These lexical items are unusual in that they do not display any u-umlaut in the singular,

(14) Examples of feminine nouns in *-an*
  ólyfjan 'poison, stench',   cf. *lyf* 'medicine'
  angan 'fragrance'   *anga* 'shed fragrance'
  líðan 'state of health'   *líða* 'pass, feel'

although they contain strong feminine stems, whereas in the plural, in the rare cases when that number is used at all, *-unum* appears in the dative case, e.g. *ólyfjunum*, with Initial umlaut. If the stem is taken to end in *an*, these nouns must be made exceptions to the requirement that u-umlaut apply at least in the non-genitive singular of strong feminine nouns. (Cf. par. 4.) On the other hand, there is no problem with the u-umlaut here if it is assumed, as it is in par. 5 below, that there is no /a/ → /ö, ʏ/ rule in the singular of the strong feminine nouns, whereas there is a comparable rule in the dative plural. A further possibility is that *an* is assigned to the desinences (either because of the strong association with the lexical items in the right column of (14), or because -*an*- is a relatively common suffix), and these words consequently form their own declension class, in which case there is no problem as far as the type of u-umlaut is concerned, for then the stems in question are monosyllabic.

Of the derived adjectives, including past participles, those in -*aður* may undergo Initial umlaut. For examples see (15). Initial umlaut is manifested, for instance, in the strong dative plural: *kölluðum, öldruð-um*, etc. However, since in most such adjectives the stems of the lexical items in the right column of (15) are readily identified with the stems

(15) Examples of adjectives in -*aður*

kallaður 'called',	cf. *kalla* 'call'
aldraður 'elderly'	*aldur* 'age'
gáfaður 'gifted'	*gáfa* 'gift'
efnaður 'well-to-do'	*efni* pl. 'means, wealth'
hugaður 'courageous'	*hugur* 'courage'

preceding -*aður*, and since -*að*- is a common suffix in the language, it is possible that at least some speakers analyze these adjectives as containing monosyllabic stems followed by *að*-initial desinences. For an example of such an analysis cf. (16). Under this analysis the adjectives in -*aður* do not display Initial umlaut and they form their own declensional class.

(16) nom. sg. m. *aldr* + aðʏr   nom. sg. f. *aldr* + ʏð
    dat. pl.   *aldr* + ʏðʏm   gen. pl.   *aldr* + aðra, etc.

A weak argument in favour of the division *aldr-aður* rather than *aldrað-ur* comes from past participles such as *parrakaður* 'kept pent in', where the u-umlauted forms contain the stem *parrök*-, e.g. nom. sg. f. *parrökuð*. If the adjectives in -*aður* contained Initial umlaut, we would expect nom. sg. f. *pörrukuð*, a non-existent form. The cut before -*aður* obliterates this difficulty: if the preceding stem is non-monosyllabic, the stem undergoes the expected Final umlaut. However, the argument is non-conclusive, for it could be argued that the adjectives like *parrak*-

aður are so few that they can be considered exceptions which do not influence the general pattern.

The situation is similar with the adjectival superlatives and ordinal numbers in *-astur,* e.g. *latastur* of *latur* 'lazy', strong dat. pl. *lötustum;* *tuttugasti* 'twentieth', pl. *tuttugustu.* At least on the face of it *lötustum* displays Initial umlaut. In reality the stem can be monosyllabic, *lat-~* *löt-,* and the case marker / + ʏstʏm/, not / + astʏm/. A weak argument in favour of analyzing *latastur* as *lat-astur* comes from superlatives such as *heilagastur* 'most holy', strong dat. pl. *heilögustum,* never *heilugust-* *um.* The argument runs parallel to the one stated above about *parrak-* *aður,* and is inconclusive for the same reasons as those given there.— The superlative *dasaðastur* 'most exhausted', dat. pl. *dösuðustum,* can contain an even longer ending in the dative plural, viz. *-uðustum.*

It might be argued that verbal forms such as the 3p. pl. pret. *kölluðu* of *kalla* 'call' (versus the 3p. sg. pret. *kallaði*) display Initial umlaut. However, it is not proved that the medial /ʏ/ is synchronically derived from /a/. It can just as well be that speakers analyze *kölluðu* as /kall + ʏ̆ðʏ/, in which case there is no sense in speaking of Initial umlaut in connection with such forms. If there is only one cut in *kölluðu,* as I assume, there is a special set of preteritival endings typically used with the *kalla* verbs: sg. *-aði, -aðir, -aði,* pl. *-uðum, -uðuð, -uðu,* and corre-spondingly in the middle voice, sg. *-aðist,* pl. *-uðumst* or *-uðustum,* *-uðuzt, -uðust.* Again, a weak argument for the cut before *-að-, -uð-* comes from verbal forms such as 3p. pl. pret. *parrökuðu* of *parraka* 'keep pent in'. If the cut is immediately after *k,* the bisyllabic stem *parrak-* can be said to have undergone the expected Final umlaut in *parrökuðu.* However, such examples are few in number, and it could be argued that they are exceptions whose idiosyncratic behaviour is due to their respective word-derivational bases, cf. pret. *kristölluðu* of *krist-* *alla* 'crystallize', and this from *kristallur* 'crystal', dat. pl. *kristöllum.*

2.4. Other types of u-umlaut. In addition to Final and Initial u-umlaut Modern Icelandic displays a third pattern, exemplified sub (17), q.v. All examples of this type known to me are bisyllabic NOUN stems. Alternative forms with Final umlaut exist as well, and are listed in (17). This and the paucity of examples testify to the marginality of this type of u-umlaut in Modern Icelandic. However, the type has a long history in the language, beginning with the dative plural of the present participle *vocǫndom* (normalized *vǫkǫndom*) of *vaka* 'be awake' in the

(17) *hafald* 'heddle of loom',   pl. *höföld(um)*,   also *haföld(um)*
    kjarald 'cask'   *kjöröld(um)*   *kjaröld(um)*
    kafald 'thick fall of snow'   *köföld(um)*   *kaföld(um)*

oldest extant Icelandic manuscript, AM 237a fol. (Benediktsson 1963a: 18); no doubt the development of the type is closely linked with the history of Final umlaut. The type deserves to be treated separately from the historical point of view. In Modern Icelandic the plurals *höföld* etc. most likely cannot be deduced from any rules of the grammar, but have to be memorized by the speakers of the language.

Another special type consists of the umlauted forms such as those adduced in (18), q.v. The example *fagur* represents a type; other in-·

(18) *fagur* 'fair': nom. sg. f. and nom./acc. pl. n. *fögur,* dat. pl. *fögrum*
    mastur n. 'mast': nom./acc. pl. *möstur,* definite form *möstrin,* dat.
        pl. *möstrum*
    sjáaldur n. 'pupil of the eye': nom./acc. pl. *sjáöldur,* definite form
        sjáöldrin, dat. pl. *sjáöldrum*
    fjöður f. 'feather', gen. sg. *fjaðrar:* dat. pl. *fjöðrum*
    klömbur f. (archaic) 'smith's vice', gen. sg. *klambrar,* dat. pl.
        klömbrum
    gröftur m. 'digging, burial', gen. sg. *graftrar:* dat. pl. *gröftrum*;
        alternatively without radical *r*

stances of the type are, *magur* 'meagre', *napur* 'cold, chilly', *dapur* 'sad', *vakur* 'ambling (of a horse)', *árvakur* 'early awake'. The stems of the nouns and adjectives of (18) all undergo vowel syncope from the synchronic viewpoint: In the non-contracted cases their stems end in C*ur*, in the contracted cases in C*r*, e.g. non-contracted *fagur-*, contracted *fagr-*. If the u-umlaut only operated in the contracted cases, these stems would be normal: *mastur, fjöður, gröftur* (the variant with radical *r*), the archaic *klömbur*, and the *fagur* type would be instances of monosyllabic stems undergoing u-umlaut, whereas *sjáaldur*, not being monosyllabic, would be undergoing the expected Final umlaut. What is unusual about the stems of (18) is their non-contracted forms, which undergo u-umlaut as if they were contracted, i.e. as if the *u* of *ur* were

166   GRIPLA

ignored by the u-umlaut. Moreover, these stems are the only ones in which a *u* that has not resulted from the u-umlaut of *a* intervenes between the umlauted vowel and the end of the stem, cf. par. 3 below. How these stems are to be treated in the descriptive grammar of Icelandic as far as u-umlaut is concerned, depends for one thing on the way that vowel syncope is treated. To mention one possibility, suppose the native learners of Icelandic analyze the stems not as losing a vowel through a rule, but as containing a special set of endings, say, /faq + Yr/, /faq + ran/, etc. In that case there would be no problem as far as u-umlaut is concerned, for the *u* of the non-contracted forms would be moved into the desinence, and thus any trace of u-umlaut operating upon vowels separated from the end of the stem by the string /C_0YC_0/, where the /Y/ does not itself result from u-umlauting, would be gone. (That a part of a stem becomes a part of an ending, is not unusual. Cf. Middle English *cheris(e* analyzed as *cheri + s*, whence a new singular *cherry*. The ultimate reason for the retraction of the morphological cut in the *fagur* type would be the learner's inability to determine where the border is between SAME and DIFFERENT in the paradigm of *fagur*.) However, the correct treatment of vowel syncope is still unknown.

2.5. A number of polysyllabic stems display sometimes Final, sometimes Initial u-umlaut, more rarely also umlaut of the *höföld* type. All such exceptional cases are listed in (19), q.v.

(19) List of stems displaying several kinds of u-umlaut

　　　héra∂ 'district': nom./acc. pl. *héru∂* (Initial umlaut) and *héröð* (Final umlaut). My impression is that *héru∂* is more common than *héröð*.[5]

　　　me∂al 'medicine, drug': nom./acc. pl. *me∂ul* (Initial umlaut) and *me∂öl* (Final umlaut). My impression is that both are equally used.

　　　líkan 'picture, model': nom./acc. pl. *líkön* (Final umlaut) and *líkun* (Initial umlaut). My impression is that *líkön* is the normal form, whereas *líkun* is rare and found in the written language only.

[5] My impressions here and below are based on the data in the OHÍ and on my work with informants.

forað 'dangerous place': nom./acc. pl. *foröð* (Final umlaut) and *foruð* (Initial umlaut). My impression is that *foröð* is the normal form, and *foruð* rare.

kastali 'citadel': dat. pl. *köstulum* (Initial umlaut), *kastölum* (Final umlaut), and *köstölum* (*höföld* type). My impression is that both *köstulum* and *kastölum* are equally used, whereas *köstölum* is rare. In the compound word *loftkastali* 'castle in Spain' Initial umlaut prevails: *-köstulum*.

óðal 'allodium': nom./acc. pl. *óðul* (Initial umlaut) and *óðöl* (Final umlaut). My impression is that *óðul* is more common than *óðöl*.

banani 'banana': dat. pl. *banönum* (Final umlaut), *bönunum* (Initial umlaut), *bönönum* (*höföld* type), possibly also *banunum*. My impression is that *banönum* and *bönunum* are equally used, *bönönum* very rarely. The form *banunum* is reported in Anderson 1969; my informants do not use it.

altari 'altar'. Here there is vacillation between the nominative/accusative plural forms *ölturu* (Initial umlaut), *öltöru* (*höföld* type), and *altari* (no umlaut). My impression is that *ölturu* is the normal form, whereas the remaining ones are rare.

vesall 'wretched': nom. sg. f. *vesöl* (Final umlaut) and *vesul* (Initial umlaut; Guðmundsson 1922:94). My impression is that *vesöl* is the normal form, whereas *vesul* is very rare.

3. The phonological environment of u-umlaut. This section describes the phonological properties of the environments in which u-umlaut shows up. It remains an open question whether the generalizations adduced in the present section are linguistically significant, for I am not aware of any arguments in favour of their significance. For a version of the Modern Icelandic u-umlaut rule in which these generalizations are expressed, and thus treated as linguistically significant, see Orešnik 1975.

Whether the reflex of Initial umlaut is /ö/ or /ʏ/ depends on stress. In stressed syllables /a/ alternates with /ö/, elsewhere with /ʏ/. Example: nom. sg. f. *gömul* of *gamall* 'old'.

In a simplex word that contains more than one u-umlauted vowel the instances of these can only be separated by consonants, i.e. such vowels

168   GRIPLA

invariably stand in successive syllables; e.g. *önnur*, *gömul* of *annar*, *gamall*. A simplex word such as *apótekari* 'pharmaceutical chemist' has dat. pl. *apótekurum*, never *öpótekurum*, because of the *ó* and *e* intervening between the stressed and unstressed *a*'s of *apótekari*.

In simplex words comprising more than two syllables "a secondary stress falls on the odd syllables, the third, the fifth, etc., e.g. '*kenna,ri* 'teacher', '*kenna,rarnir* 'the teachers', '*prófes,sorar,nir* 'the professors'" (Benediktsson 1963b:146). (Such stresses are here called RHYTHMI-CAL; the term SECONDARY stress is here reserved for the main stresses of non-initial constituents of compound words.) There is no correlation between such rhythmical stresses and the alternants /ö, Y/ of u-umlaut, cf. dat. pl. '*héröð,um* versus '*héruð,um* of *hérað* 'district'; dat. pl. '*karöt,um* of *karat* 'carat' versus '*alman,ökum* of *almanak* 'calender'. Also, *þjóð-félögin* 'the societies' contains *ö* no matter how the rhythmical and secondary stresses are distributed. (There are several possible patterns of stress, see Benediktsson ibidem.)

If the first constituent of a bipartite compound word is monosyllabic, as it often is, the second constituent often loses its constituent initial secondary accent, and the compound as a whole thus assumes the phonetic shape of a simplex word; Benediktsson 1963b:146, Kress 1963:11. An example is *samband* 'connection', without any stress on -*band*. The loss of the secondary stress under these conditions does not lead to the violation of the principle that only the inflected (normally last) constituent in any compound word undergoes synchronic u-um-laut: dat. pl. *samböndum*. On the other hand, such compound words, appearing at least optionally in the disguise of simplexes, may have been a diachronic source of Final umlaut, or at least one of its supports: *samböndum* has the rhythmic pattern of, say, *albönskum*. In fact, it is sometimes difficult, or even impossible, to decide whether a compound of the *samband* type, pronounced with one primary stress accompanied by rhythmical stresses if appropriate, is a compound or a simplex from the synchronic point of view.

Nothing HAS to intervene between a u-umlauted vowel and the end of the stem (not word!) in which it appears; cf. the 3p. pl. pret. *spjöðu* of the archaic verb *spja* 'scorn, despise'.[6] What CAN intervene in the

6 For the data on *spja* see Þórólfsson 1925:116.

said position on the systematic phonetic level, is /C₀/, or /C₀ʏr/, or
/C₀öC₀/. Actually in non-monosyllabic stems the u-umlauted vowel is
always separated from the end of the stem by at least one consonantal
segment. For examples see (20). If a vowel other than /ʏ/ or /ö/ which

(20) What can intervene between a u-umlauted vowel and the end of
the stem, on the systematic phonetic level?
(a) One or more consonants: *hundruð, folöld, bök, börn, möstr-in*
(b) One or more syllables containing /ʏr/, or /ʏ/ from /a/, or
/ö/ from /a:/: *fögur, möstur, önnur, gömul, höföld*

fulfils the conditions stated in (20b) intervenes in the said position, u-
umlaut does not take place before that vowel. Cf. the lexical items
listed in (21). It is, however, doubtful whether it can be asserted that
the intervening vowel has prevented the u-umlaut from taking place in
such cases, for the reason for the lack of u-umlaut is most probably the
circumstance that the lexical items in question would undergo Final
umlaut only.

There is reason to mention those adjectives undergoing vowel syncope of a vowel other than /a/ in some of their case forms. E.g. the
past participle *farinn* 'gone' undergoes u-umlaut, cf. dat. pl. *förn-um*;

(21) Forms lacking u-umlaut either because they are only susceptible
to Final umlaut, or because the intervening vowel is neither /ʏ/
or /ö/ fulfilling the conditions stated in (20b)
praktugur 'magnificent', dat. pl. *praktug-um*
fallegur 'beautiful'   *falleg-um*
kaktus 'cactus'   *kaktus-um*
albatros 'albatross'   *albatros-um*
aldin 'fruit'   *aldin-um*

however, its nom. sg. f., in which case form u-umlaut is expected on the
basis of such examples as *gamall* 'old' ⁓ *gömul* ⁓ *gömlum*, is *farin*,
not *förin*. On the other hand, *fagur* 'fair' follows the pattern of *gamall*:
fagur ⁓ *fögur* ⁓ *fögrum*. The relevant difference between *farinn* and
fagur is that in the former the vowel to be umlauted is followed by *i* in
the non-syncopated forms, in the latter by *ur*. However, not even in this
case can the lack of u-umlaut in *farin* be blamed on its *i* with certainty,
for the description can also be formulated in an alternative way: *fagur*

pertains to the same declension as *gamall* as far as the u-umlauting of its vowels is concerned, whereas *farinn* does not.

The stem-internal /Y/ does not trigger u-umlaut in a preceding /a/ of the same stem; cf. nom. sg. m. *fagur* (versus nom. sg. f. *fögur*), nom. sg. *akur* (dat. pl. *ökrum*), nom. sg. *mastur* (nom. pl. *möstur*). An exception is the oblique singular *föður* of *faðir* 'father'.

What phonological material can intervene between the end of the stem containing a u-umlauted vowel and the end of the word containing that stem? Nothing need intervene, see (22a). If anything does intervene, the most usual segment string immediately after the morpheme

(22) a. *börn, önnur, sumur, folöld, japönsk*
   b. *börn-um, öðr-u, folöld-um, kandídöt-um, japönsk-um, sög-u, köll-um, stör-ðu*; but cf. *pöntunar*
   c. *dal-ur, albansk-ur* (**döl-ur*, etc.)

boundary begins with /YC$_0$/, see (22b). In fact, if a lexical item contains a vowel which is susceptible to u-umlaut, that vowel invariably assumes the umlauted shape (/ö, Y/) before an ending beginning with /Y/, with the following exception: the desinence initial /Y/ of the nominative singular ending *-ur* is only accompanied by u-umlaut in the preceding stem if the u-umlaut can be ascribed to some other cause than the presence of *-ur*. For instance, there is u-umlaut in the nominative singular of the monosyllabic u-stem nouns: *skjöld-ur* 'shield', cf. gen. sg. *skjald-ar*; that this /a—ö/ has nothing to do with the *-ur* follows from the fact that those u-stem nouns which do not end in *-ur* in the nominative singular nevertheless undergo u-umlaut in that case form, e.g. *björn* 'bear', cf. gen. sg. *bjarn-ar*. For examples of lexical items that do not undergo u-umlaut before the nominative singular *-ur*, see (22c). (The fact that u-umlaut is not triggered before *-ur* is not the property of ANY ending *-ur*, only of the nominative singular case ending. The *-ur* of the nominative/accusative plural of weak feminine nouns behaves otherwise: nom./acc. pl. *sög-ur*, with u-umlaut, of *saga* 'saga'.)

The ending of the imperative singular with appended personal pronoun contains /Y/, e.g. imp. *far-ðu* of *fara* 'go, travel', *skammastu þín* of *skammast sín* 'be ashamed of oneself', yet the /Y/ of this ending does not trigger u-umlaut in the preceding stem, although the verbal stems in question otherwise are susceptible to u-umlaut; cf. 1p. pl. pres. *för-um*, *skömm-umst* ⌣ *skömm-ustum*.

If an ending does not begin with /y/, the u-umlaut generally does not take place in the stem. Exceptions:

(a) The ending of the definite dative plural of nouns can begin with *o* or *u*; there is *-onum* and *-unum* (under the influence of flámæli also *-önum*. Cf. Hægstad 1942:11 quoting Rask; Bandle 1956:65–66), e.g. *börn-onum* and *börn-unum*. The ending *-onum* ⌣ *-unum* behaves in the same way as the dative plural ending *-um* as far as u-umlaut is concerned.

(b) In general, the case forms of any Icelandic noun display two shapes, one with the postpositive article appended, and another without it. E.g. nom./acc. sg. *barn* and *barn-ið*. As far as the u-umlaut is concerned, the longer forms repeat the state of affairs that is found in the short forms: since there is no umlaut in *barn*, there is none in *barn-ið* either; and since the nom./acc. pl. *börn* displays u-umlaut, the corresponding definite form has it as well, *börn-in*. The fact that the *-in* of the definite form *börn-in* begins with /ɪ/, i.e. with a vowel other than /y/, has no influence upon the distribution of u-umlaut in the noun form with postpositive article appended to it.

In compound words only those constituents undergo u-umlaut which are morphologically inflected. Usually only the rightmost constituent, if any, is so inflected, and therefore is umlauted under the same conditions and in the same way as if it were an independent word; e.g. *aðal-dalur* 'chief valley', dat. pl. *aðal-dölum*, not *öðul-dölum* or the like. (The hyphen indicates the boundary between the constituents of the compound.) A list, probably exhaustive, of compound words in which a non-final constituent is both inflected and undergoes u-umlaut is given in (23), q.v. (These compounds are sometimes written as two words, *annar hver*, etc., yet each is considered one lexical item.) Probably this state of affairs is just a special case of the constraint that says that only inflected stems undergo u-umlaut (or ANY kind of umlaut and ablaut); another special case of this type are adjectivally used (indeclinable) present participles such as *talandi* 'speaking', and other indeclinables, e.g. *handlama* 'with paralysed hand or arm'.—For cases such as *sögu-staður* 'historical place', where *sögu-* appears to be inflected relative to the simplex *saga*, see par. 1.

172   GRIPLA

(23) *annar-hver* 'every other': nom. sg. f. *önnur-hver,* dat. pl. *öðrum-*
      hverjum

   annar-hvor 'one of two': nom. sg. f. *önnur-hvor,* dat. sg. m. *öðr-*
      um-hvorum

   annar-tveggja 'one of two': nom. sg. f. *önnur-tveggja,* dat. sg. m.
      öðrum-tveggja

   allur-saman -samall 'complete, undivided': nom. sg. f. *öll-sömun,*
      öll-sömul, dat. pl. *öllum-saman*

As is well known, Modern Icelandic distinguishes between long and
short /ö, Y, a/ (and other vowels). The phonetic differences between
the short and the long variety of each pair are not negligible, at least as
far as /ö/ and /Y/ are concerned; Pétursson (1974:105 and passim)
has ascertained experimentally that short /ö, Y/ are more open (often
considerably more open) than their respective long counterparts. Yet
from the functional point of view there is no detectable difference
between the long and the short variants of these sounds. In root-initial
syllables the u-umlaut results in /ö/ regardless of whether it alternates
with long or short /a/, and regardless of whether /ö/ is of the same
quantity as the alternant /a/. Cf. *bakari* 'baker' versus *bökurum, ax*
'ear of corn' versus *öx, gamall* 'old' versus *gamla* versus *gömul* versus
gömlu, etc. In root non-initial syllables the vocalic quantity is almost
invariably neutralized and realized as short. The structure of such
syllables does not influence the choice of the u-umlaut reflex, although
this can only be illustrated for the VC type: *héröð* versus *héruð.* With
the VCC type the illustration cannot be made because there are no
reliable examples of the reflex /Y/ alternating with /ö/ before more
than one consonant in unstressed syllables. (The alternation /au—öi/
treated in par. 6.1 involves only short /au/ and short /öi/, which is due
to the fact that the non-anterior nasal consonant appears only in closed
syllables; all other vowels are also invariably short before non-anterior
nasal.) In view of the above, the quantity problems are ignored in the
present paper as irrelevant to the matter at hand.

4. Morphological environment of u-umlaut. Both mono- and polysyllabic stems susceptible to u-umlaut undergo it in the same morphological environments. The type of umlaut (whether Initial, or Final, or
a third variety) does not depend on the morphological environment, but

on other factors. Specifically, I am not aware of any cases where one inflectional form of a lexical item would display one type of u-umlaut, e.g. Initial umlaut, and another form of the same paradigm would display another type of u-umlaut, e.g. Final umlaut. For instance, as far as I know, there is no tendency to use *héruð-* more than *héröð-* (both of *hérað* 'district') in the dative plural, and *héröð-* more than *héruð-* in the nominative/accusative plural.

U-umlaut takes place in the following morphological environments:

(I) Nouns susceptible to u-umlaut. All such nouns display u-umlaut in the dative plural: *aftan(n)* 'evening' versus *öftn-um*, *barn* 'child' versus *börn-um*, *gjöf* 'present' versus *gjöf-um* (nom. pl. *gjaf-ir*), *gata* 'street' versus *göt-um*, etc.

The nouns of the neuter gender also display u-umlaut in the nominative/accusative plural: *land* 'land' versus *lönd*, *hjarta* 'heart' versus *hjört-u*, etc.

Strong feminine nouns also display u-umlaut in the nominative, dative and accusative singular: nom./dat./acc. *gjöf* 'present', etc.; the *pöntun* nouns even in the genitive singular, e.g. *pöntunar*.

The u-stem nouns also display u-umlaut in the nominative and accusative singular (and, archaically, accusative plural): *björn* 'bear', nom. sg. *björn*, acc. sg. *björn*, archaic acc. pl. *björn-u*; the *söfnuður* nouns even in the dative singular, nominative and accusative plural: dat. sg. *söfnuði*, nom. pl. *söfnuðir*, acc. pl. *söfnuði*.

Weak feminine nouns also display u-umlaut in the oblique singular and in the nominative/accusative plural: *saga* 'history', oblique sg. *sög-u*, nom./acc. pl. *sög-ur*.

Comments on a few exceptional nouns: (a) *Faðir* 'father'. This lexical item being one of the most basic and frequent in the language, it is not unnatural that it is irregular; its oblique singular stem is *föður-*, its plural stem is *feðr-* before a vowel, *feður-* elsewhere. (b) *Regin* n. 'gods', plurale tantum, has *a* in the genitive plural, *ragna*, and *ö* in the dative plural, *rögnum*, otherwise *e*, *regin*; like *faðir*, *regin* is an exceptional noun. (c) *Altari* n. 'altar': its most usual nominative/accusative plural is *ölturu*. It is the only word of its kind as far as its inflexion is concerned, whereas the u-umlaut takes place in the same case forms as with the type *barn*: in the nominative/accusative and dative plural. (d)

In the forms of the substantivized present participles the u-umlaut does not operate, for the plural normally contains the suffix -end- and is thus not susceptible to u-umlaut. There is, however, an older dative plural in -önd-um (normal -end-um) contrasting with the singular suffix -and- (and with the older gen. pl. -and-a, normal suffix -end-a). However, the history of the u-umlaut in the present participle is complicated and requires extensive separate treatment; -öndum and -endum are not the only dative plural endings of the present participle in the history of Icelandic. This will not be discussed further here.

(II) Adjectives susceptible to u-umlaut (including past participles). All such adjectives display u-umlaut in the following strong cases: dative singular masculine/neuter and dative plural; in the following weak cases: oblique singular feminine and the plural of all three genders. E.g. valinn 'chosen': dat. sg. m. völd-um, dat. sg. n. völd-u, dat. pl. völd-um; weak oblique sg. f. völd-u, weak plural of all three genders völd-u.

In addition to this, all adjectives except those ending in -in- display u-umlaut in the strong nominative singular feminine and in the nominative/accusative plural neuter: fagur 'fair', strong nom. sg. f. and nom./ acc. pl. n. fögur. The strong nominative singular feminine and nominative/accusative plural neuter of valinn is valin, not völin; if -d- is substituted for -in-, as it sometimes is, the u-umlaut does take place: nom. sg. f. and nom./acc. pl. n. völd, not vald.

With adjectives it is necessary to distinguish (a) strong inflexion, (b) weak inflexion, (c) inflexion of the comparative, and (d) lack of inflexion. Lack of inflexion entails lack of u-umlaut, cf. afl-vana 'deficient in strength', ein-mana 'solitary', etc. Indeclinable adjectives include the adjectival usages of the present participle: talandi 'speaking'.

(III) Verbs susceptible to u-umlaut (except their participles, for which see above). All verbs display u-umlaut in the first person plural present (indicative, subjunctive, imperative) and in the preterite plural (indicative, subjunctive). E.g. kalla 'call': 1p. pl. pres. köll-um, köll-umst ⁓ köllustum, pl. pret. köll-uðum, köll-uðuð, köll-uðu; köll-uð-umst ⁓ köll-uðustum, köll-uðuzt, köll-uðust. This formulation implies that root vowels which are due to such processes as ablaut and i-umlaut are inserted into the phonological representations before u-umlaut steps in. Otherwise the above formulation predicts wrong results with the *krefja* verbs (outside plural preterite indicative), where the first person plural present is *kref-jum* (not *kröf-jum*), and preterite plural subjunctive *kref-ðum* etc. (not *kröf-ðum*); with the *vaka* verbs, i.e. with those *ē*-verbs undergoing i-umlaut in the preterite subjunctive, cf. pret. subj. *vek-tum* etc. (not *vök-tum*[7]); with the strong verbs, where the preterite contains other vowels than *ö*, e.g. *grafa* 'dig', pret. ind. *gróf-* (not *gröf-*), pret. subj. *græf-* (not *gröf-*).

Supposing that the place at which the u-umlauted vowel is inserted into the stem is determined in some independent way, the environment of u-umlaut can be stated entirely in the morphological terms listed above.

5. On /ö/ as the basic vowel of the u-umlaut alternation. The above list of morphological environments (par. 4) in which *ö, u* are found instead of *a*, is composed so as to imply that /a/ is the basic vowel from which /ö, ʏ/ are derived in appropriate contexts (presumably by aid of morphological rules of the format /a/ → /ö/ and /a/ → /ʏ/). Yet this is by no means necessarily the case. In principle /a/ can be basic in some types, /ö, ʏ/ in others. Alternatively, it may be that /a/ and /ö, ʏ/ are considered of equal standing, in some types at least. Even more complicated situations can be imagined. Different speakers might have different grammars in this respect. (It is a weak point of Orešnik 1975 that it assumes, without argumentation, that /a/ is the basic vowel of all synchronic u-umlaut alternations.)

In the following instances it is possible that /ö/ rather than /a/ is the basic vowel of the u-umlaut alternation:

Strong feminine nouns may have /ö/ as the basic vowel in the singular, and /a/ as the basic vowel in the plural. E.g. the lexical representation of *gjöf* 'present' may be: /g$_j$öv/ in the singular, /g$_j$av/ in the plural. The morphological rule /ö/ → /a/ produces the /a/ of the gen. sg. *gjaf-ar*, and the morphological rule /a/ → /ö/ produces the /ö/ of the dat. pl. *gjöf-um*.[8]

---

[7] Þorkelsson 1902:139 reports pret. subj. *vakti* (without i-umlaut in the root syllable) from Skaftafellssýslur.

[8] The hypothesis operating with two-stem lexical representations of *gjöf* nouns predicts the following concerning loanwords into Icelandic and domestic nouns

176   GRIPLA

The same type of lexical representations is likely to be valid for the
pöntun nouns. A typical lexical representation would be: /pönt/ in the
singular, /pant/ in the plural (assuming that -an-/-un- pertain to the
case desinences). The only difference from the gjöf nouns would be that
no morphological rule would apply in the genitive singular, and the /ö/
of the singular lexical representation would remain intact, pöntunar.
Nouns such as afhöfðun 'decapitation' would have /ö/ both in their
singular and plural lexical representations.

The u-stems are likely to have /ö/ in their lexical representations, at

changing declension class: If such stems originally contain /a/ as their only or
rightmost vowel, and if they join the ranks of Icelandic strong feminine nouns,
they behave in one of the following ways. EITHER such stems develop two-stem
lexical representations, with /ö/ in the singular, with /a/ in the plural, OR they
keep a one-stem lexical representation, with /a/, in which case they do not undergo any u-umlaut in the singular (there being no rule of the form /a/→/ö/ in the
singular of strong feminine nouns), but do undergo it in the dative plural (where
there operates a rule of the form /a/→/ö/). This prediction is borne out by the
facts:

Classical Icelandic nagl 'nail', root noun, masculine, became feminine in pre-
Reformation times. Its singular joined the ranks of the strong feminine nouns and
the lexical representation of the singular developed /ö/ instead of /a/, so that the
forms are now nom. sg. nögl, gen. sg. nagl-ar, just as with gjöf.

In Classical Icelandic the feminine iō-stem noun öx 'axe' contained /ö/ in all of
its case forms: gen. sg. öx-ar, dat./acc. sg. öx-i, nom./acc. pl. öx-ar, etc. In the
modern language the noun has joined the gjöf nouns as far as its root vowel is
concerned (lexical representation sg. /öx/, pl. /ax/), partially also with respect to
the endings (nom./acc. pl. öx-ar > ax-ir), so that now the nominative singular is
öx-i, gen. sg. ax-ar, dat./acc. sg. öx-i, nom./acc. pl. ax-ir, etc.

Classical Icelandic dögg 'dew', lögg 'croze', feminine wō-stems, have later been
attracted into the orbit of the gjöf nouns, i.e. they have assumed partially new
endings and developed two-stem lexical representations, sg. /dögg/, pl. /dagg/,
and sg. /lögg/, pl. /lagg/. Cf. old gen. sg. dögg-var, lögg-var, modern dagg-ar
(Bandle 1956:226), lagg-ar; old nom. pl. dögg-var, lögg-var, modern dagg-ir,
lagg-ir.

Cases of domestic and naturalized stems which manifest feminine one-stem
lexical representations. These can be illustrated with popular loanwords such as
art f. 'sort, kind' (art- undergoes u-umlaut freely otherwise, e.g. in vanartaður
'vicious', dat. pl. vanörtuðum), vakt f. 'watch' (umlauted vakt- in the sundry forms
of vakta vb. 'watch', vaktari 'guardian', etc.), forakt f. 'contempt' (umlauted -akt-
in forakta 'despise'), andakt f. 'devotion', magt, makt 'might, honour', dragt f.
'coat and skirt', which keep their /a/ unchanged in their singular inflected forms.

least in the singular. E.g. /sk$_j$öld/ 'shield'. The morphological rule /ö/ →/a/ would produce *a* in the genitive singular. I dare not state an opinion on the situation in the plural of these nouns.

/ö/ is very likely the basic vowel in the type *söfnuður*. The morphological rule /ö/ → /a/ introduces *a* into the gen. sg./pl. *safnaðar, safnaða*.

/ö/ may be the basic vowel in the weak feminine nouns, and the morphological rule /ö/ → /a/ operate in the nominative singular and in the genitive plural (nom. sg. *saga*, gen. pl. *sagna*).[9]

Moreover, when the originally neuter noun *válað* 'misery' appeared temporarily as feminine in the New Testament 1540 and Guðbrandsbiblía 1584 (see Helgason 1929:401; Bandle 1956:201), it did not umlaut its /a/ in, say, its dative singular: NT *af volad sinni*, GB *volat*, not *volöð* or *voluð*. Similarly *mann-líkan* 'idol', normally neuter, appears as feminine in Guðbrandsbiblía 1584 (Bandle ibidem), but does not undergo u-umlaut in the nominative singular: *ein Mannlijkan*, not -*ön*, -*un*.

Nouns such as *art* above undergo u-umlaut in the dative plural, if they have plural forms at all. E.g. *dragt* 'coat and skirt', dat. pl. *drögt-um*. The contrast between umlautless singular and umlauted dative plural follows if a one-stem lexical representation with the root vowel /a/ is posited.

The genitive singular /ö/→/a/ rule is occasionally dropped, with the result that /ö/ is realized on the phonetic level even in the genitive singular. This can be documented with historical facts. E.g. Bandle 1956:38 has culled the following two genitive singular case forms from Guðbrandsbiblía 1584: *Vesölldar* (normal gen. sg. *vesald-ar*, of *vesöld* 'misery') and *styriölldar* (normal gen. sg. *styrjald-ar*, of *styrjöld* 'war'). Further, the genitive singular of the feminine proper name *Ólöf*, normally *Ólaf-ar*, appears as *Ólöf-ar* in the titles of post-Reformation folk-songs, see Helgason 1962:176, 1965:105.

9 The postulation of the rule /ö/→/a/ in the nominative singular of the feminine weak nouns helps to explain the peculiar development of the words *flaga* and *amaba* in Modern Icelandic. The weak noun *fluga* 'fly' became *flöga* in the town of Hafnarfjörður (11 kms from Reykjavík) owing to flámæli, and the paradigm nom. sg. *flöga*, oblique sg. *flögu* was changed—presumably under the influence of the rule /ö/→/a/ in the nominative singular—to the paradigm nom. sg. *flaga*, oblique sg. *flögu*. (The facts were given in personal communication from Jón Helgason, April 1975.) Another example of the same kind is the learned naturalized noun *amöba* 'amoebe', which has developed a side form in the nominative singular, *amaba*, again presumably under the influence from the rule /ö/→/a/.

Baldur Jónsson has drawn my attention to the word *tölva* 'computer', originally made by Sigurður Nordal on the analogy of *völva* 'prophetess'. Instead of *tölva*, *talva* (oblique singular *tölvu*) is now often used, a form which seems to be due to

6.1. Consider now the standard Icelandic alternation /au ⌢ öi/ before a non-anterior (i.e. palatal or velar) nasal consonant. For examples see (24a). This alternation is a product of the historical processes of u-umlaut and subsequent diphthongization (*á* > [au], *ö* > [öi]) before a non-anterior nasal. The inclusion of this alternation in the present treatment of /a ⌢ ö/ and /a ⌢ ɣ/ is arbitrary, for I cannot prove that the alternations /a⌢ö/ and /a ⌢ ɣ/ on the one hand, and /au⌢öi/ on the other belong together from the synchronic point of view. A weak argument in favour of the two alternations being closer to each other than either of them to any third alternation in the synchronic grammar of Icelandic is that the two alternations occur in the same morphological

(24) a. *langur* 'long',   nom. sg. f.   *löng*
     banki 'bank',   dat. pl.   *bönkum*
   b. *banka* 'knock',   pret. pl.   *bönkuð-*
     sanka 'gather'   *sönkuð-*
     hanka 'provide with a handle'   *hönkuð-*
     tanka 'refuel'   *tönkuð-*
     ranka 'remember dimly'   *rönkuð-*
     jánka 'say *já*'   *jánkuð-*
   c. *spranga* 'walk sprightly', pret. pl. *sprönguð-*
     stanga 'goad'   *stönguð-*
     hand-langa 'hand'   *-lönguð-*
     fanga 'capture'   *fönguð-*
     banga 'hammer'   *bönguð-*
     ganga 'go',   1p. pl. pres. *göngum*
     but *anga* 'smell',   pret. pl.   *anguð-* ⌢ *önguð-*
   d. *rangla* 'stroll idly', pret. pl.   *rangluð-*
     dangla 'strike lightly'   *dangluð-*
     angra 'anger'   *angruð-*

the same kind of development as witnessed by *amöba* > *amaba* and *flöga* > *flaga* above.

Stefán Karlsson has drawn my attention to the Christian name *Marja*, oblique singular *Marju*, without any u-umlaut. This lexical item contains lexicalized /a/ in its stem: /marj+a, +ɣ/ (in contradistinction to, say, *saga*, which contains lexicalized /ö/). Since no /a/→/ö/ rule operates in the declension of weak feminine nouns, the *a* of *Marja* is never changed to *ö*.

einangra 'isolate'   *einangruð-*
hangsa 'idle'   *hangsuð-*
flangsast 'fawn and coax'   *flangsuð-*
slangra 'sling; stroll idly'   *slöngruð-* and
e. I. past participles of weak verbs   *slangr-uð*
    nom. sg. f. *jánkuð-* of *jánka*
        einangruð- of *einangra*
        etc.
  II. derivatives of verbal stems sub d
    einangrun 'isolation'
    einangrari 'insolator', dat. pl. *einangrurum*
    ranglari 'vagrant'   *ranglurum*
    hangsari 'dawdler'   *hangsurum*
    flangsari 'fawner'   *flangsurum*
  III. other non-verbs
    bangsi 'teddybear',   dat. pl.   *bangsum*
    blánka 'bleach',   oblique sg.   *blánku*
    leiðangur 'expedition', dat. pl. *leiðöngrum*,
        rarer also *leiðangrum*, cf. Helgason in Holberg 1948:296
    fanginn 'captured',   dat. pl.   *föngnum*, rarer
        also *fangnum*, cf. Helgason ibidem

environments and are in complementary distribution in the sense that /au ⁓ öi/ only takes place before a non-anterior nasal, /a ⁓ ö/ and /a ⁓ ɣ/ elsewhere.

/a⁓ö/ occurs with greater regularity than /au⁓öi/. For instance, there is *skammur* 'short', dat. pl. *skömmum*, parallel to *l*[au]*ngur* 'long', dat. pl. *l*[öi]*ngum*; on the other hand, there is *kalla* 'call', 1p. pl. pres. *köllum*, pret. pl. *kölluð-*, but *angra* 'anger', of the same conjugation, 1p. pl. pres. [au]*ngrum* (not [öi]*ngrum*), pret. pl. [au]*ngruð-* (not [öi]*ngr-uð-*). No treatment of the discrepancy of which *löngum* and *angrum* are an example has been published. As far as I can see, the alternation /au⁓öi/ occurs almost regularly (i.e. in the same contexts as the alternation /a⁓ö/) in non-verbs; a few exceptions are enumerated in (24e). In verbs, however, there is a complication in that some verbs do, and others do not, display the alternation /au⁓öi/, and a few vacillate between /au⁓öi/ and the lack of alternation. What I consider—impressionistically and on the basis of the OHÍ data—to be the more generally used form in contexts where u-umlaut is expected is adduced in the right column of (24b–e).

The alternation does occur in verbs whose present stems end in what is written *nk*, see (24b) for examples, although forms with lacking alternation can also be heard, with some verbs more, with others less often.

Verbs whose present stems end in what is written *ng* regularly experience the alternation /au—öi/. For examples see (24c). With the strong verb *hanga* 'hang', /öi/ appears in the 1p. pl. pres., *h*[öi]*ngum*, whereas it is absent from the Northern weak pret. pl. *h*[au]*ngdum* etc. (not *h*[öi]*ngdum*, Jakob Benediktsson *viva voce* in March 1975), presumably because another consonant follows *ng* in the preterite and the forms belong to the type exemplified sub (24d).

Verbs whose present stems end in what is written *ng* + consonant more often lack the alternation /au—öi/ than have it. For examples see (24d). It is difficult to see what the generalization is. No alternation before *ng* + consonant? Why then *slöngruð-* (and *slangruð-*) of *slangra*, as against *angruð-* (never *öngruð-*) of *angra*?

The historical reasons for this unusual development are also unclear. Bandle 1956:37 draws attention to the lack of u-umlaut in the relevant forms of *angra* in Guðbrandsbiblía 1584. He treats *angra* as an isolated case (because other examples of the type do not occur in his corpus), and assumes that the lack of u-umlaut may be due to the influence of verbs such as *hátta*, *mála*, which of course do not u-umlaut their root vowels. I find this explanation too general.

6.2. The diphthong [ai] usually does not participate in any u-umlaut alternations, see (25) for examples. There is, however, an exception to

(25) *grænn* 'green', nom. sg. f. *græn*, dat. pl. *græn-um*
   æra 'drive mad', 1p. pl. pres. *ær-um*, 1p. pl. pret. *ær-ðum*
   gæi 'guy', dat. pl. *gæ-jum*
   Sóraja Persian given name, oblique sg. *Sóraj-u*

this statement in standard Icelandic: In a considerable number of words there is an alternation [öi—öq—ai—aq], where the alternants beginning with [ö] appear in the environments of u-umlaut, and the [a]-initial alternants outside those environments. For examples see (26).

(26) *félag-* n. 'society', nom. sg. *félag* [-aq], definite *félagið* [-aijɪð], dat. sg. *félagi* [-aijɪ], nom./acc. pl. *félög* [-öq], definite *félögin* [-öijɪn], dat. pl. *félögum* [-öqɤm]

heilag- 'holy', nom. sg. m. *heilagur* [-aq-], weak *heilagi* [-aijɪ], nom. sg. f. *heilög* [-öq], etc.

dag- m. 'day', acc. sg. *dag* [-aq], definite *daginn* [-aijɪn], dat. pl. *dögum* [-öq-]

The following processes have cooperated in the history of the language to bring about the alternations illustrated sub (26): (a) the palatalization of velar consonants before /ɪ/-initial endings; (b) the change of palatalized /q/ to /j/; (c) u-umlaut; (d) the diphthongization of the vowel followed by /j/. The processes (a–d) are independent of each other by virtue of the fact that they are not co-extensive. One can therefore postulate the existence of a palatalization rule, a q' > j rule, a diphthongization-before-*j* rule, and a u-umlaut rule, where the rules are ordered as just given, except that the u-umlaut rule must precede the diphthongization rule, for the u-umlauted *ö* becomes *öi*, and the non-umlauted *a* becomes *ai* through diphthongization. A few sample derivations are given sub (27), q.v. (The effect of u-umlaut has been

(27)	-laq	-löq	-laq + ɪ	-löq + ɪn
palatalization	—	—	-laq' + ɪ	-löq' + ɪn
q' → j	—	—	-laj + ɪ	-löj + ɪn
diphthongization	—	—	-laij + ɪ	-löij + ɪn

incorporated into the input representations.) However, it has not been proved that the rules whose operation is assumed in (27) really are a part of Modern Icelandic descriptive grammar. Therefore further discussion of the descriptive problems raised by the alternations illustrated in (26) has to be postponed until such time that relative certainty is achieved concerning the status in Modern Icelandic grammar of the rules involved in (27).

University of Ljubljana

GRIPLA

REFERENCES

Anderson, Stephen R. 'An outline of the phonology of Modern Icelandic vowels.' *Foundations of Language* 5, 1969, pp. 53–72.

Bandle, Oskar. *Die Sprache der Guðbrandsbiblía.* Bibliotheca arnamagnæana, vol. XVII. Copenhagen, 1956.

Benediktsson, Hreinn. 'Phonemic neutralization and inaccurate rhymes.' *Acta philologica scandinavica* 26, 1963, pp. 1–18. (Referred to as Benediktsson 1963a.)

— 'The non-uniqueness of phonemic solutions: Quantity and stress in Icelandic.' *Phonetica* 10, 1963, pp. 133–53. (Referred to as Benediktsson 1963b.)

Blöndal, Sigfús. *Íslensk-dönsk orðabók.* Reykjavík, 1920–24.

Böðvarsson, Árni, ed. *Íslenzk orðabók handa skólum og almenningi.* Reykjavík, 1963.

Guðmundsson, Valtýr. *Islandsk Grammatik. Islandsk Nutidssprog.* Copenhagen, 1922.

Halldórsson, Halldór. *Íslenzk málfræði handa æðri skólum.* Reykjavík, 1950.

Helgason, Jón. *Málið á Nýja testamenti Odds Gottskálkssonar.* Safn Fræðafjelagsins um Ísland og Íslendinga gefið út af Hinu íslenska fræðafjelagi í Kaupmannahöfn, vol. 7. Copenhagen, 1929.

— ed. *Íslenzk fornkvæði. Islandske folkeviser.* Editiones arnamagnæanæ, series B. Vol. 10(1962). Vol. 14(1965). Copenhagen.

Holberg, Ludvig. *Nikulás Klím.* Translated into Icelandic by Jón Ólafsson úr Grunnavík (1745). Edited by Jón Helgason. Íslenzk rit síðari alda gefin út af Hinu íslenzka fræðafélagi í Kaupmannahöfn, vol. 3. Copenhagen, 1948.

Hægstad, Marius. *Nokre ord um nyislandsken.* Skrifter utgitt av Det Norske Videnskaps-akademi i Oslo. II. Hist.-Filos. Klasse. No number. Only proof-sheets exist. Oslo, 1942.

Kress, Bruno. *Laut- und Formenlehre des Isländischen.* Halle/Saale, 1963.

Nielsen, Karl Martin. 'Scandinavian Breaking.' *Acta philologica scandinavica* 24, 1957, pp. 33–45.

Orešnik, Janez. 'The Modern Icelandic u-umlaut rule.' *The Nordic Languages and Modern Linguistics 2*, edited by Karl-Hampus Dahlstedt. Acta Regiæ Societatis Skytteanæ, vol. 13. Stockholm, 1975.

Pétursson, Magnús. *Les articulations de l'islandais à la lumière de la radiocinématographie.* Paris, 1974.

Þorkelsson, Páll. *Beygingarreglur í íslenzku með frönskum skýringum.* Copenhagen, 1902.

Þórólfsson, Björn Karel. *Um íslenskar orðmyndir á 14. og 15. öld og breytingar þeirra úr fornmálinu.* Reykjavík, 1925.

JANEZ OREŠNIK

THREE MODERN ICELANDIC
MORPHOPHONEMIC NOTES

I. THE PRETERITE SUBJUNCTIVE
SEIGÐI OF *SEGJA* 'SAY'

The regular preterite subjunctive of the much used weak verb *segja* 'say' is *segð-* *(segði, segðir, . . .)*, as expected on the basis of the pret. ind. *sagð-*. Beside *segð-* there is also a rarer preterite subjunctive stem *seigð-*. I know of only one example in written texts, *seigdi*. It occurs in a folk ballad translated from Danish, see Helgason 1963:51, verse 29₁ (v.l. *segði*). The translation was made by Jón Ólafsson Indíafari (1593–1679), who lived, while in Iceland, in Vestfirðir. The manuscript in which *seigdi* occurs, Lbs. 449 8vo, was written in Vestfirðir in the latter half of the eighteenth century or around 1800. (These data are from Helgason 1963:XV–XVI, XVIII–XIX.) The hapax *seigdi* is thus closely connected with Vestfirðir. In March 1975 three native speakers of Icelandic told me that they use, at least occasionally, pret. subj. *seigð-* in their everyday speech. Two of these informants are from Vestfirðir (Ásgeir Blöndal Magnússon and Njörður P. Njarðvík), one from Northern Iceland (Björn Teitsson). Thus the form is still in use, and Helgason's hapax is not due to a mistake.

The root vowel *ei* of *seigð-* can only be due to the influence of the present stem *segj-*, which contains the same diphthong *ei*. *Seigð-* is not the only instance of analogy which emanates from the present stem and re-shapes the preterite subjunctive, but not the preterite indicative. Other cases in point are the verbs *þykja* 'seem' and *sækja* 'seek'.

Throughout the post-Reformation history of Icelandic *þykja* and *sækja* have had double forms in the preterite: *þykja*, pret. ind. *þótt-* and *þókt-*, pret. subj. *þætt-* and *þækt-; sækja*, pret. ind. *sótt-* and *sókt-*, pret. subj. *sætt-* and *sækt-*. The *tt*-forms are inherited, the *kt*-forms are due to analogy with the present stem, which contains a *k*, cf. the infinitives *þykja* and *sækja*. What is unusual about these preteritival forms is their eventual fate in the modern literary language. The preterite indicative is now *þótt-* and *sótt-*, i.e. *tt*-forms, whereas the preterite subjunctive is a *tt*-form, *þætt-*, with *þykja*, and a *kt*-form, *sækt-*, with *sækja*. The net result is that the paradigm of *sækja* now displays a distribution of the *tt*- and *kt*-forms which reminds one of the formation *seigð-:* the present stem and the preterite subjunctive 'go together', whereas the preterite indicative stands apart.

Why have the *kt*-forms been victorious in the preterite subjunctive of *sækja* (pret. subj. *sækt-*) and not at all in that of *þykja* (pret. subj. *þætt-*)? There is ample evidence from the post-Reformation centuries that the pret. *sókt-/sækt-* held a much stronger position in post-Reformation Icelandic (editions of even older texts have not been consulted) than the pret. *þókt-/þækt-:* in a number of texts the distribution is *sókt-/sækt-* of *sækja*, and *þótt-/þætt-* of *þykja*, whereas in a number of other texts the distribution is preponderantly *sókt-/sækt-* and preponderantly *þótt-/þætt-*, but also *þókt-/þækt-*. See, e.g., Bandle 1956:414–15; Helgason 1938:69; Helgason 1948:122, 136; Helgason in Holberg 1948:307*, 308; Helgason 1950:32, 33, 34*, 35; Jón Magnússon in Jónsson 1933:122; Sigmundsson 1965:89*. Etc. (The page references to the instances of *þókt-/þækt-* are asterisked.) The texts referred to date from the sixteenth, seventeenth, and eighteenth centuries.

In addition to the pret. subj. *þætt-* and *þækt-*, Blöndal 1920–24 s.v. *þykja* mentions another subjunctive form, *þykt-*, which he states is a Southern form. The files of the University of Iceland Dictionary Project contain three instances of *þykt-* (as of March 1975), all from Southern texts, one from the nineteenth century, two from the twentieth. The oldest examples of *þykt-* that I know of occur in the manuscript called B[4] of *Árna saga biskups*, see the variae lectiones on pp. 60, 95, 138 of Þorleifur Hauksson's edition 1972. B[4] is AM 1041 4to and is a digest of the saga composed and written by Björn Jónsson (1574–1655) á Skarðsá, Northern Iceland. Thus the subj. *þykt-* is not limited to the South of Iceland, and has a relatively long history in the language. It has arisen under the influence of the present stem *þykj-*. Preterite indicative forms of the type *þykt-* do not exist. The subj. *þykt-* is therefore a formation parallel to the subj. *seigð-*.

MORPHOPHONEMIC NOTES

II. THE 2P. SG. PRES. SUBJ. *SÉST* OF *VERA* 'TO BE'

Dr. Helgi Guðmundsson of the University of Iceland has informed me that instead of the form *sé-rt*, 2p. sg. pres. subj. of the verbum substantivum *vera*, there occurs the form *sé-st*. This form is very rare, however, and, as far as is known, only found in South Western Iceland. It is the purpose of this note to propose an explanation of *sé-st*.

I suggest that *sé-st* is due to the influence of the preterite indicative of the strong verbs, with which the pres. subj. *sé-* has all the endings in common except the second person singular:

pres. subj.	*sé*	pret. ind.	*féll* (of *falla* 'fall')
	sé-rt		*féll-st*
	sé		*féll*
	sé-um		*féll-um*
	sé-uð		*féll-uð*
	sé-u		*féll-u*

The second person singular ends in *-st* in the preterite indicative of most strong verbs (other allomorphs of the ending in question: -Ø, cf. *brast* of *bresta* 'burst'; *-t*, cf. *las-t* of *lesa* 'read'), and this desinence was introduced, in the speech of some persons, into the pres. subj. *sé-*, resulting in *sé-st*.

The form *sé-rt* is susceptible to change because it is formally isolated; other second person singular present subjunctive forms end in *-ir*, e.g. *fall-ir* of *falla* 'fall'. That *sé-rt* should be attracted to the indicative preterite of the strong verbs can likewise be explained: only the indicative preterite of the strong verbs has the same endings as the present subjunctive *sé-*. True enough, there are the present indicative of *vera (er-)* and of the future auxiliary *munu*, which show the same degree of parallelism with *sé-* in endings as the preterite indicative of the strong verbs. However, the second person singular present indicative of *vera* is *er-t*, and no changing influence can be exerted by *er-t* upon *sé-rt*; they rhyme already. *Munu* is *mun-t* in the second person singular present indicative. Under its influence *sé-rt* would become *sé-t*, and this would be an unusual form phonotactically, seeing that the ending *-t* has generally become *tt* or *ð* finally after a vowel, cf. *ný-t* > *ný-tt* of *nýr* 'new', and *spá-t* > *spá-ð* of *spá* 'prophesy'; *sé-t* would also be even more isolated morphologically than *sé-rt* is. Thus only the preterite indicative of the strong verbs remains as a source for the regularizing innovation of *sé-rt*.

It might be asked whether it is not unrealistic to assume that the preterite indicative can influence the present subjunctive. There is at least one parallel to this, which, albeit not full, is sufficiently telling. In Modern Icelandic the personal pronoun *-ðu, -tu* etc. is almost invariably suffixed to the singular imperative, e.g. *far-ðu* of *fara* 'go, travel'. This has resulted in the singular imperative of most weak verbs of the *ia*-class being formally equal to the third person plural preterite (indicative and subjunctive). E.g. imp. sg. *sendu* of *senda* 'send' equals the 3p. pl. pret. *sendu*. A consequence is that occasionally the singular imperative becomes equal to the third person plural preterite (indicative) even in those cases where there is originally a formal difference between those forms. For instance, in Icelandic folk ballads — and elsewhere — there is imp. sg. *orktu* beside the expected *yrktu* of *yrkja* 'compose poetry'. *Orktu* stems from the 3p. pl. pret. ind. *orktu*. See Helgason 1970:XLV, who also mentions imp. sg. *keyptu* beside the normal *kauptu*, under the influence of the 3p. pl. pret. *keyptu* of *kaupa* 'buy'. However, the latter parallel is less reliable, for early instances of the analogical present stem *keyp-* have been reported outside the imperative singular. Cf. Þórólfsson 1925:119, who adduces an instance of the 3p. pl. pres. ind. *keypa* from Jón Arason's poetry (sixteenth century).[1]

III. *SKILAÐU AFTUR SKINU BEINI*

In the files of the University of Iceland Dictionary Project I happened to find the following quotation from a song/poem: *Skilaðu aftur skinu beini* 'give back the withered bone'. The quotation has been culled from the anthology *Að vestan I: Þjóðsögur og sagnir*, ed. Árni

---

[1] Þórólfsson 1925:64 also mentions an early instance of analogy in the opposite direction — the spread of the present stem *kaup-* into the preterite indicative of this verb: *þau kauptu for þetta kaup*, in a charter of 1388, see now Stefán Karlsson's edition 1963:94. However, since the same charter uses the regular preterite stem *keypt-* elsewhere, the hapax *kaupt-* may be due to the influence of the noun *kaup* which follows immediately in the text.

Bjarnarson, p. 115, Akureyri, 1949. The form *skinu* is a dative singular neuter, unusual in that the expected form would be *skinnu*, with long *n*. (The spelling of the whole text in which this word occurs follows the official orthography.) It is the purpose of this note to propose an explanation of the short *n* in *skinu*. I suggest that the form *skinu* is due to analogy with adjectives, including participles, in *nninn* and in consonant + *ninn*, such as the past part. *unninn* of *vinna* 'work' and the adjective *gegninn* 'obedient'. In the contracted cases of *unninn* and other words in *nninn* three *n*'s are lumped together, but the resulting phonetic sequence is just two *n*'s, i.e. a long *n*, for Icelandic only discriminates between two consonantal quantities, long and short. The resulting long *n* is understood as pertaining to the root, with the consequence that the case endings are different from those found outside the adjectives in *nninn*. For instance, the strong dative singular neuter of *unninn* is *unnu*, which is analyzed as *unn-u:* only -*u* is the ending. In the contracted cases of *gegninn* and other words ending in consonant + *ninn* two *n*'s are coalesced into a short *n* because Icelandic only tolerates short consonantal quantity in post-consonantal position. Thus the strong dative singular neuter of *gegninn* is *gegnu*, which is analyzed as *gegn-u:* only -*u* is the ending. The rule is: The ending of the strong dative singular neuter of adjectives in *inn* is -*nu*, except after a nasal consonant, where it is just -*u*. This rule was applied to *skininn* 'withered', yielding *skinu* instead of *skinnu* in the strong dative singular neuter.

REFERENCES

Bandle, Oskar. *Die Sprache der Guðbrandsbiblia.* Bibliotheca arnamagnæana, vol. XVII. Kopenh. 1956.

Blöndal, Sigfús. *Íslenzk-dönsk orðabók.* Rvík 1920–24.

Hauksson, Þorleifur, ed. *Árna saga biskups.* Stofnun Árna Magnússonar á Íslandi, rit 2. Rvík 1972.

Helgason, Jón, ed. *Byskupa sǫgur.* Fascicle I. Kbh. 1938.

—— *Ármanns rimur eftir Jón Guðmundsson lærða (1637) og Ármanns þáttur eftir Jón Þorláksson.* Íslenzk rit síðari alda gefin út af Hinu íslenzka fræðafélagi í Kaupmannahöfn, vol. 1. Kh. 1948.

—— *Móðars rimur og Móðars þáttur.* Íslenzk rit síðari alda gefin úr af Hinu íslenzka fræðafélagi í Kaupmannahöfn, vol. 5. Kh. 1950.

—— *Íslenzk fornkvæði. Islandske folkeviser.* Editiones arnamagnæanæ. Series B. Vol. 13 (1963). Vol. 16 (1970). Kbh.

626   JANEZ OREŠNIK

Holberg, Ludvig. *Nikulás Klim.* Translated into Icelandic by Jón Ólafsson úr Grunna-
    vík. Edited by Jón Helgason. Íslenzk rit síðari alda gefin út af Hinu íslenzka
    fræðafélagi í Kaupmannahöfn, vol. 3. Kh. 1948.
Jónsson, Finnur. *Den islandske grammatiks historie til o. 1800.* Det Kgl. Danske
    Videnskabernes Selskab. Historisk-filologiske Meddelelser XIX, 4. Kbh. 1933.
Karlsson, Stefán. *Islandske originaldiplomer indtil 1450. Text.* Editiones arnamagnæanæ.
    Series A, vol. 7. Kbh. 1963.
Sigmundsson, Svavar. *Málið á 'Stutt og Einfølld Undervisun Um Christenndomenn' eftir
    Jón biskup Vidalín, Kaupmannahöfn 1729, með samanburði við nokkur bréf sama
    höfundar. — Stafsetning. — Hljóðfræði.* Unpublished cand. mag. thesis. Uni-
    versity of Iceland. Rvík 1965.
Þórólfsson, Björn Karel. *Um íslenskar orðmyndir á 14. og 15. öld og breytingar þeirra úr
    fornmálinu.* Rvík 1925.

THE AGE AND IMPORTANCE OF THE MODERN ICELANDIC WORD TYPE KLIFR

Janez Orešnik, The University of Ljubljana

In the course of its history Icelandic abolished the sound sequences of consonant + r + word boundary, of consonant + r + consonant, and, to some extent, of consonant + r + affixed definite article. This happened because an epenthetic vowel, eventually identified with u, developed before r in such environments. The insertion of the epenthetic vowel began to appear in the texts of the late thirteenth century, and took place mainly in the fourteenth century (Benediktsson 1969: 394). Examples: hafr 'buck' became hafur; hafrs, genitive singular of hafr, became hafurs; hafr-inn, the definite form of hafr, became hafurinn. This is a well known process. What is less known is that Icelandic later reintroduced words ending in consonant + word-final r, so that now the Modern Icelandic lexicon contains a number of such words. An example is klifr 'climbing', pronounced as one syllable. All the words in question are action nouns, a-stems of neuter gender. Their word-final r's belong to their stems. All of these action nouns are derived from ōn-verbs whose infinitives end in consonant + ra; e.g., klifr comes from klifra 'climb'. Word-formationally they are parallel to the formations sub (1), q.v.

(1)

grenj		grenja	'wail'
bölv	formed on	bölva	'curse'
hangs		hangsa	'dawdle'

The complete list of such nouns culled from Blöndal's dictionary, including its appendix, is stated sub (2), q.v.

(2)

{bogr / bogur}		bogra	'walk stooping'
{flögr / flögur}		flögra	'flutter, flap'
hamr		hamra	'hammer'
{klifr / klifur}	formed on	klifra	'climb'
{kumr / kumur[1]}		kumra	'bleat, neigh, etc.'
{sötr / sötur}		sötra	'suck through the teeth'
umr		umra	'growl, etc.'
vavr[2]		vafra	'toddle, roam, stroll'

Furthermore, I have a number of such nouns from miscellaneous other sources, and they are stated sub (3), q.v.

(3)

{amr / amur}		amra	'whine'
{duðr / duður}		duðra	'be busy with something easy'
{klambr / klambur}		klambra	'make clumsily'
peðr	formed on	peðra	'deal out in small portions'
{pukr / pukur}		pukra	'conceal'
snupr		snupra	'chide'
{stumr / stumur}		stumra	'totter'

Amr is mentioned by Finnur Jónsson in his edition of Jón Magnússon's grammar (Jónsson 1933: 138). Duðr is found in Halldór Kiljan Laxness' work. Klambr and peðr occur in the booklet Um ljóðalýti (Reykjavík 1942) by the amateur author Björn Bjarnarson.[3] Puðr is adduced in Bérkov and Böðvarsson's Icelandic-Russian dictionary (p. 960). Pukr and snupr are adduced in Björn Guðfinnsson's book Mállýzkur (I, 1946, p. 144). My attention has been drawn to stumr by Jón Helgason, who assumes its possible existence in Björn Halldórsson's Lexicon Islandico-Latinum (see Helgason 1967: 104).

As can be seen from lists (2) and (3), the monosyllabic forms are sometimes accompanied by bisyllabic ones, containing the epenthetic vowel. It is not known at present which of the two formations is older. Furthermore, most of the nouns in Cr have a pejorative meaning, which may have been transferred to them from their respective verbal bases. Some of my Icelandic informants associate nouns like klifr with child language and/or see nonce-formations in them. I assume that more such words are found in the spoken word than in the written language, so that my lists are incomplete.

In order to find the oldest examples of formations such as klifr I have inspected the files of the Arnamagnæan Dictionary Project in Copenhagen and the files of the University of Iceland Dictionary Project in Reykjavík. As expected, the search in the files of the Arnamagnæan Dictionary

Project proved fruitless, because the orthographic conventions of written Icelandic of the pre-Reformation times conceal the difference between, say, klifr and klifur, seeing that the epenthetic vowel is most often not indicated in the spelling. The search in the files of the University of Iceland Dictionary Project, on the other hand, brought to light that the oldest reliable examples of the type klifr occur in Jón Jónsson Rugman's booklet Mono-syllaba Is-landica, published in Uppsala in 1676. (If there are even older examples in the files, say, from the sixteenth century, they are again irretrievably lost owing to orthographic conventions.) The booklet is a 1,535-item list of Icelandic monosyllabic words in alphabetical order, with a Latin gloss added to each item. The background of the publication is stated in its Latin preface. In Rugman's time — he lived from 1636 to 1679 — and earlier, it was widely believed in scholarly circles that that language is oldest and most original which has the most monosyllabic words in its vocabulary. Rugman's patriotic purpose was obviously to secure the position of the oldest language for his mother tongue, Icelandic.

The famous eighteenth century Icelandic philologist Jón Ólafsson of Grunnavík has criticized a part of the booklet, viz. its letter a, in what is now the unpublished Arnamagnæan manuscript 977, 4to. (Cf. Helgason 1926: 97, 183). Jón Ólafsson points out that the book is full of errors: non-monosyllabic words are entered as monosyllabic, some words are misspelt, some are foreign (loans?), etc. The booklet must therefore be used with caution.

Those of Rugman's words ending in consonant + r stated sub (4), q.v., are in my opinion reliable instances of monosyllabic items, because they are known as such from elsewhere, and have already been discussed in the present paper. Dadr is stated to mean Latin 'tarditas', English 'slowness', and is therefore presumably an error for Dudr, formed on duðra 'be busy with something easy'.

(4) Amr Vagitus, ejulatio, al. labor molestus; cf. amra
Dadr Tarditas
Hamr Sonus quem malleus ad incudem cusus edit; cf. hamra
Klifr Ascensus in locum clivem; cf. klifra
Wafr Lentus gradus; cf. vafra
Umr Quærela; cf. umra

Some words adduced by Rugman can be monosyllabic in that it is always possible that he, or others he had heard, had formed ad hoc monosyllabic action nouns from the existing verbs in -ra. See (5).

(5) Blöskr Metus, trepidatio; cf. blöskra 'be shocked, shudder'
Glamr Fragor, stridor; cf. glamra 'clash, tinkle'
Gnistr Stridor; cf. gnistra 'gnash'
Lekr Stillicidium; cf. lekva 'drip'
Sladr Nugæ; cf. slaðra 'tell tales'
Slafr Loquacitas al. modus mandendi hebetibus dentibus; cf. slafra 'eat with slobbering sound'
Slidr Piger incessus; cf. slyðrast 'drag oneself'
Töfr Magia; cf. töfra 'charm'

Lekr and lekra require special comment. Neither of them is registered in printed Icelandic dictionaries. The files of the University of Iceland Dictionary Project contain two instances of the verb lekra from modern dialects, both instances from Borgarfjörður, and one instance of lekr or lekur from Matthias Saxtorph's Stutt Agrip af Yfirsetu-qvenna frædum (Copenhagen 1789).[4] One reliable instance of monosyllabic töfr is registered in the files of the University of Iceland Dictionary Project, from Gísli Brynjúlfsson's Copenhagen diary, Dagbók í Höfn (p. 287).[5]

To these items Rugman adds thirteen others, repeated here sub (6), whose citation forms can under no circumstances have been monosyllabic in his time, and therefore ought to have been omitted from his booklet. I list them here for completeness' sake.

(6) (a) Austr Sentina
Gliufr Montis ruptura aquam evomens
Klungr Terra petrosa
(b) Gildr, gild, gildt Crassus, a, um
Kræfr, kræf, kræft Fortis

(c) <u>Auðr</u> Divitiæ
<u>Brundr</u> Libido
<u>Hampr</u> Stupa
<u>Hlemr</u> Operculum doliorum aut
    similium vasòrum
<u>Laustr</u> illusio, contemtus,
    Contumelia, vituperium
<u>Nopr</u> Rivus
<u>Sytr</u> Deploratum (= plurale tantum
    fem. <u>sýtur</u>)

The existence of the type <u>klifr</u> in
Modern Icelandic is important for at least
two theoretical reasons:

(1) The type <u>klifr</u> reintroduces two
    phonotactic possibilities into
    Icelandic phonology, namely that of
    consonant + <u>r</u> + word boundary and
    consonant + <u>r</u> + consonant — the latter
    exemplified by the theoretical genitive
    singular <u>klifrs</u>.
(2) The type <u>klifr</u> seems to suggest that
    there is no epenthesis rule in the
    language any longer, for the epenthesis
    rule would obligatorily change <u>klifr</u>
    to <u>klifur</u>.

The claim that there is no epenthesis rule
in Modern Icelandic phonology encounters
strong opposition from some other facts of
the language. The main opposition comes
from cases such as <u>lifur</u> 'liver', definite
form <u>lifrin</u>, where the lack of <u>u</u> in <u>lifrin</u>
at least on the face of it cannot be due
to any synchronic vowel syncope, seeing
that generally no vowel syncope takes
place with the postpositive article as
part of its environment, cf. <u>hamar</u> 'hammer',
definite form <u>hamarinn</u>, not <u>hamrinn</u>.
Therefore the underlying representation of
the lexical item <u>lifur</u> must be monosyllabic,
/lÌvr/, and the <u>u</u> of <u>lifur</u> due to the
operation of the epenthesis rule (Orešnik
1972). However, I think it is binding to
accept the positive evidence of the type
<u>klifr</u>, and assume that there is no epen-
thesis rule in the language. In that case
examples such as <u>lifur</u>, <u>lifrin</u> have to be
dissociated from examples such as <u>hamar</u>,
<u>hamarinn</u>, and it must be assumed that
syncope of <u>u</u> <u>can</u> take place with the
postpositive article as part of its environment, in feminine and neuter nouns (except
if the <u>u</u> is a part of the ending, cf.
<u>brúð-ur-in</u>, definite form of <u>brúður</u> f.
'bride', not <u>brúðrin</u>). It is possible to

adduce some meagre evidence for this
syncope:

(a) Syncope has taken place in the
    definite nominative/accusative plural
    <u>sumrin</u> of the neuter noun <u>sumar</u>
    'summer'.
(b) Böðvarsson (1960: 5) adduces forms
    such as nominative singular <u>dóttrin</u>
    beside <u>dóttirin</u> and <u>dótturin</u>, and
    accusative singular <u>dóttrina</u> beside
    <u>dótturina</u> and <u>dóttirina</u>, of <u>dóttir</u>
    'daughter'. These forms occur in Jón
    Árnason's collection of Icelandic
    folktales. The nominative <u>dóttrin</u>
    and the accusative <u>dóttrina</u> can only
    be explained as due to syncope of the
    unstressed vowel of the stem.

Notes

1. The bisyllabic <u>kumur</u> is not adduced
in Blöndal's dictionary. I have it from
another source, Þorkelsson (1902: 8).
2. Blöndal mentions <u>vavr</u> in the phonetic
introduction, p. xxv, and in the lexical
entry on the letter <u>r</u> (p. 630).
3. My attention has been drawn to <u>duðr</u>
and to Um <u>ljóðalýti</u> by Jonna Louis-Jensen.
4. <u>Lek(u)r</u> occurs in the following
sentence: Hit <u>sídara</u> <u>beckiz</u> og <u>svo</u> <u>af</u>
<u>sífelldu</u> <u>lekri</u> <u>þvagsins</u>. I am grateful to
Ólafur Halldórsson for locating <u>lek(u)r</u>
for me in the files of the University
of Iceland Dictionary Project.
5. <u>Töfr</u> occurs in <u>getur</u> <u>þettað</u> <u>sama</u> <u>töfr</u>
<u>komið</u> <u>aftur</u>.

References

Benediktsson, Hreinn. 1969. On the inflection
    of the ia-stems in Icelandic. Afmælisrit
    Jóns Helgasonar 30. júní 1969. Reykjavík:
    Heimskringla, pp. 391 - 402.
Bérkov, Valerij P., and Árni Böðvarsson.
    1962. Íslenzk-rússnesk orðabók. Moscow:
    Gosudarstvennoe izdatel'stvo inostrannyx
    i nacional'nyx slovarey.
Blöndal, Sigfús. 1920 - 1924. Íslensk-dönsk
    orðabók. Reykjavík: Prentsmiðja Gutenberg.
Böðvarsson, Árni. 1960. Nokkrar athuganir
    á rithætti þjóðsagnahandrita í safni
    Jóns Árnasonar. Studia Islandica 18:
    5 - 21.
Guðfinnsson, Björn. 1946. Mállýzkur I.
    Reykjavík: Ísafoldarprentsmiðja H.F.

Helgason, Jón. 1926. Jón Ólafsson frá
  Grunnavík. Safn fræðafjelagsins um
  Ísland og Íslendinga gefið út af Hinu
  íslenska fræðafjelagi í Kaupmannahöfn.
  vol. V. Copenhagen: S. L. Möller.
──────────── . 1967. Björn Halldórssons
  supplerende oplysninger til Lexicon
  Islandico-Latinum. Bibliotheca arnamagnæana, vol. XXIX, pp. 101 - 160.
Jónsson, Finnur. 1933. Den islandske
  grammatiks historie til o. 1800. Det
  Kgl. Danske Videnskabernes Selskab.
  Historisk-filologiske Meddelelser XIX,
  4. Copenhagen: Levin and Munksgaard.
Orešnik, Janez. 1972. On the epenthesis
  rule in Modern Icelandic. Arkiv för
  nordisk filologi 87: 1 - 32.
Þorkelsson, Páll. 1902. Beygingarreglur í
  íslenzku med frönskum skýringum. Copenhagen: Gyldendal.

JANEZ OREŠNIK

The Modern Icelandic Epenthesis Rule Revisited

Summary

(1) There is no Epenthesis Rule in Modern Icelandic grammar. The rule must have ceased to operate in the seventeenth century at the latest, when the oldest examples of the *klifr* type appeared in the written sources. (2) The phonological boundary between a noun and an affixed article can be equated with the morpheme boundary. There is no need for an Enclitic Boundary Rule in the grammar. (3) The vowels that are deleted by the Vowel Syncope Rule must satisfy the following conditions: (a) They must be "elidible". (b) They must be followed by at most one short consonant, the morpheme boundary, and another vowel. (c) They must occur in grammatical forms that are enumerated in a list of contracted forms.[1]

1. In ANF 87 (1972) I published a Modern Icelandic Epenthesis Rule, which introduces an /ɣ/ in the context C———r{C, #}. The argumentation in favour of that rule has now to be reviewed for two reasons: (1) Since the publication of Orešnik 1972 some new facts have appeared that have some bearing on the question of the existence of the Epenthesis Rule. (2) The solution advocated in Orešnik 1972 gave rise to some difficulties, which were mostly recognised and discussed in the footnotes to that paper. It was confidently assumed that future research would contribute towards their removal. Nothing of the kind has happened since 1972, for which reason those difficulties must be discussed again. The result of this renewed look at the Modern Icelandic Epenthesis Rule is that there is no such rule in Modern Icelandic grammar.

The argumentation of Orešnik 1972 in favour of a Modern Icelandic Epenthesis Rule was divided into two parts: (1) the argumentation in favour of the nominative singular ending −*ur* being derived from underlying /+r/; (2) the argumentation in favour of many other *ur*'s being derived from underlying /r/'s.

1.1. The claim that the nominative singular ending −*ur* is derived from underlying /+r/ is now considered inconclusive, for the following reasons:

(1) It was asserted that the nominative singular desinences −*r* and −*ur* are in complementary distribution, with −*r* appearing after vowels, and −*ur* after consonants, so that any /+ɣr/ could be derived from /+r/ with the help of a simple rule: /+r/→/+ɣr/ after consonant final stems. This argument does not

[1] My thanks are due to Miss Margaret G. Davis, who has corrected my English.

by itself prove that /+r/ is more basic than /+ʏr/, but only that it is possible to derive /+ʏr/ from /+r/. The validity of the argument is uncertain, because there is a type of words in which /+ʏr/ appears after a vowel on the phonetic level. The type can be illustrated by *skógur* 'forest', where *g* is not pronounced. On the phonological level the situation can presumably be remedied by positing underlying /skóx/, with the stem final /x/ generalised from the gen. sg. *skógs* [−xs], where /x/ appears on the phonetic level. (The genitive singular is *skógs* and *skógar*.) A set of new rules would be necessary to derive the phonetic forms: one rule would delete /x/ between *ó* and *a, u* or word boundary, cf. nom. sg. *skógur*, acc. sg. *skóg*, nom. pl. *skógar*, etc.; another rule would palatalise /x/ to /j/ before /+ɪ/ in the dat. sg. *skógi* and in the definite acc. sg. *skóginn;* a third rule would change /x/ to the voiceless plosive /g/ in the definite form *skógnum* of the alternative dat. sg. *skóg*. A difficulty with this solution is that the stem final /x/ has been generalised into the stem from a highly marked case, the genitive singular, a procedure which may go counter to some universal constraint on the form of the underlying stems. The only alternative that comes to mind is to posit a vowel final stem /skó/, and have the case forms of *skógur* analysed as follows:

nom. sg.	/skó + ʏr/	pl.	/skó + ar/
gen.	/skó + xs, skó + ar/		/skó + a/
dat.	/skó + jɪ/		/skó + ʏm/
	/skó/, def. /skó + gnʏm/		
acc.	/skó/, def. /skó + jɪn/		/skó + a/

If this version is adopted, /+r/ and /+ʏr/ are not in complementary distribution on the phonological level, and the above argument in favour of /+r/→/+ʏr/ collapses.

(2) It was asserted that underlying /+r/ helps explain why no *j* appears in the nom. sg. *bylur* 'snowstorm' whereas it does appear in, say, the dat. pl. *byljum* of the same word: *bylur* would be from /bylj+r/, /j/ would be deleted between two consonants by a *j*-Deletion Rule, and then the Epenthesis Rule would produce /byl+ʏr/. However, it is unlikely that the underlying stem of *bylur* ends in /j/, for the following reason. An asset of the stem ending in /j/ is that the usual simple ending /+ʏm/ can be posited in the dat. pl. *byljum* instead of an allomorphic ending /+jʏm/: /bylj+ʏm/. If this is an advantage, the same analysis should be applied in the declension of *lyf* 'medicine', dat. pl. *lyfjum:* /lyfj+ʏm/. However, this leads to difficulties in the dative singular of *lyf*, which is *lyfi*. If the stem of *lyf* ends in /j/, the underlying representation of *lyfi* is /lyfj+ɪ/, and we are left with no means to delete the /j/, because /j/ is not generally deleted before /ɪ/, cf. 2p. pl. pres. *krefjið*, not *krefið*, of *krefja* 'require'. (This problem was mentioned in footnote 4 of Orešnik 1972.) The way out of this difficulty is to posit a stem of *lyf* that does not end in /j/, and then the dative singular ending can be /+ɪ/ (/lyf+ɪ/), and the dative plural ending must be /+jʏm/ (/lyf+jʏm/). If /+jʏm/ can be posited in the declension

of *lyf*, it can also be posited in the dative plural of *bylur* (/*byl* + jʏm/), and there is no longer any reason for the representation with / + r/ in the nominative singular, seeing that there is no /j/ to be deleted interconsonantally. Thus the argument of *bylur* in favour of / + r/ collapses.

There is a bonus in positing /j/-initial endings in the case forms in which a *j* surfaces in the phonetic representations: it is now no longer necessary to have a *j*-Deletion Rule in the grammar. As the nom. sg. *lyf* shows, the *j*-Deletion Rule is supposed to operate word-finally as well (/*lyfj*/ → /*lyf*/). This presents difficulties in cases such as *grenj* (action noun formed on *grenja* 'wail, scream'), where the word final *j* is not deleted. The difficulty disappears if there is no *j*-Deletion Rule in the grammar.

(3) The underlying representation /*söngv* + r/ of *söngur* 'song' has been posited so that, say, the dat. pl. *söngvum* could be analysed as containing the ending / + ʏm/, which occurs with many nouns, rather than as containing an allomorphic ending / + vʏm/: dat. pl. /*söngv* + ʏm/, not /*söng* + vʏm/. However, the discussion of the example *lyf* sub (2) above has shown that at least one allomorph of / + ʏm/ has to be posited, viz. / + jʏm/, and in that case / + vʏm/ is not excluded either. So if the dative plural can be analysed as /*söng* + vʏm/, the nominative singular can be analysed as /*söng* + ʏr/, because the ending / + r/ is no longer needed as part of the environment for the interconsonantal deletion of /v/.

There is a benefit in positing /v/-initial endings in the case forms in which a *v* surfaces in the phonetic representations. As noticed in footnote 6 of Orešnik 1972, a grammar which refuses to admit /v/-initial endings as allomorphs of the simpler endings without /v/, and therefore posits /v/-final stems in the pertinent lexical items, cannot explain the contrast *mör* 'suet' vs. *hverf*, first person singular present indicative of *hverfa* 'disappear'. If *mör* is derived from /*mörv*/ (cf. gen. pl. *mörva* etc.), a *v*-Deletion Rule must delete the /v/ of /*mörv*/. On the other hand, such deletion must not take place in *hverf*, where *f* is pronounced [v], and this has been a problem for the description so far. If /v/-final stems are discarded, the problem disappears, because the underlying representation of *mör* is then just /*mör*/. There is not even any need for a *v*-Deletion Rule in the grammar.

(4) It was asserted that the nom. sg. *hattur* 'hat' must be derived from the underlying representation /*hatt* + r/, so that the u-Umlaut Rule can be blocked: the rule should operate while *hattur* is still /*hatt* + r/, without /ʏ/, and therefore its operation would be blocked in this type of words. However, it is now no longer clear that the u-Umlaut Rule is a phonological rule. See Orešnik (forthcoming a) for an alternative account, in which the u-Umlaut Rule is viewed as morphological, i.e. as operating in certain morphological situations. Under this new conception of the u-Umlaut Rule the nominative singular case forms in − *ur* are not mentioned among the types of word forms which undergo the u-Umlaut Rule. Thus *hattur* can be derived from underlying /*hatt* + ʏr/.

1.2. The argumentation in Orešnik 1972 in favour of many *ur*'s which are not endings being derived from underlying /r/'s had to do with the behaviour of non-masculine nouns whose stems end in radical *r*. Examples of such nouns are *lifur* f. 'liver' and *hreiður* n. 'nest'. They lose their *u*'s before the stem final *r* whenever an ending beginning with a vowel follows: gen. sg. *lifr-ar*, dat. sg. *hreiðr-i*. The same loss occurs if the only ending is a vowel-initial form of the affixed definite article: nom. sg. *lifr-in*, dat. sg. *lifr-inni*, acc. sg. *lifr-ina*, nom./acc. sg. *hreiðr-ið*, nom./acc. pl. *hreiðr-in*. It was assumed in Orešnik 1972 that the enumerated forms with the affixed article speak in favour of the Epenthesis Rule, in the following way. If the underlying representation of the stem of, say, *lifur* were bisyllabic, /lɪvyr/, it would have to be assumed that the Vowel Syncope Rule has operated in *lifrin* etc. However, other examples show that the Vowel Syncope Rule does not operate if the affixed article is a part of its structural description. Cf. *hamar* 'hammer', definite form *hamar-inn*, not *hamrinn*, although this noun otherwise undergoes vowel syncope freely: dat. sg. *hamri*, nom. pl. *hamrar*, etc. It was therefore assumed in Orešnik 1972 that the underlying representation of the stem of *lifur* is monosyllabic, /lɪvr/, and its bisyllabic shape in *lifur* due to the operation of the Epenthesis Rule, whose existence was therefore postulated.

The recent emergence of some new facts has cast doubt upon this solution. The new facts are here summarised from Orešnik (forthcoming b).

Modern Icelandic has reintroduced words ending in consonant + word-final *r*. All such words are action nouns, *a*-stems of neuter gender, derived from *ōn*-verbs whose infinitives end in *Cra*; e.g. *klifr* 'climbing' comes from *klifra* 'climb'. Here follows my complete list of such nouns: *amr* (formed on *amra* 'whine'), *bogr* (cf. *bogra* 'walk stooping'), *duðr* (cf. *duðra* 'be busy with something easy'), *flögr* (cf. *flögra* 'flutter, flap'), *hamr* (cf. *hamra* 'hammer'), *klambr* (cf. *klambra* 'make clumsily'), *klifr* (cf. *klifra* 'climb'), *kumr* (cf. *kumra* 'bleat, neigh'), *peðr* (cf. *peðra* 'deal out in small portions'), *pukr* (cf. *pukra* 'conceal'), *snupr* (cf. *snupra* 'chide'), *stumr* (cf. *stumra* 'totter'), *sötr* (cf. *sötra* 'suck through the teeth'), *töfr* (cf. *töfra* 'charm'), *umr* (cf. *umra* 'growl'), *vavr* (cf. *vafra* 'toddle, roam, stroll'). Some of these nouns have been culled from Blöndal's (1920–24) dictionary, others from miscellaneous other sources. (For details of occurrence see Orešnik forthcoming b.) The oldest examples of such nouns occur in Jón Jónsson Rugman's booklet *Mono-syllaba Is-landica*, published in Uppsala in 1676.

The existence of the *klifr* type speaks against the existence of an Epenthesis Rule in Modern Icelandic grammar, for the Epenthesis Rule would invariably change, say, *hamr* to *hamur*.[2] Therefore examples like *lifrin* have to be dissociated from examples such as *hamarinn*, and it must be assumed that the underlying representation of the stem of *lifur* is bisyllabic after all, /lɪvyr/, so

---

[2] To be sure, some lexical items of the *klifr* type have parallel formations in *ur*, e.g. *klifr* and *klifur*. Owing to lack of documentation in the files of the University of Iceland Dictionary Project it is impossible to ascertain the historical relationship between, say, *klifr* and *klifur*. Here it is assumed that the *klifur* type stems from the time when the Epenthesis Rule was still operative.

that the Vowel Syncope Rule applies in *lifrin*, etc. This vowel syncope must be limited to the unstressed *u* of non-masculine nouns (there is no comparable syncope in masculine nouns: *akurinn* 'the acre' does not become *akrinn*), and avoids the *u* of the ending *-ur*, cf. *brúð-ur-in* 'the bride', not *brúðrin*. The evidence for this syncope is as follows:

(1) Syncope has taken place in the definite nom./acc. pl. *sumrin* of the neuter noun *sumar* 'summer'. (Pl. *sumurin* exists as well.)

(2) Böðvarsson (1960:5) adduces, from Jón Árnason's collection of folk-tales, forms such as nom. sg. *dóttrin* beside *dóttirin* and *dótturin*, and acc. sg. *dóttrina* beside *dótturina* and *dóttirina*, of *dóttir* 'daughter'. The nom. *dóttrin* and the acc. *dóttrina* can only be explained as due to syncope of the unstressed vowel of the stem.

This syncope sometimes fails to operate, resulting in substandard forms such as *lifurin* of *lifur*, pl. *blómsturin* of *blómstur* 'flower', etc. Examples of neuter gender were adduced in Orešnik 1972. I now also have comparable examples of feminine gender, culled from the files of the University of Iceland Dictionary Project. The files contain (as of April 1976) one example of *gimburin* of *gimbur* f. 'lamb of female sex', from the nineteenth century, three examples of *lifurin* of *lifur* f. 'liver', all from the twentieth century, and one example of *næfurin* of *næfur* f. 'bark of birch', from the nineteenth century.

Thus it seems that there is no Epenthesis Rule in Modern Icelandic grammar. The rule must have ceased to operate in the seventeeth century at the latest, when the oldest examples of the *klifr* type appear in the written sources.

2. In appendix B of Orešnik 1972 I discussed the nature of the boundary between a noun and the article affixed to it. The boundary in question was referred to as the AMPERSAND BOUNDARY, and this term will be used here as well. It was argued that the ampersand boundary is identical with a word boundary, only replaced by a morpheme boundary earlier in the derivations than other word boundaries. The substitution of the morpheme boundary for the ampersand boundary was postulated, executed by a special ENCLITIC BOUNDARY RULE.

The arguments in favour of the identification of the ampersand boundary with the word boundary were of two kinds. Some were supposed to show that the ampersand boundary does not behave in the same way as the morpheme boundary, and some, that it does not behave in quite the same way as the word boundary. Partially because of the above discussion of the Epenthesis Rule, I now think that there are no arguments against the identification of the ampersand boundary with the morpheme boundary. A further result is that, as the ampersand boundary can be identified with the morpheme boundary, there is no need for the Enclitic Boundary Rule in the grammar.

I propose here to review the four arguments that were supposed to show that the ampersand boundary does not behave in the same way as a morpheme boundary, and to demonstrate their invalidity.

(I) It was asserted that the Vowel Syncope Rule can operate across a morpheme boundary, whereas it cannot operate across an ampersand boundary. The above discussion of the type *lifrin, hreiðrið* brought to light that the Vowel Syncope Rule can sometimes operate even across the ampersand boundary. Thus the behaviour of the Vowel Syncope Rule says nothing about the relative strength of the ampersand and morpheme boundaries.

(II) It was asserted that the preconsonantal and word-final /j/'s and /v/'s are deleted, by the *j*-Deletion Rule and the *v*-Deletion Rule, respectively, before the ampersand boundary, but not before the morpheme boundary. It was shown above in section 1 that there is no *j*-Deletion Rule or *v*-Deletion Rule in the grammar, so that the behaviour of these rules can say nothing about the relationship between the ampersand and the morpheme boundaries.

(III) It was asserted that the u-Umlaut Rule can apply across a morpheme boundary, whereas it cannot apply across the ampersand boundary. It has already been mentioned that in my new version (Orešnik forthcoming a) of the u-Umlaut Rule that rule is not phonological, but morphological: it does not apply across any boundaries but in certain grammatical forms, irrespective of whether the postpositive article is affixed to any given noun form. The behaviour of the u-Umlaut Rule thus tells us nothing about the relationship between the ampersand and the morpheme boundaries.

(IV) It was asserted that the Vowel Truncation Rule (which deletes an unstressed vowel before another vowel) can operate across the morpheme boundary, whereas it cannot operate across the ampersand boundary. I now think that there is no Vowel Truncation Rule in Modern Icelandic phonology, and consequently the behaviour of that putative rule can tell us nothing about the relationship between the ampersand and the morpheme boundaries.[3]

To summarise, I can say that the arguments that were supposed to show that the ampersand boundary behaves differently from the morpheme boundary are not valid. In Orešnik 1972 I also published a number of arguments that the ampersand boundary behaves differently from the word boundary. Those arguments still stand. Since Modern Icelandic phonology recognises only two

---

[3] All my examples in which the putative Vowel Truncation Rule should have operated are based on the validity of the principle that the number of desinence allomorphs should be kept to a minimum. Following this principle, I assumed that the ending of the 3p. sg. pres. ind. *kallar* (of *kalla* 'call') is just -*r*, and the same -*r* was supposed to occur in, say, the 3p. sg. pres. ind. *dæmir* (of *dæma* 'judge'). Consequently the stems of *kalla* and *dæma* were set up as *kalla-* and *dæmi-*. A further consequence of this was that the first person plural present was set up as /kalla +ᵧm/ and /dæmi +ᵧm/, and it was necessary to introduce a new rule, the Vowel Truncation Rule, to delete the stem final vowels before the vowel of the person marker. Since the publication of Orešnik 1972 no proof has appeared of the principle that the number of desinence allomorphs should be kept to a minimum, and I therefore think now that that principle is premature, and that in reality the desinence of *kallar* can be -*ar*, the desinence of *dæmir* can be -*ir*, hence the respective stems can be just *kall-* and *dæm-*, and the first person plural forms underlyingly /kall +ᵧm/ and /dæm +ᵧm/, without there being any need for a Vowel Truncation Rule in the grammar.

kinds of boundaries, viz. the word boundary and the morpheme boundary, it follows that the ampersand boundary must be equated with the morpheme boundary. Words like *akurinn* are underlyingly /akur + ın/, that is, the affixed article is a desinence, just as -*s* in the gen. sg. *akurs* is a desinence, /akur + s/. There is consequently no need for an Enclitic Boundary Rule in the grammar.

3. In appendix A of Orešnik 1972 I discussed the Modern Icelandic Vowel Syncope Rule, and have stated the following conditions for vowels that are syncopated: (1) They must be marked as "elidible". (2) They must not be diphthongs or *í* (*ý*) or *ú*. (3) They must be followed by at most one short consonant, a morpheme boundary, and another vowel, in that order. (4) The short consonant which immediately follows the doomed vowel is *n, r, l, ð,* or *s.* Conditions (2) and (4) do not now seem very important to me, because they are special cases of condition (1): only such vowels are marked as "elidible" that fulfil conditions (2) and (4). Conditions (1) and (3) still stand. I can now add one further condition: The vowels which are to be syncopated must occur in morphological forms that are enumerated in a list of contracted forms. – The Vowel Syncope Rule is thus basically a morphological rule.

The list of contracted forms:

A. *Nouns:* dative singular masculine, plural masculine, nominative/accusative singular neuter, dative singular neuter, plural neuter, feminine (all case forms).

B. *Adjectives* (including participles): weak forms, comparatives, superlatives, the following strong forms: dative plural, dative singular masculine, accusative singular masculine, nominative plural masculine, accusative plural masculine, accusative singular feminine, nominative/accusative plural feminine, dative singular neuter.

C. *Verbs:* none.

Examples. Dat. sg. *akri* of *akur* 'acre', underlying representation /akur + ı/; the dative singular masculine is enumerated in the list of contracted forms; the *u* is marked as "elidible", and is followed by one short consonant, the morpheme boundary, and another vowel; therefore the syncope takes place. On the other hand, the middle vowel of the dat. sg. f. *heitinni* of *heitinn* 'deceased' is not syncopated, although this vowel satisfies the stated phonological environment (the underlying representation being /heitin + ı/[4]), and although it is "elidible"

---

[4] The following are the allomorphs of the strong adjectival dative singular feminine case ending: infix /ð/ + desinence / +ı/ in the types *seinn, sæll, mikill* (dat. sg. f. *seinni, sælli, mikilli*); desinence /+ı/ in the type *heitinn* (dat. sg. f. *heitinni*); desinence /+ ɲ/ elsewhere (e.g. *gulur,* dat. sg. f. *gulri*). There exists the possibility that the underlying representation of the dat. sg. f. *heitinni* contains a long /n/, and the lack of vowel syncope would then be ascribable to the fact that the "elidible" vowel is followed by a long consonant, not by a short one required by the phonological structural description of the Vowel Syncope Rule. The motivation for the long /n/ in *heitinni* comes from the phonetically realised long /n/ in the definite dative singular case forms such as *ánni* of *á* 'river'; the postposed definite article is basically declined in the same way as the adjectives in *inn*. In order to be able to posit long /n/ in the underlying representation of the dat. *heitinni*, we would

(cf. dat. pl. *heitnum*); the reason for the non-syncopation is that the form (strong dative singular feminine) is not enumerated in the list of contracted forms. The unstressed vowel of the acc. sg. m. *heitinn* is not syncopated, although the form (strong accusative singular masculine) is enumerated in the list of contracted forms (cf. acc. sg. m. *gamlan* of *gamall* 'old'), and although the unstressed vowel is marked as "elidible" (cf. dat. pl. *heitnum*); the reason for the non-syncopation is that the unstressed vowel is only followed by a short consonant, not also by a morpheme boundary and another vowel. The middle vowel of the dat. pl. *heimilum* of *heimill* 'at one's disposal' is not syncopated, although the strong dative plural is enumerated in the list of contracted forms (cf. dat. pl. *heitnum*), and although the middle vowel is followed by one short consonant, a morpheme boundary and another vowel; the reason for the non-syncopation is that the middle vowel is not marked as "elidible".

The forms of only one word, *sumar* 'summer', cannot be accounted for by the above system. As its contracted dat. sg. *sumri* shows, the unstressed vowel of the stem is "elidible". Yet it is not syncopated in the definite nominative/accusative singular, which is *sumarið*, not *sumrið*. Furthermore, the nominative/accusative plural is not only (the expected) *sumrin*, but also *sumurin*. This lexical item must be considered irregular, which is not surprising, seeing that it pertains to the core of the Icelandic vocabulary.[5]

References

Blöndal, Sigfús. *Íslensk-dönsk orðabók*. Reykjavík, 1920–24.

Böðvarsson, Árni. "Nokkrar athuganir á rithætti þjóðsagnahandrita í safni Jóns Árnasonar." *Studia Islandica* 18 (1960) 5–21.

Orešnik, Janez. "On the Epenthesis Rule in Modern Icelandic." *Arkiv för nordisk filologi* 87 (1972) 1–32.

– "Modern Icelandic u-umlaut from the descriptive point of view." Manuscript. Referred to as forthcoming a.

– "The Age and Importance of the Modern Icelandic Word Type *klifr*." Manuscript. Referred to as forthcoming b.

---

have to make use of the principle according to which the number of desinence allomorphs has to be reduced to a minimum in each case. However, I am not aware of any proofs of this principle, and therefore think that it is more correct to posit just / + ı/ as the desinence of *heitinni* (rather than long /n/ + /ı/), as required by the phonetic facts.

[5] The language has made two attempts at diminishing the irregularity of *sumar*: (1) Under the influence of *sumarið*, the unstressed vowel of the singular form was interpreted as not "elidible", and a non-contracted dative singular was introduced, *sumari*. The files of the University of Iceland Dictionary Project contain two instances of the dat. *sumari*, one from the eighteenth, another from the nineteenth century. (2) Under the influence of *sumri*, the unstressed vowel of the singular was interpreted as "elidible", and a contracted nominative/accusative singular *sumrið* was introduced. The files of the University of Iceland Dictionary Project contain two instances of *sumrið*, both from the nineteenth century. – These regularising attempts have not obtained a footing in the modern literary language.

ON THE MODERN ICELANDIC I-UMLAUT RULE

JANEZ OREŠNIK
University of Ljubljana

Summary. This paper reviews the discussion on the modern Icelandic i-umlaut rule. Valfells' and Anderson's formulations of the i-umlaut rule are presented, criticised, and rejected. The author concludes that there is no i-umlaut rule in modern Icelandic grammar; the i-umlaut alternations have been incorporated into the ablaut system. Orešnik's 1971 treatment of the root vowels in the modern Icelandic preterit subjunctive stems is revised so that it conforms with the hypothesis that the i-umlaut alternations are now ablaut alternations.[1]

Research on the generative phonology of modern Icelandic began in the mid-sixties, when Valfells (1967) presented her doctoral dissertation at Harvard University, her work being followed by Anderson's and Orešnik's. A prominent place in this research is assumed by the discussion of the so-called I-UMLAUT RULE. It is the purpose of this paper to review the discussion and to add the author's current opinion about the i-umlaut rule, which is that there is probably no such rule in modern Icelandic phonology.

The i-umlaut rule is supposed to account for modern Icelandic vocalic alternations which are due to the pre-historical i-umlaut. Such alternations occur in inflectional and derivational paradigms. Some examples are listed in (1), q.v.

(1) Examples of vocalic alternations due to i-umlaut

    (a) in inflectional paradigms
        dagur 'day,' dat. sg. *degi*
        köttur 'cat,' stem *katt-*, dat. sg. *ketti*
        stór 'big,' comparative *stærri*, *stærra*, superlative *stærstur*

---

1. My thanks are due to Margaret G. Davis, who has corrected my English.
GENERAL LINGUISTICS, Vol. 18, No. 4. Published by The Pennsylvania State University Press, University Park and London.

taka 'take,' lp. sg. pres. ind. *tek;* preterit stem *tók-*, pret. subj.
tæki

bók 'book,' nom./acc. pl. *bækur*

(b)   in derivational paradigms
bók 'book,' *bæklingur* 'booklet'
tók- one of the stems of *taka* 'take,' *tæki* 'device'
guð 'god,' *gyðja* 'goddess'
vanur 'accustomed,' *venja* 'custom'

1. Valfells 1967. In Valfells 1967 the modern Icelandic system of stressed vowels of (2), q.v., is set up. (The distinctive features used are those of Jakobson and Halle 1956.) Valfells points out that in her analysis the vowel system is "fully symmetrical except for the lax *ö*," and that her analysis makes it possible for the i-umlaut rule to be viewed as a simple shift of [+grave] vowels to [−grave, −flat]: $u \rightarrow i$, $a \rightarrow e$, $o \rightarrow e$, $\bar{u} \rightarrow \bar{\imath}$, $\bar{a} \rightarrow \bar{æ}$, $\bar{o} \rightarrow \bar{æ}$, $au \rightarrow ai$.

(2)   The underlying system of stressed vowels according to Valfells 1967

Phonetic symbol	Valfells' symbol	Valfells' analysis
[ɪ]	i	[−tense, +diffuse, −grave, −flat]
[ɛ]	e	[−tense, −diffuse, −grave, −flat]
[œ]	ö	[−tense, −diffuse, −grave, +flat]
[ʏ]	u	[−tense, +diffuse, +grave, +flat]
[a]	a	[−tense, −diffuse, +grave, −flat]
[ɔ]	o	[−tense, −diffuse, +grave, +flat]
[i]	ī	[+tense, +diffuse, −grave, −flat]
[u]	ū	[+tense, +diffuse, + grave, +flat]
[ai]	ǣ or ē	[+tense, −diffuse, −grave, −flat]
[au]	ā	[+tense, −diffuse, +grave, −flat]
[ou]	ō	[+tense, −diffuse, +grave, +flat]
[ei]	ai	[−diffuse, +grave, −flat] [+diffuse, −grave]
[öi]	au	[−diffuse, +grave, −flat] [+diffuse, +grave]

The structural change of Valfells' i-umlaut rule is given in (3), q.v.—The structural description of the rule consists of several parts, stated sub (4), q.v., in a slightly modified form (for instance, C_o is used instead of Valfells' ambiguous (C)). (4a) says that i-umlaut takes place in the stressed vowels if they are followed, within the stem, by $\bar{\imath}$, i, or j. Cases in point are *jan-* and *ian*-verbs, e.g. *dylja* 'conceal' and *færa* 'bring.' Valfells assumes that the j which immediately follows the root *dyl-* of *dylja* in the infinitive and present tense outside the indicative singular and imperative singular is underlyingly present in the indicative singular and imperative singular as well (and deleted in word final and preconsonantal position after the operation of the i-umlaut rule: lp. sg. pres. ind. dul + j → dil + j → dil). The consequence is that the back vowel *u* of the underlying root *dul-* (cf. the preterit stem *duld-*) is i-umlauted in all the forms of the present stem (this includes the infinitive and the present participle). As for the *ian*-verbs Valfells assumes that all their forms contain a back root vowel and the thematic vowel *i*, which is deleted whenever another syllable follows it, after the operation of the i-umlaut rule; e.g. pret. *færðum* comes from $(\text{fōr}+\text{i})_{\text{STEM}} + \text{ð} + \text{um}$.

(3) The structural change of Valfells' i-umlaut rule

$$\begin{bmatrix} +\text{voc} \\ -\text{cons} \\ +\text{stress} \end{bmatrix} \rightarrow \begin{bmatrix} -\text{grave} \\ -\text{flat} \end{bmatrix}$$

I.e. stressed vowels are fronted and unrounded.

(4) The structural description of Valfells' i-umlaut rule

(a) $\underline{\hspace{2cm}} \text{C}_{\text{o}} \left[\begin{bmatrix} -\text{cons} \\ +\text{diff} \\ -\text{grave} \end{bmatrix} \right]_{\text{STEM}}$

(b) $\underline{\hspace{2cm}} \text{C}_{\text{o}} \left[\begin{bmatrix} -\text{cons} \\ -\text{grave} \end{bmatrix} \right]_{\text{STEM}}$ in the preterit subjunctive

(c) in the present indicative singular of strong verbs

(To account for the fact that the thematic *i* of the *ēn*-verbs such as *þora* 'dare' does not cause i-umlaut although it has the same distribution as the thematic *i* of the *ian*-verbs in the forms of the present stem, Valfells assumes that the thematic vowel of the *ēn*-verbs is underlyingly *e*, raised to the phonetic *i* by a rule which operates after the application of the i-umlaut rule. Valfells generalises this solution to many other phonetic unstressed *i*'s: those that are preceded by a front unrounded vowel are underlyingly *i*, others are underlyingly *e*. E.g. *harðindi* 'difficulty' contains underlying *-end-*, whereas *kerling* 'crone' contains underlying *i*, cf. *karl* 'old man.' For unknown reasons this solution is not generalised to the desinences *-ir* and *-i* in the nominative and accusative plural of some strong nouns, i.e. these desinences are not derived from underlying *-er* and *-e* although they do not cause i-umlaut. Instead another, unmotivated, solution is suggested for these desinences by Valfells which will not be treated here.)

Environment (4b) says that stressed vowels are i-umlauted if followed, within the stem, by a front vowel or glide in the next syllable, and the form pertains to the preterit subjunctive. (The formulation correctly prevents i-umlaut from taking place in the preterit subjunctive of *ōn*-verbs, e.g. in *kallaði* of *kalla* 'call.') The formulation presupposes that a subjunctive suffix *i* is attached immediately after the verbal root in the underlying representations of the subjunctive. E.g. *fara* 'bring,' pret. subj. $(\text{fōr}+\text{i})_{\text{STEM}}+ð+\text{i} \rightarrow færði;$ *duga* 'avail,' pret. subj. $(\text{dug}+\text{i})_{\text{STEM}}+ð+\text{i} \rightarrow dygði.$

Environment (4c) says that i-umlaut takes place in the indicative present singular of strong verbs. E.g. *fara* 'go, travel,' present stem *far-*, sg. pres. ind. *fer, ferð, fer*.

2. Criticism of Valfells 1967. The main critical remark that can be made in retrospect is that Valfells postulates a number of what have been called ABSOLUTE NEUTRALISATIONS by Kiparsky 1968b. (However, it must be kept in mind that Kiparsky 1968b, the chief work attacking absolute neutralisations, is more recent than Valfells 1967. At that time absolute neutralisations were legitimate and much employed in phonological descriptions of the generative vein, and continued as such in the work of some linguists long after Kiparsky 1968b began to circulate.) Kiparsky 1968b characterises absolute neutralisations in the following way:

> Let us term the merger of distinct representations *neutralization*. The present theory of generative grammar allows phonological distinctions which are never realized on the phonetic surface to appear in the lexical representations of morphemes. I will term this kind of neutralization, which takes place regardless of environment, *absolute neutralization*, in order to distinguish it from the more usual *contextual neutralization*, in which an underlying distinction is lost only in a specific environment and retained elsewhere.
>
> Absolute neutralization is a consequence of setting up underlying distinctions for the sole purpose of classifying segments into those that do and those that do not meet the structural analysis of a rule. In a commonly posited type of absolute neutralization identical segments are assigned different underlying representations because they function differently as environments of some rule.

The absolute neutralisations to be found in Valfells' work are mostly of the type described in the last sentence of the quotation. An example: As mentioned above, Valfells accounts for the presence vs. lack of i-umlaut in *færa* vs. *þora* by positing the present stems fōr+i vs. þor+e, and adding a late rule changing underlying unstressed *e* to *i*. (Whenever the thematic vowel surfaces in *færa* and *þora*, e.g. in the 1p. sg. pres. ind. *færi, þori*, it is *i*.)

There is some evidence against positing a rule changing unstressed *e* to *i*, and thus against underlying unstressed /e/ as the source of phonetic [ɪ]. The evidence—not mentioned by Valfells—consists of the words containing an unstressed *e* on the phonetic level. Such words are relatively many; they include (a) a number of native lexical items such as *Noregur* 'Norway,' *faðerni* 'fatherhood,' *móðerni* 'the mother's side,' *bróðerni* 'brotherhood,' (b) one class of native grammatical forms, viz. the plural of all substantivised present participles that have a plural, e.g. *leikandi* 'actor,' plural stem *leikend-*, (c) a number of pre-Reformation loanwords such as *akkeri* 'anchor,' *fangelsi* 'prison,' *reykelsi* 'incense,' *stúdent* 'student,' *manneskja* 'man,' *pláneta* 'planet,' *Alexander* man's name, (d) a great number of more recently naturalised words, e.g. the month names *september, október, nóvember, desember*, further *prófessor* 'professor,' *algebra* 'algebra,' *fröken* 'Miss, waitress,' *apótek* 'pharmacy,' *inflúensa* 'flu.' All such words would be exceptions to the rule changing unstressed *e* to *i*.—Also speaking against the rule changing unstressed *e* to *i* is the circumstance that there exists no such evidence in favour of the rule as would be independent of the parts of grammar that have caused the postulation of the rule.

One would think that Valfells would treat pres. subj. *taki* (of *taka* 'take'; without i-umlaut) vs. pret. subj. *tæki* (with i-umlaut) in the same way, that is, that she would posit tak+e vs. tōk+i. Valfells does mention this solution, but rejects the rule that embodies it (her rule (XII)) with the words:

> The validity of the rule (XII) would have to be justified by attempting to find a special feature of the stem forming *i* and the subjunctive-forming *i* that would particularly distinguish these two naturally from all other affixes with *i* that do not cause fronting and unrounding of the immediately preceding root-vowel. This is not possible without arbitrary assumptions. For there are countless affixes that are formed with an *i* as phonological constituent that never cause fronting of the root-vowel, and to define the distinction between these affixes and the subj. affix is not possible in any logical manner. Thus we must consider rule (XII) unsatisfactory in that it does not have any clearly justifiable basis within the general framework of the grammar.

This is valid reasoning. On its basis Valfells ought to have rejected

all her solutions employing absolute neutralisations, not just pres. subj.
tak+e vs. pret. subj. tōk+i.

The absolute neutralisations postulated by Valfells can be divided
into those concerning underlying distinctive features and into those
concerning underlying segments.

The absolute neutralisations involving distinctive features include
the following: *u* [y] is [+grave] instead of [−grave], *æ* [ai] is a monophthong and [−grave] instead of a diphthong and [+grave], *ā* [au] and
ō [ou] are monophthongs instead of diphthongs, in *ai* [ei] the initial
portion of the diphthong is *a* rather than *e*, in *au* [öi] the initial portion
of the diphthong is [+grave, −flat] instead of [−grave, +flat], and the
final portion of the diphthong is *u* rather than *i*. Once these deviations
from phonetic facts are done away with, there is no way in which the
segments undergoing i-umlaut could be combined into a natural class,
a fact that Valfells recognises, even if we disregard the complicating
i-umlaut alternations of *o* ~ *i* (*þoldi* ~ *þyldi*), *ö* ~ *e* (*slökkva* ~ pret.
subj. *slekkti* beside *slökkti*), *ja* ~ *i* (*fjarðar* ~ *firði*), *jö* ~ *ý* and *jú* ~
ý (*frjósa* ~ *frýs*, *ljúga* ~ *lýg*), which Valfells ought to have incorporated
into the i-umlaut rule seeing that they occur in (some of) the same
environments as the remaining i-umlaut alternations. (Valfells tries to
account for some of these alternations with ad hoc rules, see this section ad finem.)

Valfells' absolute neutralisations involving underlying segments
include the following: (a) Whenever the derivational suffixes *-sk-*,
-sn-, *-sl-*, and some others, are preceded by a front vowel within the
word, Valfells postulates underlying *-isk-*, *-isn-*, *-isl-*. E.g. *bernska*
'childhood,' which is word-formationally related to *barn* 'child,' is
derived from barn+isk+a. The *i* of this representation never surfaces
in phonetic representations. To delete it, Valfells posits an ad hoc rule
here repeated sub (5), q.v. The rule is uncontradictory as far as native words are concerned (with the proviso, not mentioned by Valfells,
that it is assumed—as it plausibly can be—that the *i* of the frequent
suffix *-ing-* is underlyingly tense (thus not subject to rule (5)), but
fails the test of applicability with naturalised words in *-ism-i* (e.g.
súrrealismi 'surrealism'), *-ist-i* (e.g. *húmanisti* 'humanist'), *-isk-ur* and
-istisk-ur (e.g. *kommúniskur* and *kommúnistiskur* 'communist'). Valfells
does not mention these cases; to get around them she would have to
say that these items are exceptions to rule (5), or to postulate underlying *e* instead of the critical *i*. The latter solution, however, would
clash with the fact, mentioned above, that unstressed *e* is usually not
raised to *i* in naturalised words.

(5)   Valfells' rule deleting i in *bernska* and similar words

$i \rightarrow \emptyset$ / [$\overline{\text{=stress}}$] [+cons] [+cons]]$_{\text{STEM}}$ +

I.e. any unstressed i is deleted before two stem-final consonantal segments.

(b) Whenever the comparative and the superlative of an adjective contain i-umlauted root vowels and the endings *-ri* and *-st-*, respectively, Valfells posits an underlying i immediately after the root, and a rule deletes this i after the application of the i-umlaut rule so that it never surfaces. E.g. *stór* 'big': its comparative *stærri* is derived from stōr+i+ri, and its middle i is deleted by the vowel syncope rule here repeated sub (6), q.v. The superlative of *stór*, *stæ rst-*, is derived from stōr+i+st, and its i is deleted by rule (5) after the application of the i-umlaut rule.

(6)   Valfells' vowel syncope rule

$i \rightarrow \emptyset$ / VC$_{\text{o}}$——C$_{\text{o}}$VC$_{\text{o}}$

I.e. any unstressed i is deleted if followed by another syllable.

Valfells' formulation of rule (6) cannot be considered final. On the one hand, the rule is too general, seeing that in reality not all i's are deleted in its environment. Cf. *heimill* 'at one's disposal,' dat. pl. *heimilum*, without syncope, as against *mikill* 'big, great,' dat. pl. *miklum*, with syncope. On the other hand, the rule is too specific seeing that it ought to apply at least also to underlying a and u, cf. *hamar* 'hammer,' dat. sg. *hamri*, *djöfull* 'devil,' dat. sg. *djöfli*. Moreover, Valfells says that the syllable following the doomed vowel must not pertain to the affixed definite article, seeing that the doomed vowel is not syncopated in such environments, cf. *hamar-inn*. This is only partly true; the typical counter-examples may be represented by *lifr-in* and *hreiðr-ið*, the definite forms of *lifur* 'liver' and *hreiður* 'nest' (vs. *akurinn*, the definite form of *akur* 'acre'). For a formulation of the vowel syncope rule which takes this data into account see Orešnik MSa.

(c) In the preterit subjunctive of verbs Valfells posits a suffix i immediately after the root which never surfaces in the weak verb forms. E.g. the pret. subj. *dygði* of *duga* 'avail' is derived from (dug+i)+ð+i, and the pret. subj. *dyldi* of *dylja* 'conceal' from (dul+i)+ð+i. The i in question is deleted by the vowel syncope rule (6) after the application of the i-umlaut rule.

So much about absolute neutralisations in Valfells' treatment of i-umlaut. There follow some other critical remarks. (a) Valfells does not treat examples such as dat. sg. *ketti* of *köttur* 'cat,' dat. sg. *firði* of *fjörður* 'fjord,' nom./acc. pl. *bækur* of *bók* 'book,' and the plural *-end-* of the substantivised present participles, e.g. *leikandi* 'actor,' pl. *leikend-*. While *ketti* could be "rescued" if it were assumed that the normal dative singular desinence is the non-umlauting *e*, and that the desinence is the umlauting *i* in *ketti*, I can see no way of accounting for the i-umlaut in the remaining examples within Valfells' system. All the examples represent types.

(b) In some of her derivations, e.g. in the 1p. sg. pres. ind. *dyl* (of *dylja* 'conceal') ← dul+j, Valfells operates with a *j*-deletion rule which deletes *j* word finally and preconsonantally. There is some evidence that there is no such rule in modern Icelandic grammar, see Orešnik MSa.

(c) Valfells derives the past participle stem *færð-* of *færa* 'bring' (this example represents the *ian*-verbs) from (fōr+i)+ð, but she does not state how she would delete the *i* in those forms of the past participle in which the stem is not followed by a vowel initial desinence, as in the gen. pl. *færð-ra*, in the gen. sg. m./n. *færð-s*, etc.

(d) Valfells' environment (4c) is too general in that it does not prevent the i-umlaut from taking place in the singular present indicative of the strong verb *hanga* 'hang,' cf. 1p. sg. pres. ind. *hangi*. On the other hand, the environment is too specific in that it does not predict i-umlaut in the singular present indicative of the weak verbs (some of them have strong forms as well) *ljá* 'lend,' *ná*, 'reach,' *slökkva* 'extinguish,' *hafa* 'have,' *flá* 'flay,' *núa* 'rub,' *þvo* 'wash,' cf. 1p. sg. pres. ind. *ljæ, næ, slekk, hef, flæ, ný, þvæ*.

(e) It has already been mentioned above passim that Valfells postulates several ad hoc phonological rules. To those can be added the rule that changes underlying *o* to underlying *u* in the preterit subjunctive of such verbs as *þola* 'suffer' (the derivation of the pret. subj. *þyldi* is, þol+i+ð+i → þul+i+ð+i → þil+i+ð+i → þil+ð+i), and the rule which changes underlying *ū* to underlying *ō* in the present stem of such verbs as *frjósa* 'freeze' (the derivation of the present stem *frjós-* is, presumably, friūs → friōs).

3. *Anderson 1969 a,b.* Valfells 1967 was followed by Anderson 1969 a and b. The latter two works contain a number of points in common with Valfells 1967; the author, Stephen Anderson, states (1969a:71) that he has arrived at such features independently. It is the purpose of this section to sketch Anderson's treatment of modern Icelandic

i-umlaut. Since 1969b contains later views than 1969a, I will deal with
1969b only.

In Anderson 1969b the modern Icelandic system of stressed vowels
of (7), q.v., is set up. The distinctive features used are those of
Chomsky and Halle 1968.

(7) The underlying system of stressed vowels according to Anderson
     1969b

Phonetic symbol	Anderson's symbol	Anderson's analysis
[ɪ]	i	[−tense, +high, −back, −round]
[ɛ]	e	[−tense, −high, −low, −back, −round]
[œ]	−	produced by the i-umlaut rule
[ʏ]	u	[−tense, +high, +back, +round]
[a]	a	[−tense, +low, +back, −round]
[ɔ]	o	[−tense, −high, −low, +back, +round]
[i]	í	[+tense, +high, −back, −round]
[u]	ú	[+tense, +high, +back, +round]
[ai]	−	produced by the i-umlaut rule
[au]	á	[+tense, +low, +back, −round]
[ou]	ó	[+tense, −high, −low, +back, +round]
[ei]	ai	a + i
[öi]	au	a + u
[jɛ]	é	[+tense, −high, −low, −back, −round]

Anderson's i-umlaut rule is given sub (8), q.v. In comparison with
Valfells' i-umlaut rule, Anderson's i-umlaut rule can be characterised
as an attempt at reducing even the structural description of the rule
to a single generalisation.

(8) Anderson's i-umlaut rule

$$[+\text{back}] \rightarrow \begin{bmatrix} -\text{back} \\ -\text{round} \\ <\alpha\text{low}> \end{bmatrix} / \begin{bmatrix} +\text{syll} \\ <-\text{high}> \\ \alpha\text{tense} \end{bmatrix}$$

$$/ \begin{bmatrix} {}_a \langle \begin{Bmatrix} -\text{low} \\ +\text{tense} \end{Bmatrix} \rangle {}_a \end{bmatrix}_b <C_o>_b \begin{bmatrix} +\text{high} \\ -\text{back} \\ {}_c<-\text{cons}>_c \end{bmatrix}$$

Condition: if a, then b and c

I.e. any back vowel is fronted and unrounded before /i/ or /í/ in
the following syllable; any resulting /é/ is lowered to /ǽ/, and

any resulting /æ/ is raised to /e/. Any /a/ is fronted also if immediately followed by a fronted velar consonant. (Later rules change /æ/ to [ai].)

I have had to construct several examples illustrating the operation of Anderson's i-umlaut rule myself, for Anderson adduces the underlying representations of only two forms undergoing i-umlaut, viz. those of *bækur* and *degı*.

Nom./acc. pl. *bækur* of *bók* 'book': underlying representation /bók+i+r/. Here the i-umlaut rule (8) operates first: under the influence of /i/ the root vowel /ó/ is changed to /æ/ (and further to /ai/ by later rules). Then the rule repeated here sub (9), q.v., deletes the umlaut causing /i/. The epenthesis rule inserts /u/ between /k/ and /r/.

(9) Anderson's vowel deletion rule

$$
\begin{bmatrix} +\text{syll} \\ +\text{high} \\ -\text{tense} \\ -\text{stress} \end{bmatrix} \rightarrow \emptyset \ / \ \underline{\hspace{1.5cm}} [+\text{coronal}]_0
$$

I.e. any unstressed lax /i/ is deleted if immediately followed by any number of coronal consonants and the word boundary, or if immediately followed by the word boundary.

Dat. sg. *degi* of *dagur* 'day': underlying representation /dag+e/. Here the palatalisation rule (alluded to, but not formulated by Anderson) first palatalises /g/ (i.e. /γ/, I assume) to /g'/. Then the i-umlaut rule (8) applies and changes the root vowel /a/ to /e/ under the influence of the front /g'/. Later rules diphthongise the root vowel and change /g'/ into a glide: [dei:jı].

Dat. sg. *ketti* of *köttur* 'cat': underlying representation /katt+í/. Here the i-umlaut rule (8) changes the root vowel /a/ to /e/ under the influence of /í/. Then /í/ is laxed by the vowel reduction rule here repeated sub (10), q.v. This rule (a) laxes unstressed vowels, and (b) raises unstressed /e/ to /i/ and unstressed /o/ to /u/. Function (a) can be illustrated by *ketti* from /katt+í/, function (b) by *degi* from /dag+e/.

(10) Anderson's vowel reduction rule

$$
[+\text{syll}] \rightarrow \begin{bmatrix} +\text{high} \\ -\text{tense} \\ \alpha\text{back} \end{bmatrix} \ / \ \begin{bmatrix} \alpha\text{round} \\ -\text{stress} \\ -\text{low} \end{bmatrix}
$$

I.e. any non-low unstressed vowel becomes high and lax; the value of its backness feature is assimilated to the value of its roundness feature. (Rule (10) follows rule (9) in the ordering.)

1.3.p. sg. pres. ind. *fer* of *fara* 'go, travel'; underlying representation /far+i+r/. Here the i-umlaut rule (8) changes the root vowel /a/ to /e/ under the influence of /i/. Then /i/ is deleted by the vowel deletion rule (9). Later rules simplify /rr/ to /r/.

Sg. pres. ind. middle *ferst* of *fara* 'go, travel': underlying representation (presumably) /far+i+st/. The derivation proceeds as with *fer* above. The example illustrates the deletion of /i/ before two coronal consonants.

4. Criticism of Anderson 1969a,b. The main critical remark that can be made in retrospect is that Anderson, like Valfells, postulates a number of absolute neutralisations. These are of two kinds: one type concerns underlying distinctive features, the other type underlying segments.

The absolute neutralisations involving distinctive features include the following: /u/ [ʏ] is [+back] instead of [−back], /á/ [au] and /ó/ [ou] are monophthongs instead of diphthongs, /é/ [jɛ] is a monophthong instead of bisegmental (/je/), /ai/ [ei] has a low back initial portion instead of [−low, −high, −back], /au/ [öi] has a non-round initial portion instead of a round one. The rule that is the essential step in the production of the diphthongs out of the monophthongs *á, ó, é* (Anderson's rule 7.1) is ad hoc; it is also too general in that it diphthongises—incorrectly—/í/ and /ú/ to /íi/ and /úu/, respectively. (The diphthong /ai/ is changed to /ei/ by the i-umlaut rule, and /au/ to /öu/ by the u-umlaut rule. The fronting of the final portion of /öu/ is not discussed.)

Concerning /u/ [ʏ], Anderson offers as evidence suggesting that it is not a front vowel at every stage of its history in derivations the fact that the palatalisation rule does not apply before [ʏ]. This argumentation is a circulus vitiosus: first Anderson formulates the palatalisation rule so that a velar consonant is fronted if immediately followed by a front vowel, and then the conclusion is drawn that /u/ [ʏ] cannot be a front vowel throughout its derivation. In reality the palatalisation rule applies to velar consonants followed by [−back, −round] vowels, and the failure of /u/ [ʏ] to cause velar fronting follows from the fact that it is round. In addition to this there is some evidence that the palatalisation rule in the form envisaged by Anderson does not exist at all, see Orešnik MSb.

Anderson posits a rule, here repeated sub (11), q.v., which fronts

/u/ to /ʏ/. He claims that the rule is not ad hoc, for it is needed to front that /o/ to /ö/ which is ultimately derived from /a/ via u-umlaut. Anderson derives /ö/ from underlying /a/ in the following way: /a/ becomes /ɔ/ by the u-umlaut rule, /ɔ/ is raised to /o/ by a raising rule (which simultaneously lowers /o/'s of other origin to /ɔ/), and /o/ is fronted to /ö/ by rule (11). Briefly, /a/ → /ɔ/ → /o/ → /ö/. The weakest link of this chain is /a/ → /ɔ/. Anderson does not adduce any arguments in its favour, but only draws attention to the fact that the u-umlauting of /a/ resulted in /ɔ/ in Old Icelandic. The raising of /ɔ/ to /o/ is not motivated in any way. Incidentally, experimental investigations of modern Icelandic vowels published later than Anderson 1969b have shown that modern Icelandic /ö/ is a low vowel (Pétursson 1972). This fact speaks against the raising rule. I conclude that Anderson has not adduced any motivation for rule (11) and thus for the putative fronting of /u/ to /ʏ/.

(11)   Anderson's fronting rule

$$\begin{bmatrix} +syll \\ -low \\ -tense \end{bmatrix} \rightarrow [-back]$$

I.e. any lax non-low vowel is fronted.

Another absolute neutralisation is constituted by the underlying unstressed /e/, which is in all cases raised to /i/ after the application of the i-umlaut rule (8). This matter was critically discussed above in section 2. The rule which raises unstressed /e/ to /i/ also raises unstressed /o/ to /u/. There are many counter-examples to this part of the rule. They include the definite dative plural noun forms, in which the ending -unum can be pronounced [ʏnʏm] or [ɔnʏm], and a number of naturalised words, such as *prófessor* 'professor,' *rektor* 'rector,' *mótor* 'motor,' *doktor* 'doctor,' *nælon* 'nylon,' *badminton* 'badminton.'

Absolute neutralisation is also involved in Anderson's +/−tense unstressed vowels. Anderson's vowel reduction rule (10) laxes all tense unstressed vowels. The laxing part of the rule is ad hoc. It also has many exceptions, seeing that tense vowels are quite common in unstressed position, mostly in loanwords. Böðvarsson 1963 abounds in such cases: *dínamít* 'dynamite,' *kandídat* 'graduate,' *negatífur* 'negative,' *bríarí* 'propensity to experiment,' *kardínáli* 'cardinal,' *klarínetta* 'clarinet,' *latína* 'the Latin language,' etc. (I have culled only some of such examples in which Anderson's i-umlaut rule (8) ought to apply as well, but does not.) A very old loanword is *Stefán* man's name.

(/á/ is a monophthong in Anderson's framework.)   More and more words like this are entering the language.

Absolute neutralisations involving segments are to be found in those underlying representations containing unstressed /i/'s which are deleted by the vowel deletion rule (9) after the application of the i-umlaut rule (8). By way of example cf. the derivations of *bækur* and *fer(st)* in section 3.

Other critical remarks: (a) Monosyllabic second person singular present indicative verbal forms add a dental at the end of the word, cf. *ferð* of *fara* 'go, travel,' *nærð* of *ná* 'reach,' *lest* of *lesa* 'read' (the only exception: *vex* of *vaxa* 'grow'). The environment for the addition of the dental is counter-intuitive in Anderson's framework.   Consider *ferð*, the 2p. sg. pres. ind. *færir* of *færa* 'bring,' and the 2p. sg. pres. ind. *vakir* of *vaka* 'be awake.' The underlying representations before the addition of the dental are /far+i+r/, /fōr+í+r/, and /vak+e+r/, respectively. This shows that the rule governing the addition of the dental in the second person singular present indicative must refer to the underlying tenseness and height of the unstressed vowel: if that vowel is lax and high, and consequently syncopated by rule (9), the dental is added, otherwise not. (The assumption here is that the dental is added before the operation of the phonological rules.)

(b) Anderson posits a vowel syncope rule which is here reproduced sub (12), q.v. Rule (12) can be criticised: Like Valfells' vowel syncope rule (6), it is too general in that it does not exclude cases such as dat. pl. *heimilum* of *heimill* 'at one's disposal.' On the other hand, it is too specific, because it does not account for *höfuð* 'head,' dat. sg. *höfði*, with syncope before *ð* (Orešnik 1971:159), and for cases such as *náinn* 'near, close,' contracted form *nán-*, with syncope of *i* although no consonant immediately precedes it. Furthermore, there is the problem of *akurinn* vs. *lifrin, hreiðrið*.

(12)   Anderson's vowel syncope rule (Anderson 1973:4)

$$\begin{bmatrix} +\text{syll} \\ -\text{stress} \end{bmatrix} \rightarrow \emptyset \ / \ C\underline{\hspace{2em}} \begin{bmatrix} +\text{coronal} \\ +\text{sonorant} \\ \left\{ \begin{bmatrix} +\text{continuant} \\ -\text{voice} \end{bmatrix} \right\} \end{bmatrix} \ + \ V$$

I.e. any unstressed vowel is deleted between a consonant and a coronal sonorant (*r, l, n*) or *s* before an inflectional ending beginning with a vowel.

Also problematical is the interaction of rule (12) with the vowel deletion rule (9). Just as he posits underlying unstressed lax /i/'s which are deleted by the vowel deletion rule (9) after the application of the i-umlaut rule (8), Anderson also posits underlying lax /u/'s that are deleted by rule (9) after the application of the u-umlaut rule (which will not be treated here). Such a /u/ is posited, e.g., in the nom./acc. pl. *börn* (of *barn* 'child'); its underlying representation is /barn+u/. This shows that in Anderson's framework neuter strong nouns have the desinence /+u/ in the nominative/accusative plural. Another example is the nom./acc. pl. n. *hvöss* (of *hvass* 'sharp'); its underlying representation is /hvass+u/. That is, in Anderson's framework the strong nominative/accusative plural neuter forms of adjectives have the desinence /+u/. Consider now a part of the derivation of the dat. pl. *förnum* (of *farinn* 'gone'), nom/acc. pl. n. *farin*, and the nom./acc. pl. *höfuð* 'head.' See (13), where the ordering of the rules is Anderson's; notice in particular that the ordering of the vowel syncope rule and the u-umlaut rule is feeding in the sense of Kiparsky 1968a. It will be seen that two of the derivations yield unacceptable results.

(13) Partial derivations of *förnum*, *farin*, pl. *höfuð*

	far+en+um	far+en+u	havúð+u
vowel syncope rule	far+n+um	far+n+u	havð+u
u-umlaut rule	för+n+um	för+n+u	hövð+u
vowel deletion rule	—	förn	höfð
	förnum	*förn*	*höfð*

(c) Anderson does not deal with a number of i-umlaut alternations: [ɔ] ~ [ɪ] (*þoldi* ~ *þyldi*), [œ] ~ [ɛ] (ind. *slökkti* subj. *slekkti* beside *slökkti*), *jú, jó* ~ *ý* (*ljúga, frjósa* ~ *lýg, frýs*), [ja] ~ [ɪ] (dat. sg. *firði*, stem *fjarð-*, of *fjörður* 'fjord'), and [ɛ] ~ [ɪ] (*sitja* 'sit,' which in Anderson's framework contains the root /set/).

(d) Anderson does not say how he would treat derivatives such as *bernska* 'childhood' (whose derivational base is *barn* 'child'). He cannot start from the underlying representation /barn+isk+a/ (as Valfells can), seeing that /sk/ is not word final in /barn+isk+a/ and it contains a non-coronal consonant; Anderson posits no rule deleting /i/ before such a consonant cluster. Another theoretically possible underlying representation is /barn+sk+i+a/; this would become /bern+sk+i+a/ by the i-umlaut rule (8), and further /bern+sk+j+a/ by a rule not treated here (Anderson's rule 7.5); there is no rule for the deletion of the glide /j/ after velar in Anderson's framework. A third possibility is /barn+sik+a/, but this does not work either, seeing that

Anderson posits no rule syncopating vowels (here /i/) before non-coronal consonants (here /k/). In /barn+sk+a+i/ the /i/ can be deleted, but the structural description of the i-umlaut rule is not satisfied.

(e) The i-umlaut rule (8) is rather complicated because Anderson has insisted on accounting for the example *degi* with it and because his system of underlying stressed vowels contains the segment /é/ instead of /je/. As for *degi*, it is the only noun form of its kind; it could either be derived from the underlying representation /dag+í/ (for /+í/ cf. *ketti* of *köttur* 'cat') or be treated as an exception. As for the type *tekinn* (past participle of *taka* 'take'), which I add to *degi*, it can pertain to the ablaut series *a* − *ō* − *ō* − *e* (*taka, tók, tókum, tekinn*), and thus need not have anything to do with i-umlaut (any longer). Notice that the past particle of *auka* 'increase' is *aukinn*, not *eykinn*.

(f) The inclusion of provisions for *degi* into the i-umlaut rule (8) causes Anderson an ordering problem that he resolves by appealing to the principle of local ordering, which he has formulated. The principle of local ordering will not be treated here. The reader can get some idea of it from the following quotation from Anderson 1969b dealing with the ordering problem just mentioned:

> "A problem arises with this formulation; the vowels that are produced by umlaut are front vowels; as such they cause velar fronting. Thus, velar fronting must follow umlaut; but if umlaut is at least partially conditioned by the frontness of a following velar, the velar fronting rule must also *precede* umlaut. Both of these are feeding orders, however, and the result is that the correct results will be obtained (on the assumptions adopted here) simply by not stating an ordering constraint."

Seeing that *degi* is the only form in which the i-umlaut is "conditioned by the frontness of the ... velar," the ordering problem disappears if *degi* is treated as an exception or given some other underlying representation than /dag+e/, as suggested sub (e) above. Thus the modern Icelandic i-umlaut rule cannot be invoked as a reliable instance of the application of the principle of local ordering.

5. When the absolute neutralisations of Valfells and Anderson are eliminated, the structural change of the i-umlaut rule becomes a LIST of structural changes, and the structural description of the rule becomes (partly stays, from the standpoint of Valfells 1967) a LIST of structural descriptions, which are morphological. See (14). The rule (if there is such a rule) expresses no single generalisation. In its form it resembles ablaut rules (if there are such rules). My conclusion is

that there is no independent i-umlaut rule in modern Icelandic grammar, and that the phenomena that this rule is supposed to handle are
best treated as ABLAUT.

(14)   i-umlaut rule (morphological)

$$\left\{\begin{matrix} a \rightarrow e \\ y \rightarrow i \\ \vdots \end{matrix}\right\} / \left\{\begin{matrix} \text{in the sg. pres. ind. of strong verbs} \\ \text{in the pret. subj. of strong verbs} \\ \vdots \end{matrix}\right\}$$

I can think of three ways in which modern Icelandic ablaut can be
treated in a generative description:

(1) Words undergoing ablaut of the root vowel contain an empty
place instead of the root vowel segment in the lexicon. E.g. *taka*
'take' would be lexically /t^h ... k/, where the ellipsis indicates the
place at which the rules insert the sundry ablaut vowels. The ablaut
rules operating in the forms of *taka* would be approximately as follows:

[ ] → e in the sg. pres. ind. and in the past participle
[ ] → a in the forms of the present stem outside the sg. pres. ind.
[ ] → ou in the pret. ind.
[ ] → ai in the pret. subj.

The first and the last rules are a part of the i-umlaut rule in Valfells'
and Anderson's frameworks.

(2) Words undergoing ablaut of the root vowel contain a basic vowel
in the lexicon. E.g. *taka* would be lexically /t^hak/, and the phonological rules would replace /a/ with other vowels in the appropriate
contexts. The ablaut rules operating in the forms of *taka* would be as
follows:

/a/ → /e/ in the sg. pres. ind. and in the past part.
/a/ → /ou/ in the pret. ind.
/a/ → /ai/ in the pret. subj.

(3) Words undergoing ablaut of the root vowel contain roots which
are suppletive formations; all the different roots are listed in the lexicon, in the case of *taka* as follows:

/t^hek/ in the sg. pres. ind. and in the past participle
/t^hak/ in the forms of the present stem outside the sg. pres. ind.
/t^houk/ in the pret. ind.
/t^haik_j$/ in the pret. subj. (Notice the palatal guttural.)

Solutions of type (1) are popular in generative studies of Semitic ablaut, those of type (2) are used, e.g., for English in Chomsky and Halle 1968, and type (3) has not, to the best of my knowledge, been proposed for any language so far. Yet it is exactly type (3) that deserves special attention because it takes into account even the irregularities of consonantism which tend to accompany the vocalic ablaut, e.g. the alternation *k* ~ *kj* above, *v* ~ Ø in *hverfa* 'disappear' ~ *hurfu horfinn*, *nn* ~ *nd* in *fann* ~ *fundum* of *finna* 'find,' etc. However, rules could be written for these additional irregularities, so that they do not constitute a decisive argument in favour of type (3). We lack an evaluation measure which would allow us to choose among these three treatments of ablaut.

A weak verb such as *dylja* 'conceal,' pret. *duldi*, whose vocalic alternation /ɪ/ ~ /ʏ/ is due to the historical i-umlaut, can be treated in the following alternative ways:

(1) Lexical stem /d ... l/ and the following rules:

[ ] → ɪ in the forms of the present stem and in the pret. subj.
[ ] → ʏ elsewhere
(2) Lexical stem /dɪl/ and the following rule:
ɪ → ʏ in the pret. ind. and in the past participle

(3) Lexical stems /dɪl/ and /dʏl/ with the following distribution:

/dɪl/ in the forms of the present stem and in the pret. subj.
/dʏl/ elsewhere.

6. Orešnik 1971. Orešnik 1971, which deals, among other things, with the i-umlaut reflexes in modern Icelandic preterit subjunctive forms, accepts some aspects of Valfells' and Anderson's i-umlaut rule: the existence of underlying non-umlauting unstressed /e/ vs. umlauting unstressed /i/; /j/ is also umlauting; no vowel may intervene between the vowel to be umlauted and the umlauting /i, j/. The reader is referred to Orešnik 1971 for fuller information. It is now necessary to replace the treatment of i-umlaut in the preterit subjunctive forms of Orešnik 1971 with a new treatment which would be independent of Valfells' and Anderson's i-umlaut rule, and compatible with i-umlaut alternations viewed as ablaut.

Two kinds of preterit subjunctive forms were distinguished in Orešnik 1971. In one type the root vowel of the preterit subjunctive stem is identical with the root vowel of the present tense stem; every preterit subjunctive stem of this type is called a 'PRESENT STEM'

FORMATION. Example: *krefja* 'require' has the present stem *kref-*, the preterit indicative stem *krafð-*, and the preterit subjunctive stem *krefð-;* both the present stem and the preterit subjunctive stem contain the same root vowel, *e*, so subj. *krefð-* is a 'present stem' formation. In the other type the root vowel of the preterit subjunctive stem is an i-umlauted version of the root vowel in the preterit indicative stem; every preterit subjunctive stem of this type is called a 'PRETERITIVAL.' FORMATION. Example: *þykja* 'seem' has the present stem *þykj-*, the preterit indicative stem *þótt-*, and the preterit subjunctive stem *þætt-;* the *æ* in *þætt-* is the i-umlauted reflex of *ó* in *þótt-*, so *þætt-* is a 'preteritival' formation.

The following verbs contain 'preteritival' formations: all strong verbs, all preterit-present verbs, a few other irregular verbs, such as *þykja* 'seem' (pret. subj. *þætt-*); *ēn*-verbs such as *vaka* 'be awake' (pret. subj. *vekt-*), although many *ēn*-verbs contain 'present stem' formations.

The following verbs contain 'present stem' formations: all weak verbs except a few *ēn*-verbs, *sækja* 'seek' (pret. subj. *sækt-*), *þykja* 'seem' in dialect, when its preterit subjunctive is *þykt-* instead of the normal *þætt-* (for *þykt-* see Blöndal 1920–24 s.v. *þykja* and Orešnik MSc).

(15) Some weak verb paradigms

        kalla 'call,' pret. ind. *kallað-*, pret. subj. *kallað-*
        blasa 'lie open'   *blast-*   *blast-*
        færa 'bring'   *færð-*   *færð-*
        krefja 'require'   *krafð-*   *krefð-*
        sækja 'seek'   *sótt-*   *sækt-*
        þykja 'seem'   *þótt-*   dial. *þykt-*

On the basis of paradigms such as those given in (15), q.v., the speakers of Icelandic have subconsciously formulated rule (16) for the formation of weak preterit subjunctive stems:

(16) Preterite subjunctive stem = present stem + dental suffix

It is well known that weak verbs have formally influenced some of the strong verbs in the history of Icelandic so that some strong verbs now have weak forms also. One way in which weak verbs have influenced the strong verbs is through rule (16): some strong verbs have formed—in dialect—new preterit subjunctive stems according to rule (16), without at the same time forming weak preterit indicative stems.

(17) Examples of weak preterit subjunctive stems formed according to rule (16) in otherwise strong verbs

(a) 'Northern' forms

nema 'take,' pret. ind. *nam-, nám-,* pret. subj. *næm-* and *nemd-* (13 examples)

syngja 'sing,' pret. ind. *söng-, sung-,* pret. subj. *syngj-* and *syngd-* (1 example)

bera 'carry,' pret. ind. *bar-, bár-,* pret. subj. *bær-* and *berð-* (1 example)

(b) 'Southern' form

hlæja 'laugh,' pret. ind. *hló(g)-,* pret. subj. *hlægj-* and *hlæð-* (3 examples)

Such cases are treated in detail in Orešnik 1971, where the relevant philological evidence is also presented in toto and discussed. Examples are given sub (17), q.v. (The number of examples (of the weak preterit subjunctive forms) adduced in Orešnik 1971 is given in parentheses.)

The 'southern' form *hlæð-* has been a source of further 'southern' innovations. It was interpreted as the preterit subjunctive stem *hlægj-* + dental suffix. This gave rise to the weak preterit subjunctive stems enumerated sub (18), q.v. These forms were in turn occasionally interpreted as the consonantism of the present stem + *æð*. This gave rise to the weak pret. subj. *sjæð-* (10 examples) of *sjá* 'see,' pret. ind. *sá-,* regular pret. subj. *sæ-.* The chronology of these weak preterit subjunctive stems, as it was presented in Orešnik 1971, does not contradict the above assumptions, but is not very helpful either, seeing that all the 'southern' weak preterit subjunctive stems but *læð-* appeared at the beginning of the nineteenth century. *Læð-* is a twentieth century formation.

(18)   *slá* 'strike,' pret. ind. *sló(g)-,* pret. subj. *slægj-* and *slæð-* (6 examples)

draga 'draw,' pret. ind. *dró(g)-,* pret. subj. *drægj-* and *dræð-* (3 examples)

deyja 'die,' pret. ind. *dó-,* pret. subj. *dæ-* and *dæð-* (11 examples)

liggja 'lie,' pret. ind. *lá(g)-,* pret. subj. *lægj-* and *læð-* (1 example)

REFERENCES

Anderson, Stephen R.   An outline of the phonology of modern Icelandic vowels. *Foundations of Language* 5 (1969) 53–72.—Referred to as Anderson 1969a.

———.   *West Scandinavian Vowel Systems and the Ordering of Phonological Rules.* M.I.T. doctoral dissertation, 1969.—Referred to as Anderson 1969b.

——— U-umlaut and skaldic verse. *A Festschrift for Morris Halle*, ed. by Stephen R. Anderson and Paul Kiparsky, New York, 1973, pp. 3–13.

Blöndal, Sigfús. *Íslensk-dönsk orðabók*. Reykjavík, 1920–24.

Böðvarsson, Árni, ed. *Íslenzk orðabók handa skólum og almenningi*. Reykjavík, 1963.

Chomsky, Noam, and Morris Halle. *The Sound Pattern of English*. New York, 1968.

Jakobson, Roman, and Morris Halle. *Fundamentals of Language*. The Hague, 1956.

Kiparsky, Paul. Linguistic universals and linguistic change. *Universals in Linguistic Theory*, ed. by Emmon Bach and Robert T. Harms, New York, 1968.—Referred to as Kiparsky 1968a.

———. How abstract is phonology? Mimiographed, M.I.T., 1968.—Referred to as Kiparsky 1968b.

Orešnik, Janez. On some weak preterit subjunctives of otherwise strong verbs in modern Icelandic. *Arkiv för nordisk filologi* 86 (1971) 139–78.

———. The modern Icelandic epenthesis rule revisited. Forthcoming.—Referred to as Orešnik MSa.

———. On the modern Icelandic palatalisation rule. Forthcoming.—Referred to as Orešnik MSb.

———. Three modern Icelandic morphophonemic notes. Forthcoming.—Referred to as Orešnik MSc.

Pétursson, Magnús. Peut-on interpréter les données de la radiocinématographie en fonction du tube acoustique à section uniforme? Réflexions à propos de l'analyse du système vocalique de l'islandais moderne. *Travaux de l'Institut de Phonétique de Strasbourg* 4 (1972) 18–111.

Valfells, Sigrid. *"Umlaut"-Alternations in Modern Icelandic*. Harvard University doctoral dissertation, 1967.

Orešnik MSa has been published in *Arkiv för nordisk filologi* for 1978, MSb in the festschrift for K.-H. Dahlstedt (Umeå, 1977), and MSc in the festschrift for Jakob Benediktsson (Reykjavík, 1977).

Janez Orešnik (Ljubljana):

ON THE MODERN ICELANDIC CLIPPED IMPERATIVE

Icelandic has a SHORT imperative singular, consisting of only the root or the stem of the verb (e.g. kom,
kalla, statt, þegi), and a LONG imperative singular,
which equals the short imperative + the suffixed þú (e.
g. kondu, kallaðu, stattu, þegiðu). In addition to the
short and long imperatives INFORMAL modern Icelandic
possesses an imperative singular ending in a dental,
e.g. kond of koma, látt of láta, rádd of ráða. The type
will be called the CLIPPED IMPERATIVE here. In the modern language, clipped imperatives seem always to be accompanied by an emphatic þú, in constructions such as
Lest Þú bókina, ekki HANN "YOU read (imp.) the book,
not HE" (where capitalisation indicates emphasis). To
get hold of the clipped forms I enlisted the help of a
number of informants. The results of my work with the
informants can be summarised as follows: (1) The shape
of the elicited clipped imperatives is such as if they
were formed with the help of the following rule: delete
the final u of the long imperative. E.g. taktu minus u
yields takt. (2) I could not elicit clipped imperatives
of verbs in which the final dental would be preceded by
a vowel. Examples of probably non-existent clipped imperatives: kallaᴧ, þegið, sjáᴧ. (3) The existence of
the clipped imperatives ending in a consonant + ᴧ seems
to be less certain than the existence of the clipped
imperatives whose final dental is realised as a plosive.
Thus, while all my informants are sure of the existence

of forms such as kond ÞÚ, takt ÞÚ, some of them are less sure of the existence of forms such as gerð ÞÚ, leggð ÞÚ. (4) Speakers of Icelandic can always avoid using the clipped imperative. Two typical ways out are, (a) the use of the short imperative + ÞÚ, the predominant form in formal Icelandic, and (b) the paraphrase with the modal auxiliary skulu, e.g. lest ÞÚ bókina, ekki HANN can be paraphrased as ÞÚ skalt lesa bókina, ekki HANN.

The age of the clipped imperatives. (In what follows the spelling of the examples is partly normalised. The examples immediately followed by a vowel-initial word are to be used with caution, because of the possibility of elision. The fact that I have seen/found some of the examples in the files of the Arnamagnæan Dictionary is hereby acknowledged once for all.) The oldest examples of the type are, 2x vest of vesa, sett of setja, kjóst of kjósa, and kennd of kenna (Larsson 1891 s. vv. vesa, setja, kjósa, kenna; the vest of Plácítusdrápa is, however, philologically uncertain, Helgason 1932-33:152-53), veitt of veita (Widding 1952:145), hirt of hirða (Gíslason 1860:472), blótt of blóta and grátt-attu of gráta (the two last mentioned occur in the Codex Regius of the older Edda). Fourteenth century: sent of senda (Þorláksson 1881:16) and hent of henda (Kålund 1908:64). Fifteenth century: vert (Þórólfsson 1925:110, Holm-Olsen 1945:121, Foote 1962:15, Kirby 1976:321), sent (Larsson 1893:39), dreypt of dreypa (Helgason 1936:169), hirt (Widding 1960:88). Sixteenth century, Catholic times: vert (Loth 1969:112, 266; 1970:88, 260, 315, 390; Sig-

mundsson 1977:210-12; the unedited Codex Vindobonensis
2713:28v, 41r, 57v, 58v, 60v), sent (Loth 1969:381; 1970:
141, 157, 160, 267, 364), flýtt of flýta (Helgason 1936:
226), bítt of bíta (marginal note in AM 147 4°, p. 138;
Jonna Louis-Jensen viva voce), -lítt of -líta (Sigmundsson 1977:211). Sixteenth century, Lutheran times: for
vert, sent, gyrt of gyrða, virt of virða, sækt of sækja,
hellt of hella, látt of láta, see Þórólfsson 1925:110-11,
Helgason 1929:92, Bandle 1956:388; further there is gakkt
of ganga (Westergård-Nielsen 1955:122, 294), seld of selja (ibidem 287), vert (ibidem, 17 exx.; Widding 1960:
151). Seventeenth century: vert (Pjetursson 1924:156,
Friðriksson 1848:52, Kålund 1906-11:14, Helgason 1936:
222, 1960ᵃ:230), hirt (Pjetursson 1924:47, Helgason 1978:
397), takt of taka (Helgason 1962:54), gakkt (Helgason
1978:125), hljótt of hljóta (Helgason 1960b:24), ?leggð
of leggja (spelled legda = leggð á, Helgason 1936:15³).
Eighteenth century: no examples. Nineteenth century: 2x
ljúkt of ljúka, 2x rádd of ráða, komd of koma (Helgason
1968:127; 1970:143, 174, 184). Twentieth century: I have
only examples of vert followed by emphatic þú from Hagal-
íns novel Kristrún í Hamravík (e.g. Sæl vert þú, móðir
mín, answer: Sæll vert þú, sonur vor). Further I have
seen one example of kond þú in a private letter.

The origin of the clipped imperative. Kock 1891 explained the imperatives blótt and grátt- as due to a
faulty analysis of the corresponding long imperatives.
This explanation is repeated for the clipped imperatives
of the 15th and 16th centuries in Þórólfsson 1925:110.
Bandle 1956:388 tentatively connected the clipped imper-

atives of the 15th and 16th centuries with the early
imperative vest. On the other hand, the modern clipped
imperatives have never been discussed in this, or any
other, connection, to the best of my knowledge.

The original way of forming the two oldest variants
of the imperative singular, say kjós and kjóstu, must
have been as follows: kjós was probably abstracted from
the finite present tense forms of the verb, and kjóstu
formed from kjós through the affixation and modification
of þú. Thus kjós was the basic variant of the imperative.
By the beginning of the literary period this situation
had been reversed, at least optionally, in the sense
that the type kjóstu began to be treated, at least optionally, as the basic variant of the imperative, that
is, that process began to assert itself which eventually
established the type kjóstu as the basic imperative variant, witness the state of affairs in modern Icelandic.
That the long imperative could be the basic imperative
variant, at least optionally, even in Old Icelandic,
can be seen from the following statistics, which are extremely rough, due to several factors, partly of a philological, partly of a stylistic nature, that hinder exact computation. In the Icelandic Book of Homilies 55%
of all imperatives are long imperatives. In the Old Icelandic and Old Norwegian biblical quotations as collected and edited in Kirby 1976, about a half of all occurring imperatives are long imperatives. It can be assumed
that the share of the long imperatives was even greater
in the less conservative spoken language of the time. -
In those instances when the basic variant was kjóstu,

kjós was formed from it through CLIPPING. There arose
several clipping processes, depending on the morphonological characteristics of the verbs. For instance, with
the majority of the verbs whose long imperatives ended
in -ðu or -du, the rule was, remove -ðu or -du: kallaðu
minus -ðu gave kalla, brenndu minus -du gave brenn. With
most, and the most used, imperatives in -tu, however,
the rule was, remove just u. This rule was established
on the basis of pairs such as haltu : halt, stattu :
statt, bittu : bitt, further giftu : gift and more than
75 other verbs whose roots end in Ct. In the 14th century the rule was reinforced by all the middle voice imperatives, e.g. forðastu : forðast. In all these cases
the short imperative was formed from the long one through
the removal of the final u. The rule gained momentum
with time, when the status of the long imperative as the
basic imperative variant became more and more established. This widely used truncation of u in imperatives ending in -tu was applied even outside its proper domain,
in the earliest cases to the long imperatives in -tu
that did not participate in the formulation of the rule.
The overgeneralisation was facilitated, even called for,
by imperatives such as sentu, láttu, taktu, from which
there was no straightforward way of deriving send, lát,
tak because of the internal sandhi complications. The
result of the overgeneralisation was forms such as sent,
látt, takt. The clipping of just the final u was then
further extended even to the long imperatives ending in
-du: thus arose seld, kond. This stage in the development of the clipped imperative must have been achieved

by the time of the oldest preserved manuscripts. The
next step was the overgeneralisation of the rule to the
long imperatives ending in C+ðu: thus arose gerð, leggð.
The reason why the overgeneralisation affected long imperatives ending in C+ðu, but not long imperatives ending in V+ðu, may be that in the former there are some
ambiguities and sandhi complications from which the latter are completely free: ráddu : ráð, bregðu : bregð,
leggðu : legg, but kallaðu : kalla.

The derivation of the clipped imperatives from the
long imperatives was an attempt to form the short imperative in a novel way. Therefore the clipped and the
short imperatives were functionally equivalent. By the
beginning of the literary period the clipped imperatives
had begun to combine with þú just like, and to the same
extent as, the functionally equivalent short imperatives
combined with þú. I assume that the accompanying þú was
sometimes emphatic, sometimes not, depending on syntax
and meaning. In the further development the clipped imperative, just like the short imperative, had to retreat
before the long imperative because the long imperative
was a better linguistic sign than the clipped and the
short imperatives, for within the morphology, in whose
domain the formal development of the imperative was
taking place, the long imperative was most clearly of
the three morphological imperative variants marked as a
second person singular. (The 2p. singular imperative
can be encoded primarily as an imperative singular, in
which case it tends to be as short as possible; or it
can be primarily encoded as a second person singular, in

which case it tends to have an ending.) In the modern
language the clipped imperative has survived only where
it was superior to the long imperative, i.e. in its
usage with emphatic þú. The short imperative has had an
even worse fate than the clipped imperative: barring
certain fixed expressions it has been abolished in the
non-biblical uses, probably because from the morphological point of view it was less good a linguistic sign
than even the clipped imperative: it bore no indication
of being a second person singular.

The clipped imperative existed in Old Norwegian as
well. Further there were parallel developments in the
2p. singular present indicative in Icelandic (e.g. lest,
ferð of lesa, fara), in Faroese, and in the old West
Germanic languages.

References:

Bandle, Oskar 1956: Die Sprache der Guðbrandsbiblía.
     Bibliotheca arnamagnæana Vol. XVII. Munksgaard,
     Copenhagen.

Foote, Peter ed. 1962: Lives of saints. Early Icelandic
     Manuscripts in Facsimile Vol, 4. Rosenkilde & Bag-
     ger, Copenhagen.

Friðriksson, Halldór K. ed. 1848: Sagan af Þórði hreðu.
     Nordiske Oldskrifter Vol. VI. Det nordiske Litera-
     tur-Samfund, Copenhagen.

Gíslason, Konráð ed. 1860: Fire og fyrretyve Prøver af
     oldnordisk Sprog og Literatur. Gyldendal, Copen-
     hagen.

Helgason, Jón 1929: Málið á Nýja testamenti Odds Gott-

skálkssonar. Safn fræðafjelagsins um Ísland og Íslendinga gefið út af Hinu íslenska fræðafjelagi í
Kaupmannahöfn Vol. VII. S. L. Møller, Copenhagen.

Helgason, Jón 1932-33: Til Skjaldedigtningen. Acta philologica scandinavica Vol. 7, 150-68.

Helgason, Jón ed. 1936: Íslenzk miðaldakvæði. Munksgaard,
Copenhagen.

Helgason, Jón 1960a: Den danske Lykkebog pa Island. Opus-
cula I. Bibliotheca arnamagnæana Vol. XX, 213-46.

Helgason, Jón 1960b: Kvæðabók séra Gissurar Sveinssonar.
AM 147, 8VO. B. Inngangur. Íslanzk rit síðari alda
Vol. 2 B. Hið íslenzka fræðafélag, Copenhagen.

Helgason, Jón ed. 1962: Íslenzk fornkvæði I. Editiones
arnamagnæanæ, Series B, Vol. 10. Munksgaard, Copenhagen.

Helgason, Jón ed. 1968: Íslenzk fornkvæði VI. Editiones
arnamagnæanæ, Series B, Vol. 15. Munksgaard, Copenhagen.

Helgason, Jón ed. 1970: Íslenzk fornkvæði VII. Editiones
arnamagnæanæ, Series B, Vol. 16. Munksgaard, Copenhagen.

Helgason, Jón ed. 1978: Byskupa sǫgur. Editiones arnamagnæanæ, Series A, Vol. 13, 2. Reitzel, Copenhagen.

Holm-Olsen, Ludvig ed. 1945: Konungs skuggsjá. Dybwad,
Oslo.

Kirby, Ian J. ed. 1976: Biblical quotation in Old Ice-
landic-Norwegian religious literature. Vol. I: Text.
Stofnun Árna Magnússonar á Íslandi Vol. 9. Ísafold-
arprentsmiðja, Reykjavík.

Kock, Axel 1891: Fornnordiska kvantitets- och akcentfrågor. Arkiv för nordisk filologi Vol. 7, 334-77.

Kålund, Kristjan ed. 1906-11: Sturlunga saga. 2 vols.

Gyldendal, Copenhagen.

Kålund, Kristjan ed. 1908: Alfræði íslenzk I. Samfund

til Udgivelse af gammel nordisk Litteratur, Copen-

hagen.

Larsson, Ludvig 1891: Ordförrådet i de älsta islänska

handskrifterna. Ph. Lindstedt, Lund.

Larsson, Ludvig ed. 1893: Sagan ... om Friðþjófr hinn

froekni. Samfund til Udgivelse af gammel nordisk

Litteratur, Copenhagen.

Loth, Agnete ed. 1969: Reykjahólabók I. Editiones arna-

magnæanæ, Series A, Vol. 15. Munksgaard, Copenhagen.

Loth, Agnete ed. 1970: Reykjahólabók II. Editiones arna-

magnæanæ, Series A, Vol. 16. Munksgaard, Copenhagen.

Pjetursson, Hallgrímur 1924: Passíusálmar. Ed. by Finnur

Jónsson. S. L. Møller, Copenhagen.

Sigmundsson, Svavar 1977: Handritið Uppsala R:719. Opus-

cula septentrionalia. Festskrift til Ole Widding,

207-20. Reitzel, Copenhagen.

Þorláksson, Guðmundur ed. 1881: Gyðinga saga. Samfund

til Udgivelse af gammel nordisk Litteratur, Copen-

hagen.

Þórólfsson, Björn Karel 1925: Um íslenskar orðmyndir á

14. og 15. öld og breytingar þeirra úr fornmálinu.

Fjelagsprentsmiðjan, Reykjavík.

Westergård-Nielsen, Christian ed. 1955: Gissur Einars-

sons islandske oversættelse af Ecclesiasticus og

Prouerbia Salomonis. Bibliotheca arnamagnæana Vol.

XV. Munksgaard, Copenhagen.

Widding, Ole 1952: Et fragment af Stephanus saga (AM
655, 4° XIV B), tekst og kommentar. Acta philologica scandinavica Vol. 21, 143-71.

Widding, Ole ed. 1960: Alkuin i norsk-islandsk overle-
vering. Editiones arnamagnæanæ, Series A, Vol. 4.
Munksgaard, Copenhagen.

JANEZ OREŠNIK

On the Dental Accretion

*in Certain 2nd p. sg. Verbal Forms of Icelandic, Faroese,
and the Old West Germanic Languages*

0. *Summary*

Certain 2. p. sg. pres. ind. verbal forms of Icelandic, of Faroese, and of the old West Germanic languages have developed a dental accretion, e. g. Icelandic *les-t*, *fer-ð* of *lesa*, *fara*, Faroese *ger-t*, *býr-t* of *gera*, *búgva*, Old English *gǣs-t* of *gān*, Old High German *tuos-t* of *tuon*. Such forms arose from the corresponding forms containing the suffixed personal pronoun *þú, tú, thu, du*, through the removal of the final vowel, e. g. Icelandic *lestu* minus *u* gave *lest*. Evidence for this comes from the history of the Icelandic imperative singular.

Section 1 deals with the origin of the modern Icelandic 2. p. sg. pres. ind. and imperative singular forms ending in a dental, e.g. 2. p. *lest*, *ferð*, imp. *kond*, *takt*. Section 2 discusses parallel phenomena in Faroese and in the old West Germanic languages. In section 3 the paper is summed up.[1]

1.

1.1

This section discusses the origin of the modern Icelandic 2. p. sg. pres. ind. forms such as *lest* of *lesa*, *ferð* of *fara*, and *færð* of *fá*. The oldest paradigms of the present indicative singular of the three verbs were those given here sub (1), q.v. (spelling modernised and normalised):

(1)			
1.	les	fer	fæ
2.	less, lestu	ferr, ferðu	fær, færðu
3.	less	ferr	fær

Every 2. p. sg. verbal form of Icelandic has two morphological vari-

[1] My thanks are due to Höskuldur Þráinsson for important remarks, to Magnús Pétursson for help with §1.2, and to Margaret G. Davis for the correction of my English.

ants, one with, and the other without, the suffixed pronoun *þú*, e.g. *fær* and *færðu* of *fá* (Cleasby-Vigfusson 1957: xxvi–vii). The forms without the suffixed *þú* will here be called the **short** forms. The forms with the suffixed *þú* will be called the **long** forms. Thus *fær* is a short second person singular, and *færðu* a long one.

The geminates that occur in the above oldest paradigms of *lesa* and *fara* were simplified already in pre-Reformation Icelandic (Noreen 1923:210), and the resulting paradigms were as shown in (2):

(2) 1. les   fer   fæ
   2. les, lestu   fer, ferðu   fær, færðu
   3. les   fer   fær

The next, and so far last, step in the development of these paradigms consisted in the addition of a dental at the end of the three short 2. p. sg. forms: *les > lest, fer > ferð, fær > færð* (Arpi 1904). The added dental is either *t* or *ð*; *t* is added to any short second person singular if that form is monosyllabic and ends in V*s*; *ð* is added to any short second person singular if that form is monosyllabic and ends in V*r*, where the *r* either pertains to the root (as in *fer-ð*), or to the ending (as in *fæ-rð*).

I will refer to forms such as *lest* as the **lest type**, and to forms such as *ferð, færð* as the **ferð type**. The common name for the short forms expanded with a dental will be the **clipped** forms (this in anticipation of the historical explanation to be suggested below).

The oldest known example of the *lest* type occurs in *Donatus Hoc est Paradigmata partium orationis Latino – Isl.* (Hafniæ 1733, p. 62) where the form is *lest* (Jón Þorkelsson 1888–94:5), and in Jón Magnússon's grammar of Icelandic dated from the same time, where the form is *eyst* of *ausa* (Björn K. Þórólfsson 1925:112, cf. Finnur Jónsson 1933: 114). The oldest known example of the *ferð* type is to be found in Rask's *Kortfattet Vejledning til det oldnordiske eller gamle islandske Sprog* (København 1832, p. 60) where the form is *ferð* (Björn K. Þórólfsson 1925:112).

At least since Arpi (1904) the *lest* and the *ferð* types have been explained as due to a faulty analysis of the corresponding long forms, cf. *lestu* and *ferðu*. This idea is undoubtedly correct, and will be elaborated in what follows.

I assume that in the much used preterite-present verbs, further in *vera* and *vilja*, and in the strong preterites, the long forms such as *skaltu, ertu, viltu, hélstu*, etc., were the basic variants[2] of the 2. p. sg. pres. ind., from the morphological point of view,[3] and the corresponding short forms, *skalt, ert,*[4] *vilt, hélst*, etc., were derived from the long forms through the clipping of the final *u* of the respective long forms: *skaltu* minus *u* = *skalt*, *ertu* minus *u* = *ert*, etc. I further assume that from such examples the clipping of *u* spread to long forms of verbs other than those mentioned at the beginning of this paragraph, and thus clipped forms came into being which were not identical with the corresponding short forms: the long form *lestu* minus *u* gave the clipped form *lest*, and soon thereafter the long form *ferðu* minus *u* gave the clipped form *ferð*, and similarly with all the instances of the *lest* and *ferð* types.

The above explanation of the *lest* and *ferð* types can be couched in the following more general terms. The sundry morphological forms of the 2. p. sg. that any verb has (e. g. *skalt* and *skaltu* of *skulu*) are morphological variants of the 2. p. sg; sometimes—depending on the morphological structure of the variants involved—one of the variants comes to be considered their basic variant (for the notion of **basic variant** cf. footnote 2); the remaining variants begin to be made from their basic variant. E.g. in the 2. p. sg. pres. ind. of *skulu, skaltu* becomes the basic variant, from which the remaining variant, *skalt*, begins to be made. The rules by aid of which the non-basic variants (in our example *skalt*) are derived from their basic variants (in our example *skaltu*) are deduced from a number of pairs of forms, each of which

---

[2] The **basic variant** is here defined as the variant which is the best linguistic sign in a set of variants.

[3] The phrase, „from the morphological point of view", is essential here, because the 2.p.sg. of Icelandic verbs also has syntactic variants. For instance, beside the 2.p.sg.pres.ind. *kallar* and *kallarðu* (these are the morphological variants of the 2.p.sg.pres.ind. of *kalla*; they are called morphological because they consist of one word each) there are also the syntactic variants *þú kallar* and *kallar þú* (they are called syntactic because they consist of more than one word each). The syntactic variants have been ignored in what follows, except in footnote 8, where it is also pointed out that such a procedure is legitimate.

[4] *Est* (>*ert*) and the subjunctive *sért* may be early cases of the clipping of *u*. This, however, does not prejudice their later role as models for other forms.

Janez Orešnik

pairs comprises the basic variant and a non-basic variant (in our example the basic variant *skaltu* and the non-basic variant *skalt*). The rules are formulated so that the non-basic variants are derived from the basic variant (in our example *skalt* is derived from *skaltu* by the clipping of the final *u* of *skaltu*). If some derivational rule of this provenance is applied to a verbal form that did not participate in the original formulation of the rule, a new form may come into being as a result. (E.g. if the rule formulated above on the basis of *skaltu* and *skalt* is applied to the long form *lestu*, a new form *lest* is produced.)

1.2

To lend plausibility to the above account, the crucial part of which is the assertion that the long forms (e.g. *skaltu*) are the basic variants of the 2. p. sg., I will now discuss a morphological case similar to *lest* and *ferð*, viz. the so-called **clipped imperative**.[5]

In Icelandic it is necessary to distinguish between morphological and syntactic variants of the imperative singular. The morphological variants consist of only one word each, e.g. *kalla(ðu)*, whereas the syntactic variants consist of a morphological variant accompanied by the non-suffixed pronoun *þú*, e. g. *kalla þú*. We will concentrate on the morphological variants.

There are three morphological variants of the imperative singular: the **short**, the **long**, and the **clipped** imperatives.

The short imperative has no ending; it consists of the verbal root or stem alone. Examples: *kom, tak, kalla, þegi* of *koma, taka, kalla, þegja*.

The long imperative = the short imperative + the suffixed personal pronoun *þú*. Examples: *kondu < komdu, taktu, kallaðu, þegiðu*. The long imperative is the prevailing imp. sg. form of modern informal Icelandic. (Also of modern formal Icelandic, with special provisos for biblical language, for other very formal usage, and for certain standing expressions, where the short imperative is also to be found.)

The clipped imperative = the long imperative minus its final *u*. Examples: *kond, takt, gerð, leggð* of *koma, taka, gera, leggja*.[6]

---

[5] What follows about the imperative is in some respects a summary of Orešnik 1980, which paper should also be consulted for the philological detail concerning the clipped imperatives.

[6] Imperatives such as *kallað, þegið* probably do not exist. The clipped impera-

The basic variant of the imperative singular is the long imperative. This assumption must be made in order to account for the fact that the long imperative has prevailed over all other imperative variants in the informal language, to a lesser extent in the formal language. By prevailing over the remaining imperative variants the long imperative has proved that it is more resistant than the remaining imperative variants against „attacks" upon itself. Its resistance must be due to the circumstance that the long imperative is a better linguistic sign, from the morphological point of view, than the remaining imperative variants.[7] The „betterness" of the long imperative is in my opinion ascribable to its being better than the remaining imperative variants characterised as a second person singular: the suffixed *þú* is the most universal Icelandic 2. p. sg. ending, and as such best of all the **morphological** signs denotes the second person singular.[8]

The long imperative, which we have now established as the basic imperative variant of Icelandic (from the morphological point of view) on the evidence of its eventual rise above all other imperative variants, has been the base from which the short imperatives gradually, and at least optionally, came to be formed in the last thousand years or so in

---

tives can only be formed from the long imperatives that end in CD*u*, where C = any consonant, D = *t, d*, or *ð*; the long imperatives *kallaðu, þegiðu*, etc. lack the C of the formula.

[7] This Darwinian reasoning owes much to Willi Mayerthaler's lectures at the Linguistic Society of America Summer Institute in Salzburg, 1979.

[8] It is questionable whether the long imperative would win the title of the basic imperative variant if the contest among the imperative variants were conducted on the **syntactic** level. In that case the contestants would include the short imperative + the non-suffixed *þú*, e. g. *kalla þú*. However, it never came to a contest among the imperative variants on the syntactic level: the type exemplified by *kalla þú* did not disappear because it was less good a linguistic sign than *kallaðu*, but because its integral part, the short imperative *kalla*, lost the battle against the long imperative *kallaðu* on the morphological level. (For the difference between the morphological and syntactic variants of the 2.p.sg. see footnote 3 above.) — That linguistic changes can occur within one component only of the grammar, is commonplace: remember by way of example that sound laws can operate blindly and create highly irregular morphological forms. The psychologically real, pronounced compartmentalisation of grammars into components has been known for a long time, and has now led Wolfgang U. Dressler to posit his polyzentristische Theorie des Sprachsystems, see Dressler 1977:60 and passim.

the history of Icelandic. The rule for the formation of the short imperative was formulated on the basis of the many pairs such as the long
imperative *haltu* versus the short imperative *halt* (of *halda*): the long
imperative minus *u* = the short imperative. This clipping rule was then
generalised to cases which did not participate in the formulation of the
rule to begin with, with the result that clipped imperatives such as *kond,
takt, gerð, leggð* arose from the long imperatives *kondu, taktu, gerðu,
leggðu*, respectively.—Under the pressure from the long imperatives
(e. g. *kondu*), which are the basic imperative variants, the clipped imperatives (e.g. *kond*) are losing ground, just like the short imperatives
(e.g. *kom*), except in the one usage in which the long imperative (e.g.
kondu) was of no avail: when the clipped imperative (e.g. *kond*) was
followed by **emphatic** *þú*, e. g. *Lest* ÞÚ *bókina, ekki* HANN.—The formal
style has kept the short imperative + þú in this function—except with
vert of *vera* and *verða*[9]—so that the clipped imperatives—barring *vert*
—now occur in informal style only.

The above aspects of the history of the imperative singular support
my parallel account of the history of the *lest* and *ferð* types. In particular, the history of the imperative singular shows that any 2. p. sg.
form ending in suffixed *þú* is the basic morphological variant of that
second person singular, and that the remaining variants of that second
person singular are derived from their basic variant in suffixed *þú*
through clipping.

1.3

I assume that the clipped 2. p. sg. forms *lest* and *ferð* were optional
variants of the old short forms *les* and *fer* to begin with. But gradually
the innovations (*lest, ferð*) prevailed over the inherited forms *(les, fer)*
because the innovations (*lest, ferð*) were more than the inherited forms
(les, fer) similar to their basic variants, the long forms (*lestu, ferðu*).
Also, the process by which the clipped forms (*lest, ferð*) came into being
is still active, and keeps producing the clipped forms. Another reason
for the success of the clipped forms may be this. Most Icelandic verbs

[9] The clipped form *vert* penetrated the formal style probably because it was
more frequent than other clipped imperatives in the texts of the past centuries, and
was therefore supported by the written tradition. More on this in Orešnik 1980.

are conjugated in the active voice singular of both tenses and moods, except in the indicative present of the non-preterite-present verbs (roughly speaking), in such a way that the 2. p. sg. is longer than the first and third persons. E.g. the indicative preterite of the strong verb *lesa* is, 1. *las*, 2. *last*, 3. *las*; of the weak verb *kalla*, 1. *kallaði*, 2. *kallaðir*, 3. *kallaði*. Etc. The clipped forms such as *lest*, *ferð* follow this prevailing model: the old paradigm was, 1. *les*, 2. *les*, 3. *les*, the new, 1. *les*, 2. *lest*, 3. *les*.—When *lest*, *ferð* had prevailed in the spoken language, the written language also accepted them, as unofficial variants to begin with, and only in the twentieth century as the normal official forms (Arpi 1904).

To the best of my knowledge, only four modern Icelandic monosyllabic short second persons singular—not including the short imperative—remained without a dental ending after *lest*, *ferð* had prevailed in the spoken and written language: *skín* of *skína*, *hvín* of *hvína*, *hrín* of *hrína*, and *vex* of *vaxa*. I cannot offer any explanation of this state of affairs. The situation is all the more perplexing because the same verbs can form the clipped imperative, according to my informants: *skínd*, etc. (e.g. *skínd þú, blessuð sólin*).

An interesting question is why the clipping of *u* has not spread to the 2. p. sg. verbal forms ending in *-urðu*, so that *-urð* would result, e.g. a clipped *krefurð* beside the long form *krefurðu* of *krefja*. (Words in *urð* are commonplace in Icelandic, cf. *megurð, fegurð, lipurð*, so that the prohibition cannot be due to restrictions on the pronunciation.) The following explanation can be suggested. In all those pairs of long and corresponding short verbal forms that originally participated in the formulation of the clipping rule, the long form was dissyllabic and the short form monosyllabic. In contradistinction, the long forms in *-urðu* are at least trisyllabic. The implication is that the statement concerning the number of syllables is a part of the clipping rule.[10]

The oldest example of the *lest* type, from the former half of the eighteenth century (see § 1.1 above), shows that the clipping rule must have begun to spread outside imperatives around 1700 at the latest. I have nothing to say about why the clipped forms of the *lest* type began to appear precisely in the eighteenth century. The oldest example of the

---

[10] This suggests that morpho(no)logical rules can be sensitive to the number of syllables in the words on the basis of which such rules are formulated.

ferð type, from the former half of the nineteenth century (see § 1.1 above), shows that the clipping rule must have begun to spread to dissyllabic long forms in *-ðu* around 1800 at the latest.

Why did the *ferð* type come into being later than the *lest* type? I think because *lest* requires the formulation, „delete the *u* of *tu*", whereas *ferð* requires the generalised formulation, „delete the *u* of dental + *u*." The process of generalising (simplifying) a rule tends to take some time, as such pertinent examples as described in the literature testify. (See, e.g., Höskuldur Thráinsson 1980.) This has obviously also been the case with the clipping rule, and has caused the time difference that separates the earliest occurrence of the *lest* type from that of the *ferð* type.

1.4

I now continue with a comparison of the fate, in the informal language, of the clipped imperatives and of the clipped indicatives. Why has the long imperative scored such success in the informal language, whereas the long indicative could not prevail over the clipped indicative? Answer: The functional difference between the variants of the imperative was essentially less than the functional difference between the variants of the indicative. With one exception (the use with emphatic *þú*) the difference between the variants of the imperative was stylistic at most. On the other hand, the difference between the variants of the indicative is first of all grammatical: *lestu* is used with inversion, e.g. in interrogative sentences, *lest* elsewhere.[11] This accounts for the difference in treatment alluded to in the above question. When the short indicative *les* was joined by the clipped indicative *lest*, between which there was at most a stylistic difference, one of them, viz. *les*, disappeared entirely, as expected on the basis of the similar situation in the imperative. If the indicative forms *les(t)* and *lestu* were stylistic variants at most, I predict that *lest(t)* would be on the way out of the language under the pressure from *lestu*.

Let us compare the fate of the clipped imperative with the fate of the clipped indicative in the modern formal language: the clipped imperative could not penetrate the formal language (barring *vert*, cf.

---

11 More precisely, *Þú lest margar bækur*, *Lestu margar bækur?* and *Lest þú margar bækur?* are acceptable sentences, whereas *Þú lestu margar bækur* is not.

Orešnik 1980, the clipped indicative could. I will explain this as follows. The use of the clipped imperative must have been quite limited when the modern norm was being established in the nineteenth century, and that limited usage was not noticed, or not taken seriously, by the prescriptive grammarians, so that the incorporation of the clipped imperative into the modern norm has not even been discussed, witness the lack of pertinent statements in the grammatical literature of the nineteenth and twentieth centuries. On the other hand, the clipped indicatives had such essential usage in the informal language that one could not fail to notice them. Therefore the incorporation of the clipped indicatives into the modern norm was discussed (for an unsympathetic attitude see Guðbrandur Vigfússon 1857:163), and eventually answered affirmatively (as any twentieth century grammar of modern Icelandic witnesses).

2.

2.0

The assumption that the long form is the basic variant of the Icelandic imperative singular and of the 2. p. sg. pres. ind., has helped us understand the origin of the dental accretion in the so-called clipped forms of Icelandic. I will now use this same idea to try and explain some typologically related phenomena of Faroese and the old West Germanic languages.

2.1

In modern Faroese, the monosyllabic 2. p. sg. pres. ind. verbal forms end in -t, e. g. *gert* of *gera*, *býrt* of *búgva*, etc. (see Zachariasen 1977).[12] Zachariasen sees in the -t an innovation of Faroese, due to the gradual movement, within verbal forms such as *ger*, *býr* to which the personal pronoun *tú* had been added enclitically, of the *t* of the pronoun to the end of the preceding verbal forms. The movement has been promoted by the 2. p. sg. pret. ind. of the strong verbs, which ends in -(s)t, e.g. *fórt*, *gekst*, and by the 2. p. sg. pres. ind. of the preterite-present verbs, which also ends in -(s)t, e.g. *skalt*, *kanst*.

Originally each second person singular form (barring the imperative) had two morphological variants, one, the **long** form, ending in enclitical

---

[12] My attention has been drawn to this paper by Björn Hagström.

-*tú*,[13] and another, the **short** form, not ending in -*tú*. E.g. *ger* was the short, and *gertú* the long, form of *gera*. The facts of Icelandic suggest that the long form was the basic variant of the second person singular, from which the corresponding short form was made by aid of a **clipping** rule: remove the -*tú* of the long form. E.g. *gertú* minus *tú* gave *ger*. However, there was also a competing clipping rule in the language, formulated on the basis of the 2. p. sg. verbal forms that had already ended in *t*. The rule was, remove the final *ú* of the long form. E.g. *kanstú*, *fórtú* minus *ú* gave *kanst*, *fórt*. This clipping rule, formulated on the basis of certain dissyllabic long and monosyllabic short forms, was generalised to ALL dissyllabic long forms, with the result that new monosyllabic short forms in -*t* (here called the **clipped** forms) arose. E.g. *gertú* minus *ú* gave *gert*. One of the reasons why the clipped forms (e. g. *gert*) replaced the corresponding old short forms (e.g. *ger*) may be that the clipped forms (e.g. *gert*) are more than the corresponding original short forms (e.g. *ger*) similar to the corresponding long forms (e.g. *gertú*), i.e. to their respective basic variants. The process by which the clipped forms came into being is still active and produces the clipped forms all the time. After the clipped forms had come into being, all monosyllabic 2. p. sg. verbal forms of Faroese (barring the imperative) ended in *t* (Zachariasen 1977).

As Zachariasen points out, the clipped forms are not used in southern Faroese. (For instance, the 2. p. sg. pres. ind. of *gera* is *ger*, not *gert*.) From the descriptive point of view this is as it should be. For while southern Faroese does know the long forms such as *gertú*, it does not possess the model for the formulation of the rule that produces the clipped forms (*gert*, etc.): the 2. p. sg. pres. ind. of the preterite-present verbs and the 2. p. sg. pret. ind. of the strong verbs do not (any longer) end in -*(s)t* in southern Faroese, but are without endings. (E.g. *tú kann*, *fór*, not *tú kanst*, *fórt*.) How this state of affairs is to be accounted for historically is a different problem, most probably one that will never be solved with certainty, given the paucity of the available information on the Faroese of the previous centuries.[14]

[13] In contradistinction to Icelandic this *tú* is never written together with the verbal form that immediately precedes it; I will, however, resort to this spelling device here to facilitate the exposition.

[14] I thank Kaj Larsen for a discussion of southern Faroese.

2.2

In this section I shall discuss a similar phenomenon of the old West Germanic languages: the addition of *t* to the final *s* of the 2. p. sg. of verbs. E.g. OE *gǣs* > *gǣst* of *gān*, OHG. *tuos* > *tuost* of *tuon* (Sievers 1951:297–98; Braune 1975:258). The ensuing discussion will be limited to Old English and Old High German, where this matter has been best documented and investigated.

The facts of the Old English case, as reported in this paragraph, are taken from Sievers (1951:297–98). The oldest Old English 2. p. sg. desinence in the present of the non-preterite-present verbs and in the preterite of the non-strong verbs was (ended in) *s*, e.g. *bindes, dēmes*, pret. *dēmdes, sceoldes*. The *s* was used in the early texts „oft noch fast ausschlieszlich", so that there can be no question of *-st* being inherited from pre-literary times. Younger texts have mostly *-st*. Its *t* is due to a faulty analysis of the *s*-forms to which the personal pronoun *þū* had been added enclitically. E.g. *gǣs þū* > *gǣstu* (such long forms do occur in the texts), and from the latter *gǣst* arose. The *st*-forms appeared earliest in the monosyllabic 2. p. sg., more precisely, in the 2. p. sg. pres. ind. of the contracted verbs and of the verbs in *-mi*.

The facts of the Old High German case, as reported in this paragraph, are taken from Braune (1975:258). The oldest Old High German 2. p. sg. desinence in the present of the non-preterite-present verbs and in the preterite of the non-strong verbs was (ended in) *s*, e.g. pres. *nimis, salbōs*, pret. *salbōtōs, scoltōs*. Since this desinence is the only one used „in den ältesten Quellen", there can be no question of *-st* being inherited from pre-literary times. In the ninth century a *t* began to occur after *s*, first in Franconian, then, in the tenth century, in Upper German. „Entstanden ist die Endung *st* aus den Formen mit enklitisch angefügtem *thu, du*." (The long forms in suffixed *thu, du* occur already in early texts.) *-st* is due to a faulty analysis of the long forms, probably under partial influence of *bist*[15] and of the 2. p. sg. pres. ind. of the preterite-present verbs. This idea goes back to Scherer (1878:331).

The faulty analysis mentioned in the two preceding paragraphs can be made more explicit with the help of the analogous Icelandic development, discussed earlier in the present paper.

[15] *Bist* is either an early clipped form, or its *t* stems from the 2.p.sg.pres.ind. of the preterite-present verbs, or is analogy after *ist*, according to the handbooks.

206   *Janez Orešnik*

The earliest Old English and Old High German had non-imperative
short forms in *s* and long forms in *stu*. The short and the corresponding
long forms were morphological variants of the 2. p. sg., with the long
forms having the status of the basic variants. Therefore the short forms
tended to be made from the corresponding long forms by aid of a
clipping rule: the long form minus *tu* = the short form. E.g. OE.
gǣstu minus *tu* = *gǣs*, OHG. *tuostu* minus *tu* = *tuos*. However, there
was also another clipping rule in the language, formulated on the basis
of the short and long forms in the preterite-present verbs and in the
verb „to be" (OE. *eart, earð, arð*, OHG. *bist),* in Old English also in
the verb *willan* (*wilt*). The short forms of these verbs were, OE. *wāst,
canst, eart, wilt*, etc., OHG. *weist, kanst, bist*, etc. The corresponding
long forms were, OE. *wāstu, canstu, eartu, wiltu*, etc., OHG. *weistu,
kanstu, bistu*. Here again the long forms were the basic variants, from
which the short forms were made by aid of the following rule: the long
form minus *u* = the short form. E.g. OE. *wāstu* minus *u* = *wāst*, OHG.
weistu minus *u* = *weist*.

This clipping of *u*, whose position was relatively strong because it
had been abstracted from forms of much used verbs, began to compete
with the clipping of *tu*. In Old English, the competition was to begin
with limited to dissyllabic long forms (e.g. *gǣstu*), because the clipping
of *u* had been abstracted precisely from dissyllabic long (and monosyllabic short) forms (e.g. from *canstu, canst*). In Old High German,
the competition was to begin with limited to the pres. ind. sg., no doubt
because the verbal forms from which the clipping of *u* had been abstracted (e.g. *kanstu, kanst*) also pertained to the pres. ind. sg.[16] Examples of the operation of the clipping of *u* outside its original domain:
OE. *gǣstu* minus *u* yielded *gǣst*, OHG. *tuostu* minus *u* yielded *tuost*.
For a time forms such as the inherited OE. *gǣs* and OHG. *tuos* on the
one hand, and the innovations OE. *gǣst* and OHG. *tuost* on the other,
competed with each other, until the clipped forms (e.g. OE. *gǣst*, OHG.
tuost) won the day, presumably because they were more than the
original short forms (e.g. OE. *gǣs*, OHG. *tuos*) similar to their respective basic variants (e.g. to OE. *gǣstu*, OHG. *tuostu*). The implication is

[16] There is no indication that in Old High German the competition between
the two clipping rules was originally limited to dissyllabic long forms, as was the
case in Old English.

that non-basic morphological variants tend to become similar to their respective basic morphological variants, under favourable conditions. (See section 1.3 for a similar discussion of Icelandic.) The next, and last, step in the Old English development consisted, I think, either in the gradual analogical spread of *st* from the monosyllabic clipped forms (e.g. *gæst*) to the polysyllabic short forms (e.g. *dēmes > dēmest*), or in the generalisation of the clipping of *u* to more-than-dissyllabic long forms (e.g. to *dēmestu*). The analogous step in the Old High German development consisted, I assume, either in the analogical spread of *st* from the sg. pres. ind. (e.g. from *tuost, salbōst*) to the remaining 2. p. sg. forms (e.g. *salbōtōs > salbōtōst*), or in the generalisation of the clipping of *u* to non-present-indicative long forms (e.g. to *salbōtōstu*). I cannot choose among these alternatives. At any rate, the process was aided, as earlier, by the universal tendency of non-basic morphological variants to become similar to their respective basic morphological variants.[17]

3.

To sum up, it is necessary to distinguish between **long** and **short** 2. p. sg. verbal forms in Icelandic: the long forms end in the suffixed personal pronoun *þú* (e.g. *krefurðu* of *krefja*), the short forms do not (e.g. *krefur*). Some monosyllabic short forms have developed a dental accretion, e.g. *lest* of *lesa*, *ferð* of *fara*, *færð* of *fá*. This accretion arose in the last stage of the development shown sub (3), q.v. In Stages 1 and 2

---

[17] A marginal problem is the situation in Northumbrian, where the *st*-forms were indeed used (and spread even into the preterite of the non-strong verbs), but did not eventually prevail over the *s*-forms (Brunner 1962:177). I assume that this must somehow be connected with the well known, although not well understood, Northumbrian replacement of almost all present indicative endings with a new ending *s*. If this assumption is correct, one would expect more *st*-forms in the Northumbrian preterites, where no comparable spread of the new *s* took place, than in the corresponding presents. This prediction seems to be borne out: Sievers (1951:298) mentions that in the two main Northumbrian texts, the Lindisfarne Gospels and in the Durham Ritual, *st*-forms occur more often in the preterite than in the present. This fact has hitherto been unexplained.

I assume that Gothic did not develop the clipped *st*-forms because it lacked the long *stu*-forms (the latter are not mentioned in any handbook on Gothic).

208   *Janez Orešnik*

(3) Stage 1:   less, lestu   ferr. ferðu   fær, færðu
    Stage 2:   les, lestu   fer, ferðu   fær, færðu
    Stage 3:   lest, lestu   ferð, ferðu   færð, færðu

the short forms *less/les, ferr/fer,* and *fær* did not end in a dental, in Stage 3 they do. The dental accretion *t/ð* stems from the corresponding long 2. p. sg. pres. ind. forms, *lestu, ferðu, færðu,* which have been **clipped** to yield *lest, ferð, færð.* The model for the clipping was provided by the long and short 2. p. sg. pres. ind. forms of the preterite-present verbs, of *vera* and *vilja,* and by the long and short 2. p. sg. pret. ind. forms of the strong preterites, whose long dissyllabic forms ended in *-tu,* and whose short monosyllabic forms ended in *-t,* e.g. *skaltu* and *skalt.* In such pairs of long and short forms the long form was considered basic, and the short form was made from it through the clipping of the final *u: skaltu* minus *u = skalt.* This clipping process was first generalised to all dissyllabic long 2. p. sg. pres. ind. forms ending in *-tu* (except *vextu* of *vaxa*), and there arose, e.g., *lest* from *lestu.* After some time the clipping process was further generalised to all dissyllabic long 2. p. sg. pres. ind. forms ending in *-ðu,* and there arose, e.g., *ferð* from *ferðu, færð* from *færðu.*

That it is the long forms (e.g. *skaltu*) that are basic, is corroborated by the history of the Icelandic imperative singular. Any imperative singular form had a short and a long form (e.g. *kom* and *komdu*) to begin with. In the further development the long form (e.g. *komdu*) prevailed almost completely so that it is now the dominant form of the imperative singular. This development can only be understood if it is assumed that the long form of the imperative singular (e.g. *komdu*) has been the basic variant of the imperative singular. The basicness of the long form (e.g. *komdu*) may be due to its being more explicitly than the short form (e.g. *kom*) characterised as a 2. p. sg. (through the suffixed pronoun *þú*). I assume that the same relationship between the short and the long forms obtains in the 2. p. sg. verbal forms outside the imperative.

The same clipping process took place in Faroese. From the long 2. p. sg. pres. ind. forms such as *gertú* (official spelling *gert tú*) of *gera* the clipped forms such as *gert* were made on the analogy of the pairs of long and short forms in which the short form ended in *-t.* E.g. on the basis of pairs such as *kanstú* and *kanst*, where the long form was the basic variant (on the evidence of the Icelandic imperative singular), the following rule was established: the short form = the long form minus the final *ú*. (E.g. *kanst* = *kanstú* minus *ú*.) This rule was generalised to all dissyllabic long forms in *-tú*, e.g. to *gertú*, from which it produced a new clipped form *gert*. Nowadays all monosyllabic 2. p. sg. pres. ind. forms end in *-t* in Faroese.

Also in the old West Germanic languages the short 2. p. sg. pres. ind. developed a dental accretion (e.g. OE. *gǣs* of *gān* was replaced by *gǣst*, OHG. *tuos* of *tuon* was replaced by *tuost*). I see the origin of the new *-t* of the 2. p. sg. pres. ind. in the same kind of clipping as has been posited above for Icelandic and Faroese: on the basis of pairs such as OE. *canstu*, *canst*, OHG. *kanstu*, *kanst*, where the long form was the basic variant (on the evidence of the Icelandic imperative singular) the following clipping rule arose: the short form = the long form minus the final *u*. E.g. OE *canst* = *canstu* minus *u*, OHG. *kanst* = *kanstu* minus *u*. This clipping rule was generalised to all long 2. p. sg. pres. ind. forms, e.g. to OE. *gǣstu* (and there arose *gǣst*) and to OHG. *tuostu* (and there arose *tuost*). Subsequently the dental accretion spread even to the 2. p. sg. forms outside the present indicative.

University of Ljubljana,
Yugoslavia

REFERENCES

Arpi, Rolf. 1904. Anmärkningar till nyisländsk gramatik. *Nordiska studier tillegnade Adolf Noreen*, pp. 70–77. K. W. Appelberg, Uppsala.

Björn K. Þórólfsson. 1925. *Um íslenskar orðmyndir á 14. og 15. öld og breytingar þeirra úr fornmálinu.* Fjelagsprentsmiðjan, Reykjavík.

Braune, Wilhelm. 1975. *Althochdeutsche Grammatik.* 13th edition, by Hans Eggers. Max Niemeyer, Tübingen.

Brunner, Karl. 1962. *Die englische Sprache. Ihre geschichtliche Entwicklung.* Vol. 2. 2nd edition. Max Niemeyer, Tübingen.

Cleasby, Richard and Gudbrand Vigfusson. 1957. *An Icelandic–English dictionary.* 2nd edition. Clarendon Press, Oxford.

Dressler, Wolfgang U. 1977. *Grundfragen der Morphonologie.* Österreichische Akademie der Wissenschaften, Wien.

Finnur Jónsson. 1933. *Den islandske grammatiks historie til o. 1800.* Det Kgl.

210   *Janez Orešnik*

Danske Videnskabernes Selskab. Historisk-filologiske Meddelelser, XIX, 4. Levin & Munksgaard, København.

Guðbrandur Vigfússon. 1857. Um stafrof og hneigíngar. *Ný félagsrit gefin út af nokkrum Íslendíngum* 17.

Hovdhaugen, Even (ed.). 1980. *The Nordic Languages and Modern Linguistics* [4]. Universitetsforlaget, Oslo.

Höskuldur Thráinsson. 1980. Sonorant Devoicing at Lake Mývatn: A Change in Progress. In E. Hovdhaugen (ed.):355–364.

Jón Þorkelsson. 1888–94. *Beyging sterkra sagnorða í íslensku.* Reykjavík.

Noreen, Adolf. 1923. *Altisländische und altnorwegische Grammatik (Laut- und Flexionslehre) unter Berücksichtigung des Urnordischen.* 4th edition. Max Niemeyer, Halle (Saale).

Orešnik, Janez. 1980. On the Modern Icelandic Clipped Imperative. In E. Hovdhaugen (ed.):305–314.

Scherer, Wilhelm. 1878. *Zur Geschichte der deutschen Sprache.* 2nd edition. Weidmann, Berlin.

Sievers, Eduard. 1951. *Altenglische Grammatik.* 2nd edition of the adaptation by Karl Brunner. Max Niemeyer, Halle (Saale).

Zachariasen, Ulf. 1977. Eitt sindur um ljóðyvirflyting í føroyskum. *Fróðskaparrit* 25:101–04.

ÚTDRÁTTUR

Í þessari ritgerð gerir höfundur greinarmun á **löngum** og **stuttum** orðmyndum í 2. p. sagna. Löngu myndirnar enda á viðskeyttu fornafni 2. p. *þú* (t. d. *krefurðu* af *krefja*), stuttu myndirnar ekki (sbr. *krefur*). Sumar einkvæðar stuttar myndir hafa bætt við sig tannhljóði, t. d. *lest* af *lesa*, *ferð* af *fara*, *færð* af *fá*. Þessi viðbót var þriðja og síðasta stig þeirrar þróunar sem sýnd er í (3) hér að framan, þ. e. á fyrsta og öðru stigi enda stuttu myndirnar ekki á tannhljóði en því hefur verið bætt við á þriðja stiginu.

Þessi tannhljóðsviðbót (*-t* eða *-ð*) á rót sína að rekja til samsvarandi langra mynda í 2. p. et. nt. fh., svo sem *lestu*, *ferðu*, *færðu*, en þær hafa verið **stýfðar** þannig að útkoman verður *lest*, *ferð*, *færð*. Fyrirmyndin að þessari stýfingu var sótt til 2. p. et. nt. fh. af núþálegum sögnum, sögnunum *vera* og *vilja*, og til langra og stuttra mynda í 2. p. e. þt. fh. af sterkum sögnum. Í þessum tilvikum enduðu löngu tvíkvæðu myndirnar á *-tu* og stuttu einkvæðu myndirnar á *-t*, sbr. *skaltu*, *skalt*; *viltu*, *vilt*; *ertu*, *ert*; *tók(s)tu*, *tók(s)t*. Slík þör voru túlkuð þannig að langa myndin varð eins konar grunnform og stutta myndin leidd af henni á þann hátt að *u* var stýft af. Þessi stýfing breiddist fyrst út til allra tvíkvæðra langra mynda í 2. p. et. nt. fh. sem enduðu á *-tu* (nema *vextu* af *vaxa*) og af því leiddi myndir eins og *lest* af *lestu*. Nokkru síðar breiddist þessi stýfing út til allra tvíkvæðra langra mynda í 2. p. et. nt. fh. sem enduðu á *-ðu* og upp komu myndir eins og *ferð* af *ferðu* og *færð* af *færðu*.

Sú skoðun að löngu myndirnar séu grunnform í þessum skilningi fær stuðning af þróun boðháttar í eintölu í íslensku. Þar voru líka til bæði langar og stuttar myndir í fyrstu, svo sem *kom* og *komdu*. Þróunin varð sú að löngu myndirnar náðu yfirhöndinni og eru nú nær alls ráðandi. Þá þróun er aðeins hægt að skýra á þann veg að löngu myndirnar hafi verið grunnform boðháttarins. Það kann að stafa af því að löngu myndirnar (t. d. *komdu*) hafi verið ótvíræðari eða greinilegri annarrar persónu myndir (vegna viðskeytisins sem leitt var af 2. p. fn. *þú*). Í þessari grein er gert ráð fyrir að samsvarandi afstaða hafi ríkt milli stuttra og langra sagnmynda í öðrum formum 2. p. et. en boðhætti — þ. e. að löngu myndirnar hafi þar líka verið túlkaðar sem grunnform.

Sams konar stýfing hefur átt sér stað í færeysku. Af löngum sagnmyndum eins og *gertú* (sem venjulega er ritað *gert tú*) af sögninni *gera* voru leiddar stýfðar myndir eins og *gert* fyrir áhrif frá sögnum þar sem stutta myndin endaði á *-t*. Á grundvelli para eins og *kanstú* og *kanst*, þar sem langa myndin var grunnformið (sbr. íslensku þróunina) var mynduð reglan: stutta myndin er eins og langa myndin þegar *ú* hefur verið stýft af. Þessi regla breiddist síðan út til allra tvíkvæðra langra mynda sem enduðu á *-tú*, t. d. til *gertú*, þannig að upp kom ný stýfð mynd *gert*. Nú enda allar einkvæðar myndir 2. p. et. nt. fh. á *-t* í færeysku.

Tannhljóði var einnig bætt við stuttar myndir 2. p. et. nt. fh. í fornum vestur-germönskum málum. Þannig komu fram myndir eins og *gæst* í stað *gæs* af *gān* í fornensku, og *tuost* í stað *tuos* af *tuon* í fornháþýsku. Hér er því haldið fram að þetta hafi gerst við sams konar stýfingu og átti sér stað í íslensku og færeysku. M. ö. o., til voru þör eins og *canstu*, *canst* í fornensku og *kanstu*, *kanst* í fornhá-þýsku og af þeim voru leiddar stýfingarreglur, sem síðar voru látnar ná til allra langra mynda í 2. p. et. nt. fh., og enn síðar breiddist svo tannhljóðsviðbótin til annarra forma í 2. p. et.

JANEZ OREŠNIK

On Some Icelandic Irregular Imperative Singular Forms

Spoken modern Icelandic possesses a few irregular imperative singular (= imp. sg.) forms, some of which will be discussed in the present paper. They include, *keyptu* of *kaupa* 'buy' (section 1), *attu* of *etja* 'egg on' (section 2), *kýs(tu)* of *kjósa* 'choose' (section 3), and (Old Icelandic) *sé(ðu)* of *vera* 'be' (section 4).[1]

1. The regular imp. sg. of *kaupa* 'buy' is *kauptu*. While this form does exist, it is more and more common to say *keyptu* instead of *kauptu* (Jón Friðjónsson 1978:320). The imp. *keyptu* is an irregular formation containing the non-present stem *keyp-* (cf. the 1p. sg. pret. ind. *keypti*), rather than the expected present stem *kaup-* (cf. the 1p. sg. pres. ind. *kaupi*).

The oldest examples of *keyptu* known to me occur in the manuscript Add. 11.177 (British Museum), from the latter half of the seventeenth century (most probably the manuscript originates from Vestfirðir). For the examples see Jón Helgason 1962a:54 v. l.; for the dating and provenance of the manuscript see *ibidem*, XVI.

The origin of the imp. *keyptu* has been briefly discussed by Jón Helgason (1970:XLV), who writes concerning the language of the manuscript Lbs. 276 fol (from 1861–68): "Imperativ af 'yrkja' er *orktu* 194 (efter præt. plur. 3. person, som i en række verber havde samme form som imperativ med tilføjet subjekt, jfr. at man nu kan høre en imp. 'keyptu' for 'kauptu')." Jón Helgason's terse explanation will here be freely interpreted as follows. A number of Icelandic verbs (i. e. most *ian-* and *ēn-*verbs, more than 700 in all, to judge by the lists in Valtýr Guðmundsson 1922:137ff.) have long imp. forms formally identical with the 3p. pl. pret. ind. of those verbs.[2] E.g. the imp. *heyrðu* of *heyra*

---

1 My thanks are due to Miss Margaret G. Davis, who has corrected my English.
2 The term LONG IMPERATIVE refers to the variant of the imp. sg. containing the affixed personal pronoun *þú*. The term SHORT IMPERATIVE, which occurs elsewhere in the main text, refers to the variant of the imp. sg. containing

212   *Janez Orešnik*

'hear' is formally identical with the 3p. pl. pret. ind. *heyrðu* of the same verb. This situation led to the introduction of rule (1), q.v. This rule was in a few cases applied outside its original domain of regular *ian-* and *ēn-*verbs. Thus two imp. sg. forms came into being which, while identical with the 3p. pl. pret. ind. of the verbs in question, were not equal to the present stem + affixed *þú*: *keyptu* and *orktu*.

(1) To form the long imp. sg., take the 3p. pl. pret. ind. of the verb.

A few further examples of the type can be added to *keyptu* and *orktu*, see Table (2). The sources of the new imperatives given in (2c-f): *sóttu* and *studdu* are from Jón Friðjónsson 1978:111 (*ibidem* 112 it is stated that both forms are rarely used; the remaining present stem forms of *styðja* contain *y* in *o. c.*), *spurðu* is from Páll Þorkelsson 1902:136 (who has *y* in the remaining present stem forms of *spyrja*),[3] the existence of *numdu* was confirmed by Magnús Pétursson *per litteras* 1979, in answer to my express question. (Is Valtýr Guðmundsson's imp. *nimdu/nymdu* (1922:136) meant to have the pronunciation [nʏmḍʏ]?) — The imp. *studdu* and *spurðu* are not reliable examples of the type: they may be remnants of *stuðja* and *spurja*, see Valtýr Guðmundsson 1922:5. — A further example *attu* will be treated in section 2 below.

(2)	infinitive	old imperative	3p. pl. pret. ind.	new imperative
(a)	*kaupa*	*kauptu*	*keyptu*	*keyptu*
(b)	*yrkja*	*yrktu*	*orktu*	*orktu*
(c)	*sækja*	*sæktu*	*sóttu*	*sóttu*
(d)	*styðja*	*styddu*	*studdu*	*studdu*
(e)	*spyrja*	*spyrðu*	*spurðu*	*spurðu*
(f)	*nema*	*nemdu*	*numdu*	*numdu*

A great many examples possibly belonging here have been left out of Table (2), namely those *ian-*verbs whose dental suffix in the non-present forms is an inorganic *t*, and whose affixed *þú* begins with an inorganic *t* in the imp. sg. (E.g. *herða* 'harden', imp. sg. and 3p. pl. pret. ind. *hertu*.) The introduction of the *t* into the imp. sg. proceeded independently of the introduction of the *t* into the non-present forms, as can be

---

only the root or the stem of the verb. For instance, *kalla* is the short, *kallaðu* the long, imp. of *kalla* 'call'.

[3] My attention has been drawn to Páll Þorkelsson 1902 by Professor Jón Helgason.

seen from the fact that the inorganic *t* was also introduced into the imp. sg. of a number of strong verbs, where it was of course not supported by some *t* of the non-present forms. (E.g. there is the imp. sg. *bregtu* beside *bregðu* of the strong verb *bregða* 'move quickly.') However, in the modern language, the *ian*-verbs that have an inorganic *t* in their imp. sg. always have it in their non-present forms also, and v. v. I assume that this uniformity in the distribution of the inorganic *t* in the *ian*-verbs, in as much as it is not accidental, is due to the activity of rule (1). As the matter is totally unexplored, I leave it out of account here.

Jón Helgason's explanation of the imp. *keyptu* as parallel with *orktu* was tentatively questioned by Orešnik (1977:624), who drew attention to the one-time existence of a verb *keypa* 'buy', culled by Björn Karel Þórólfsson (1925:119) from Jón Arason's poetry (sixteenth century): the imp. *keyptu* could be a remnant of the now obsolete *keypa*.

Thus there are two hypotheses concerning the origin of *keyptu*, one that builds on the identity of the imp. *keyptu* with the 3p. pl. pret. ind. *keyptu*, and the other that sees in *keyptu* a remnant of the verb *keypa*. How can we choose between these hypotheses? My strategy has been to look for ways in which the new imperatives such as *orktu* differ systematically from the old imperatives such as *yrktu*, and to try to determine whether the imp. *keyptu* behaves like the imp. *orktu* or like the imp. *yrktu*.

I have found one such systematic difference: the old imperatives such as *yrktu* have short imperatives beside them (i.e. there is *yrk* beside *yrktu*), whereas the new imperatives such as *orktu* are not thus coordinated with short forms (i.e. there is no *ork* beside *orktu*), as shown schematically in (3), q.v.

(3) long imperative   short imperative
    yrktu   *yrk* (*þú*)
    orktu   *ork* (*þú*)

The inherited imp. *kauptu* parallels the imp. *yrktu*: there is also *kaup* (*þú*). The new imp. *keyptu* parallels the imp. *orktu*: there is no *keyp* (*þú*) in the language, according to my informants (although there exists *keypt þú*, a form clipped from *keyptu* in the way explained in Orešnik 1980a, b). Consequently, the imp. *keyptu* is not a present stem formation based on the verb *keypa*, but is to be explained as *orktu*.

(The imp. *studdu* and *spurðu* could be checked in the same way, and the results interpreted as follows. For speakers who can use the short imp. *stuð* and *spur,* as they can use other forms of *stuðja* and *spurja,* the imp. *studdu* and *spurðu* pertain to *stuðja* and *spurja,* and are not parallel with *keyptu, orktu.* For speakers who do not use the short imp. *stuð* and *spur,* or other forms of *stuðja* and *spurja,* the imp. *studdu* and *spurðu* are of the same origin as *keyptu, orktu,* or are preserved due to the forces that have brought about *keyptu, orktu.*)

The moral of the present section is an old one: when a morphological form is investigated linguistically, it should not be observed in isolation, but together with all the other forms cooccurring in the same inflexional paradigm. With which other forms a form F cooccurs — or conspicuously does not cooccur — in an inflexional paradigm is as important as what shape F possesses.

2. Beside the regular imp. sg. *ettu,* the Icelandic verb *etja* 'egg on' possesses an irregular imp. sg. *attu.* The present section discusses the origin of *attu.*

The oldest example of the imp. *attu* that I have seen in print occurs in Páll Þorkelsson 1902:132, where the author describes the form as used in the district of Skaftafell, South-Eastern Iceland. My informants produce this form without hesitation, in response either to the question, "What is the imp. sg. of *etja?*" or to the question, "Do you use the imp. sg. *attu?*" Thus the imp. *attu* is at least eighty years old, and is still used in spoken Icelandic. The origin of this form has never been discussed in print, as far as I know.

I assume that the imp. *attu* contains the vowel of the pret. *att-* of *etja,* and that this fact is to be explained in the same way as the corresponding facts of the new imp. *orktu, keyptu,* etc. of Table (2). However, Jón Helgason's explanation adduced in the previous section cannot be adopted for the imp. *attu* without change: the 3p. pl. pret. ind. of *etja* is *öttu,* so that Jón Helgason's explanation predicts the innovation imp. sg. *öttu,* which does not exist.

Jón Helgason's explanation has to be made slightly abstract to accommodate both the new imperatives of Table (2) and the imp. *attu.* Speakers must have noticed that, in a great number of verbs (most *ian-* and *ēn*-verbs), the part of the imp. sg. that precedes the final *u* is identical with the dental stem of the verb. Consequently the rule for the formation of the long imp. sg. became in such cases (4), q.v. Example:

the imp. sg. *heyrðu* of *heyra* 'hear' was interpreted as the dental stem *heyrð-* + *u*. Rule (4) was overgeneralised to the verbs listed in Table (2), so that new imp. forms such as *orktu, keyptu* arose, and to the verb *etja*, with the result that the imp. *attu* came into being.

(4) To form the long imp. sg., take the sg. pret. ind. dental stem of the verb and add (non-umlauting) *u*.

Formulation (4) supersedes formulation (1) above.

The example *attu* shows that it is the shape of the dental stem used in the SINGULAR pret. ind. that must be mentioned in rule (4): the dental stem *att-* + *u* = *attu*. That the singular shape of the dental stem is thus used is understandable: the new imperatives of Table (2) are also singular forms. (In order to constrain the theory of analogy as much as possible, I will assume in what follows that it is the shape of the dental stem in the SECOND PERSON sg. pret. ind. that is used in the formation of the new imperatives of Table (2) and of *attu*. This assumption, made possible by the fact that the imp. sg. is also a second person form, has no consequences for the actual shapes of the new imperatives.)

For the theory of morphology, the example *attu* shows, as a first approximation, that it is easier for speakers to notice the (substantial) PARTIAL formal identity of semantically/functionally MORE related forms than the TOTAL formal identity of semantically/functionally LESS related forms. In our case, speakers were quicker to notice the partial formal identity between, say, the imp. sg. *heyrðu* and the 2p. sg. pret. ind. *heyrðir*, than to notice the total formal identity between the imp. sg. *heyrðu* and the 3p. pl. pret. ind. *heyrðu*. If it were the other way round, *attu* would probably not have come into being.

3. On the basis of the very many pairs consisting of an imp. sg. and a corresponding 2p. sg. PRESENT ind., where these two forms contain identical roots, one would expect that the rule for the formation of the imp. sg. would at least optionally be (5), q.v. For instance, the imp. sg. *gefðu* and the 2p. sg. pres. ind. *gefur* of *gefa* 'give' contain the same form of the root. The semantic/functional similarity between the imp.

(5) To form the imp. sg., take the root of the 2p. sg. pres. ind. (and add affixed *þú*).

sg. and the 2p. sg. PRESENT ind. is at least as great as the semantic/ functional similarity between the imp. sg. and the 2p. sg. PRETERITE ind., i.e. in the pairs of forms discussed in sections 1 and 2 above. Consequently we expect imp. sg. formations containing the vowel of the (2p.) sg. pres. ind. instead of the inherited vowel of the imp., in the cases when the two vowels are not identical. There are ca. eighty verbs of this kind in the language, judging by the lists in Valtýr Guðmundsson 1922. But the only forms of the type that I have found are the imp. sg. *kýs(tu)*, beside the regular imp. sg. *kjóstu*, of *kjósa* 'choose' (cf. the 2p. sg. pres. ind. *kýs*), and the imp. sg. *veld*, beside the regular imp. sg. *vald*, of *valda* 'cause' (cf. the 2p. sg. pres. ind. *veldur*). The origin of *kýs(tu)* and *veld* has never been discussed in print, as far as I know.

The oldest example of the imp. *kýs(tu)* that I know of — and the only one that I have seen in print — occurs in the manuscript Ny kgl. sml. 1141 fol., from the latter half of the eighteenth century. (For the example see Jón Helgason 1962b:157 v. 1., for the dating of the manuscript, which is a copy of a lost manuscript from 1699–1700, see Jón Helgason 1962a:IX, XX.) My informant Miss Aldís Sigurðardóttir told me in 1978, in the course of an investigation of the imp. sg. forms, that she and the then Icelandic priest in Copenhagen, a Northern man, used the imp. *kýstu*. Magnús Pétursson (*per litteras* 1981) is of the opinion that the imp. *kýstu* is more common than the imp. *kjóstu*, in the modern spoken language.

The imp. *veld* was furnished by Miss Aldís Sigurðardóttir in 1978 in response to the question, "What is the imp. sg. of *valda*?" Magnús Pétursson (*per litteras* 1981) states that the imp. *veld* is not used in the spoken language. It is notorious that speakers have difficulties forming the imp. sg. of *valda* 'cause'.

4. There is also substantial formal and semantic/functional similarity between the imp. sg. and the 2p. sg. pres. SUBJUNCTIVE. E.g. imp. sg. *gefðu* of 'gefa' and the 2p. sg. pres. subj. *gefir* contain the same root. On the basis of the very many such pairs, one expects rule (6), q.v., for the formation of the imp. sg. Rule (6) can lead to a new result only in

(6) To form the imp. sg., take the root of the 2p. sg. pres. subj. (and add affixed *þú*).

the verbs in which the forms of the pres. subj. contain a root different from the root in the imp. sg. (In all other verbs rule (6) supports the inherited imp. sg.) There is only one such verb in Icelandic, viz. *vera* 'be', whose pres. subj. is *sé, sért* (old form *sér*), *sé*, etc. The expected innovation is the imp. *sé(ðu)*. I know this form only from pre-Reformation Icelandic. My oldest examples are from the manuscript AM 623 4° (written probably about or not long after the middle of the thirteenth century, see Hreinn Benediktsson 1965:xxxvii): *lofaþr se þv* (ed. Finnur Jónsson 1927:9³, 27¹³). I have culled my most recent examples from the Reykjahólabók (written in the former half of the sixteenth century, see the introduction in ed. Loth 1969): *lofaþr sie þv* and *Heill sie þv* (ed. Loth 1969:151¹⁶, 306²⁴). — The Old Norwegian Book of Homilies contains two instances of the imp. *se þu*, see Holtsmark 1955, column 704, where both instances are classified as 2p. sg. pres. subj. forms.

That the effects of rule (6) appeared earlier than the effects of rules (4) and (5), is understandable: the similarity between the imp. sg. and the 2p. sg. pres. subj. is especially close, both in terms of the number of verbs involved in the formulation of rule (6) (all the verbs that possess an imp. sg. are involved) and in terms of the semantic/functional affinity between the imp. sg. and the 2p. sg. pres. subj.

The imp. *sé(ðu)* disappeared relatively early because it had to compete with the subj. form *sér(t)*, whose range of usage included the range of usage of *sé(ðu)*.

REFERENCES

Björn Karel Þórólfsson. 1925. *Um íslenskar orðmyndir á 14. og 15. öld og breytingar þeirra úr fornmálinu*. Fjelagsprentsmiðjan, Reykjavík.

Finnur Jónsson, ed. 1927. *AM 623, 4°. Helgensagaer*. Samfund til udgivelse af gammel nordisk litteratur, København.

Holtsmark, Anne, ed. 1955. *Ordforrådet i de eldste norske håndskrifter til ca. 1250*. Jacob Dybwad, Oslo.

Hreinn Benediktsson. 1965. *Early Icelandic Script*. The Manuscript Institute of Iceland, Reykjavík.

Jón Friðjónsson. 1978. *A Course in Modern Icelandic*. Tímaritið Skák, Reykjavík.

Jón Helgason, ed. 1962a. *Íslenzk fornkvæði*. Vol. I. Editiones arnamagnæanæ, series B, vol. 10. Ejnar Munksgaard, København.

Jón Helgason, ed. 1962b. *Íslenzk fornkvæði*. Vol. III. Editiones arnamagnæanæ, series B, vol. 12. Ejnar Munksgaard, København.

Jón Helgason, ed. 1970. *Íslenzk fornkvæði*. Vol. VII. Editiones arnamagnæanæ, series B, vol. 16. Munksgaard, København.

218   *Janez Orešnik*

Loth, Agnete, ed. 1969. *Reykjahólabók.* Vol. I. Editiones arnamagnæanæ, series A, vol. 15. Munksgaard, København.

Orešnik, Janez. 1977. Three modern Icelandic morphophonemic notes. *Sjötíu ritgerðir helgaðar Jakobi Benediktssyni 20. júlí 1977,* pp. 621–26. Stofnun Árna Magnússonar, Reykjavík.

Orešnik, Janez. 1980a. Um stýfðan boðhátt í íslensku. *Skíma* 3, 3:7–9.

Orešnik, Janez. 1980b. On the modern Icelandic clipped imperative. *The Nordic languages and modern linguistics* (ed. Even Hovdhaugen), pp. 305–14. Universitetsforlaget, Oslo.

Páll Þorkelsson. 1902. *Beygingarreglur í íslenzku með frönskum skýringum.* Gyldendal, Copenhague.

Valtýr Guðmundsson. 1922. *Islandsk Grammatik.* H. Hagerups Forlag, København.

EFNISÚTDRÁTTUR

Í greininni er fjallað um uppruna nokkurra óreglulegra boðháttarmynda: *keyptu* af *kaupa, attu* af *etja, kýs(tu)* af *kjósa, sé(ðu)* af *vera* og fáeinna fleiri. Þessar beygingarmyndir koma allar fyrir í mæltu máli nema *sé(ðu)* sem einungis er að finna í fornu máli.

Í fyrsta hluta greinarinnar er rætt um orðmyndina *keyptu*. Uppruna hennar er að leita til þess að löng boðháttarmynd og 3.p.ft.þt.fh. eru eins (*keyptu*(bh.):(þeir) *keyptu*) í mörgum sagnorðum. Af þessum líkindum leiddi eftirfarandi reglu: „til að mynda langa bh.-mynd skal taka 3.p.ft.þt.fh. af sagnorðinu". Önnur skýring, sú, að *keyptu* sé leifar af so. *keypa* 'kaupa', getur ekki verið rétt því að ekki er til bh.-myndin *keyp*(þú) í málinu en einmitt þetta atriði skipar bh.-myndinni *keyptu* á bekk með bh.-myndum (í et.) sem efalaust eiga rót sína að rekja til þt.fh. (í ft.), sbr. *orktu* (af *yrkja*) þar sem ekki er til neitt *ork*.

Í öðrum hluta greinar er fjallað um *attu*. Upphafs-*a*-ið stafar frá et.fh. í þt. af *etja*. Eigi að skýra *attu* á sama hátt og *keyptu* verður að gera regluna hér að framan lítið eitt sértækari: „til að mynda langa bh.-mynd skal taka sagnstofninn í et.fh. í þt. ásamt tannhljóðinu og bæta við *u*-i sem ekki veldur hljóðvarpi". Af þessari reglu sprettur *keyptu* ekki síður en *attu*.

Í þriðja hluta er fjallað um *kýs(tu)*. Sérhljóðið *ý* stafar frá et.fh. í nt. af sögninni og hlýtur að eiga rætur að rekja til reglunnar: „til að mynda bh.et. skal taka rót sagnorðsins í et.fh. í nt. (og skeyta við *þú*)". Þessi regla hlýtur að vera sprottin upp meðal hinna mörgu sagnorða þar sem rót bh. í et. og et.fh. í nt. eru eins.

Fjórði hluti fjallar um forníslensku bh.-myndina *sé(ðu)*. Þessi mynd sprettur af reglunni: „til að mynda bh.et. skal taka rót sagnorðsins í et.vh. í nt. (og skeyta við *þú*)". Þessi regla hlýtur að vera til komin af því að rætur reglulegra bh.-mynda í et. og et.vth. í nt. eru ætíð eins.

BIBLIOGRAPHY

This bibliography contains all the work by Janez Orešnik about the Icelandic language published before October 1983. (For the contents of the publications, see the Index below.) The bibliographical data on the papers reprinted in the present volume are preceded by +.

1965 – Review of: *Sravnitel'naja grammatika germanskix jazykov,* vol. IV, Moscow, 1966. – *Linguistica* 7, pp. 169–75. Ljubljana.

1966–68 – On the perfect stem of the strong and the preterit-present verbs in Proto-Germanic and in the old Germanic languages. *Linguistica* 8, pp. 123–39. Ljubljana.

1969 – A philological miscellany on the Icelandic verbs *kefja, ljá, œxa, skepja, sýsa. Linguistica* 9, pp. 49–52. Ljubljana.

+ 1971 a – On some weak preterite subjunctives of otherwise strong verbs in modern Icelandic. *Arkiv för nordisk filologi* 86, pp. 139–78. Lund.

+ 1971 b – On the phonological boundary between constituents of modern Icelandic compound words. *Linguistica* 11, pp. 51–9. Ljubljana.

+ 1972 a – On the Epenthesis Rule in modern Icelandic. *Arkiv för nordisk filologi* 87, pp. 1–32. Lund.

1972 b – Morphophonemic notes on the modern Icelandic imperative singular. *Studies for Einar Haugen Presented by Friends and Colleagues* (ed. E. S. Firchow et al.), The Hague: Mouton, pp. 450–9.

+ 1972 c – Four modern Icelandic devoicing rules. *Linguistica* 12, pp. 137–56. Ljubljana.

1973 – Old Icelandic Consonant Lengthening Rule and modern Icelandic infixation of /ð/. *Linguistica* 13, pp. 229–61. Ljubljana.

1975 a – Moderne islandsk generativ fonologi – et eksempel. *Selskab for nordisk filologi. Årsberetning for 1971–73,* København, pp. 32–33.

1975 b – The modern Icelandic u-Umlaut Rule. *The Nordic Languages and Modern Linguistics 2* (ed. K.-H. Dahlstedt), Stockholm: Almqvist & Wiksell, pp. 621–30, discussion pp. 630–3.

1975 c – Review of: Magnús Pétursson, *Les articulations de l'islandais à la lumière de la radiocinématographie,* Paris: Librairie C. Klincksieck, 1974. – *General Linguistics* 15, pp. 120–7. University Park, Penna.

1976 a – Ueber die Lautalternationen im neuisländischen Typus *veggur. Skandinavistik* 6, pp. 110–6. Kiel.

1976 b – Inflection of modern Icelandic nouns, adjectives and adverbs. *Linguistica* 16, pp. 97–118. Ljubljana.

1977 a – On the modern Icelandic Palatalisation Rule. *Dialectology and Sociolinguistics. Essays in Honour of Karl-Hampus Dahlstedt* (ed. C.-C. Elert et al.), Umeå Studies in the Humanities, vol. 12, Umeå, pp. 137–45.

1977 b – (with Magnús Pétursson as co-author) Quantity in modern Icelandic. *Arkiv för nordisk filologi* 92, pp. 155–71. Lund. – Only the phonological part indexed in the Index below.

+ 1977 c – Modern Icelandic u-Umlaut from the descriptive point of view. *Gripla II* (ed. Jónas Kristjánsson), Stofnun Árna Magnússonar á Íslandi, rit 16, Reykjavík, pp. 151–82.

+ 1977 d – Three modern Icelandic morphophonemic notes. *Sjötíu ritgerðir helgaðar Jakobi Benediktssyni 20. júlí 1977* (ed. Einar G. Pétursson and Jónas Kristjánsson), Stofnun Árna Magnússonar á Íslandi, rit 12, Reykjavík, pp. 621–6.

1978 a – Inflection of modern Icelandic verbs and pronouns. *Linguistica* 17, pp. 91–122. Ljubljana.

+ 1978 b – The age and importance of the modern Icelandic type *klifr*. *The Nordic Languages and General Linguistics 3* (ed. J. Weinstock), Austin: The University of Texas at Austin, pp. 468–71.

1978 c – Review of: Magnús Pétursson, *Drög að hljóðkerfisfræði*, Reykjavík: Iðunn, 1978. – *Nordic Linguistic Bulletin* 2.3, pp. 22–9. Uppsala.

+ 1978 d – Modern Icelandic Epenthesis Rule revisited. *Arkiv för nordisk filologi* 93, pp. 166–73. Lund.

+ 1978 e – On the modern Icelandic i-Umlaut Rule. *General Linguistics* 18, pp. 181–200. University Park, Penna.

1978 f – Modern Icelandic preaspiration from the phonological point of view. *Linguistica* 18, pp. 141–66. Ljubljana.

1978 g – Review of: Magnús Pétursson, *Isländisch*, Hamburg: Helmut Buske, 1978. *Linguistica* 18, pp. 261–4. Ljubljana.

1979 – On the pronunciation of modern Icelandic rövl(a) and slafneskur. *Íslenskt mál* 1, pp. 225–32. Reykjavík.

+ 1980 a – On the modern Icelandic clipped imperative. *The Nordic Languages and Modern Linguistics* (ed. E. Hovdhaugen), Oslo: Universitetsforlaget, pp. 305–14.

1980 b – Um stýfðan boðhátt í íslensku. *Skíma* 3.3, pp. 7–9. Reykjavík.

+ 1980 c – On the dental accretion in certain 2nd p. sg. verbal forms of Icelandic, Faroese, and the old West Germanic languages. *Íslenskt mál* 2, pp. 195–211. Reykjavík.

1980 d – On the lack of palatalisation before -*end*- in the plural of Icelandic nominalised present participles such as *leikandi*. *Linguistica* 20, pp. 245–59. Ljubljana.

+ 1981 – On some Icelandic irregular imperative singular forms. *Afmæliskveðja til Halldórs Halldórssonar 13. júlí 1981* (ed. Guðrún Kvaran et. al.), Reykjavík: Íslenska málfræðifélagið, pp. 211–8.

1982 – An Old Icelandic dialect feature: iæ for æ. *Gripla V* (ed. Jónas Kristjánsson), Stofnun Árna Magnússonar á Íslandi, rit 23, Reykjavík, pp. 183–96.

LIST OF MANUSCRIPT REFERENCES

Den arnamagnæanske samling,
København. Stofnun Árna Magnússo-
nar á Íslandi, Reykjavík:

AM 53 fol. 82 : 184n, 186
AM 61 fol. 82 : 184n
AM 66 fol. 82 : 184n, 186
AM 122 a fol. 82 : 186, 190, 193–4
AM 132 fol. 82 : 187–9
AM 162 f fol. 82 : 187–8
AM 180b fol. 82 : 190–2
AM 237a fol. 77c : 165
AM 126 4to 82 : 192n
AM 147 4to 80a : 307
AM 173 c 4to 82 : 188
AM 273 I 4to 82 : 184
AM 396 4to 82 : 190–2
AM 415 4to 82 : 191
AM 420 b 4to 82 : 188
AM 561 4to 82 : 191
AM 566 b 4to 82 : 187
AM 573 4to 82 : 188
AM 619 4to 81 : 217
AM 623 4to 81 : 217
AM 713 4to 80d : 251n
AM 732 b 4to 82 : 191
AM 764 4to 82 : 188–9, 194
AM 977 4to 78b : 469
AM 1041 4to 77d : 622
AM Dipl. Isl. Apogr. nr. 4885 82 : 185
AM Dipl. Isl. Apogr. nr. 5278 82 : 185
AM Dipl. Isl. Fasc. V 28 82 : 184
AM Dipl. Isl. Fasc. LIX 23 82 : 185

Landsbókasafn Íslands, Reykjavík:

Lbs 276 fol. 81 : 211
Lbs 290 fol. 71a : 150
Lbs 68 4to 71a : 149
Lbs 1319 4to 71a : 149–50
Lbs 420 8vo 71a : 144
Lbs 423 8vo 71a : 145
Lbs 449 8vo 77d : 621
Lbs 2083–4 8vo 71a : 146
Lbs. fragm. 5 82 : 189

Þjóðskjalasafn Íslands, Reykjavík:

AM Dipl. Isl. Fasc. I 6 82 : 194n
AM Dipl. Isl. Fasc. II 11 82 : 184
AM Dipl. Isl. Fasc. X 4 82 : 184
AM Dipl. Isl. Fasc. XIII 18 82 : 184
AM Dipl. Isl. Fasc. XXXIII 28
  82 : 185
AM Dipl. Isl. Fasc. XXXVIII 4
  82 : 185

Det kongelige bibliotek, København:

Ny kgl. sml. 1141 fol. 81 : 216
Ny kgl. sml. 3262 4to 71a : 141
Add. 627 c 4to 71a : 142

Kungliga biblioteket, Stockholm:

Perg. fol. nr 3 81 : 217
Perg. fol. nr 5 82 : 187, 189, 190
Perg. fol. nr 12, fragm. VI 82 : 191–2
Perg. 4 : o nr 16 82 : 189, 193
Perg. 4 : o nr 18 82 : 191

British Museum, London:

Add. 11, 177 81 : 211

Österreichische Nationalbibliothek,
Wien:

Cod. Vind. 2713 80a : 307

INDEX

This index contains references to all those points considered to be of interest in the work listed in the Bibliography. Persons have only been indexed if their published scholarly views are criticised in the references to them, or if they have contributed unpublished opinion/material to the work listed in the Bibliography, or if they acted as informants. Unless otherwise stated, the entries (barring the names of persons) refer to modern Icelandic phenomena; for instance, "phonology" means "modern Icelandic phonology."

The papers indexed here are designated by the last two digits of their year of publication, plus a letter of the alphabet, if necessary; for instance, "78f" refers to the publication under 1978f in the Bibliography. The alphabetisation is according to Icelandic custom: ð follows d, and Þ, ö, æ, œ follow z, in that order.

/q/ means voiced velar fricative.

For reasons of economy, there are no intentional cross-references. Persons searching for particular information are advised to read the whole Index.